OTTOLENGHI

THE COOKBOOK

OTTOLENGHI
THE COOKBOOK

Yotam Ottolenghi & Sami Tamimi

with Tara Wigley

EBURY
PRESS

10 9 8 7 6 5 4 3 2

Ebury Press, an imprint of Ebury Publishing,
20 Vauxhall Bridge Road,
London, SW1V 2SA

Ebury Press is part of the Penguin Random House
group of companies whose addresses can be found
at global.penguinrandomhouse.com

Penguin
Random House
UK

This updated edition first published by Ebury Press
in 2016

Originally published in 2008 as *Ottolenghi:
The Cookbook* (ISBN 9780091922344)

www.penguin.co.uk

A CIP catalogue record for this book is available
from the British Library

Design: Here Design
Photography: Richard Learoyd

ISBN: 978 178503 4 770

Colour origination by Altaimage London

Printed and bound in Italy by Graphicom S.r.l

Penguin Random House is committed to a
sustainable future for our business, our readers and
our planet. This book is made from
Forest Stewardship Council® certified paper.

MIX
Paper from
responsible sources
FSC
www.fsc.org FSC® C018179

To Ruth, Michael and Karl
– Yotam

To Na'ama, Hassan and Jeremy
– Sami

Photography by Richard Learoyd

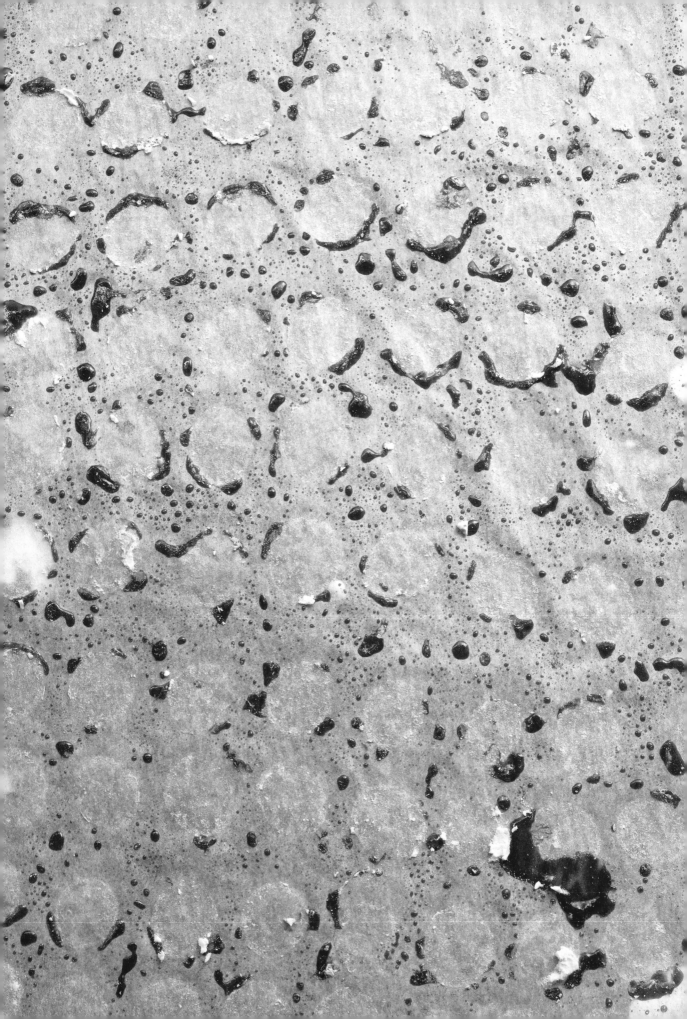

Contents

Introduction 12

Vegetables, pulses and grains   26

Meat and fish   110

Baking and pâtisserie   164

Larder   282

Index 296

The Ottolenghi people 302

Acknowledgements 304

It was under a decade ago that we started
testing recipes for the Ottolenghi cookbook.
So much has happened in this period:
four more books published, restaurants
opened, new cuisines explored, ingredients
discovered, techniques unravelled,
a dedicated test kitchen set up, chefs
coming through the door and sharing their
tricks with us. A sea of change in what
seems like a pretty short amount of time.

It is probably fair to say that this one-off project – a modest cookbook to satisfy our desire to spread our word out a little and give our customers tools to cook Ottolenghi at home – has taken on a life of its own and, by and by, transformed ours.

These days, testing recipes, putting them together, writing related stories, packaging them into magazine articles or beautiful books, going on tours to sell them – have very much become part of our day job. Our books and our constant dialogue with the readers inform the way we think about food, how we cook, and what we serve to our customers.

From this perspective, it is pretty hard not to feel stupidly nostalgic when we go back and flick through our first book: our very first dish using sumac, and that aubergine with saffron yoghurt which we've cooked a thousand times since; much younger and better-looking versions of ourselves; the old Notting Hill kitchen team; our cake display circa 2007, and that cute dog that's always parked outside.

As always, when going through old photo albums, this one offers plenty of reasons for embarrassment: what were we thinking placing that cable between the fennel gratin and the camera? Or suggesting serving crusty bread with almost every dish (had we not heard of gluten-free)? Or garnishing everything with pomegranate seeds? Couldn't the two roasted chicken dishes (arguably the most popular recipes in the book) be made to look just a little bit nicer?

In all truth, though, we are very pleased of our first attempt at a cookbook. A year of Friday night dinners at Sami's, in which a group of friends got together to eats lots, argue with passion and suggest endless improvements, yielded a bunch of dishes which we are still extremely happy to cook; dishes which are, in a sense, the blueprint for all the ones that have followed.

This new edition celebrates those dishes with great pride in a new package that fits in better with the books that came after it. We wanted to modernise the look and update the introductions while still keeping the particular texture of the original. We very much hope that it works for the old devotees as well as for new ones.

Yotam Ottolenghi and Sami Tamimi
September 2016

Introduction

Our feast is, literally, a feast of bold colours and generous gestures. It is driven by an unapologetic desire to celebrate food and its virtues, to display abundance in the same way that a market stallholder does: show everything you've got and shout its praise wholeheartedly.

We got started in July 2002, not really sure what was ahead of us, when we opened Ottolenghi – food shop, pâtisserie, deli, restaurant, bakery. A place with no single description but at the same time a crystal-clear reflection of our obsessive relationship with food. In a small shop in Notting Hill we began to cook and bake.

We did it while the white paint on the walls was still drying. Together with a small group of friends, and alongside some newly acquired staff (quickly turned friends), we began our experiment with food.

Our partner and designer, Alex Meitlis, supplied us with a blank canvas: 'A white space with white shiny surfaces is what's going to make your concoctions stand out,' he said. We argued a little but were soon persuaded. The white background turned out to be the perfect setting for our party. And we did not intend to be shy about it.

Our food impulse

We wanted to start this book with the quip, 'If you don't like lemon or garlic... skip to the last page.' This might not be the funniest of jokes, but, considering lemon and garlic's prevalence in our recipes, it is as good a place as any to start looking for a portrait of our food. Regional descriptions just don't seem to work; there are too many influences and our food histories are long and diverse. True, we both come from a very particular part of the world – Israel/Palestine – with a unique culinary tradition. We adore the food of our childhoods. We both ate lots of fresh fruit and vegetables: oranges from Jericho, used only to make the sweetest fresh juice; crunchy little cucumbers, full of the soil's flavours; heavy pomegranates tumbling from small trees that can no longer support their weight; figs, walnuts, wild herbs... the list is endless.

We both ate a lot of street food – literally, what the name suggests. Vendors selling their produce on pavements were not restricted to 'farmers' markets'. There was nothing embarrassing or uncouth about eating on the way to somewhere. Sami remembers frequently sitting bored in front of his dinner plate, having downed a few grilled corns-on-the-cob and a couple of busbusa (coconut and semolina) cakes bought at street stalls while out with friends.

However, what makes lemon and garlic such a great metaphor for our cooking is the boldness, the zest, the strong, sometimes controversial, flavours of our childhood. The flavours and colours that shout at you, that grip you, that make everything else taste bland, pale, ordinary and insipid. Cakes drenched with rosewater-scented sugar syrup; piles of raw green almonds on ice in the market; punchy tea in a small glass with handfuls of mint and sugar; the intense smell of charred mutton cooked on an open fire; a little shop selling 20 types of crumbly ewe's and goat's milk cheeses, kept fresh in water; apricot season, when there is enough of the fruit lying around each tree to gorge yourself, the jam pot and the neighbourhood birds.

These are the sources of our impulse. It is this profusion of overwhelming sensations that inspires our desire to stun with our food, to make you say 'wow!' even if you're not the expressive type. The colours, the textures and finally the flavours that are unapologetically striking.

Our food philosophy

Like the market vendor, we make the best of what we have and don't interfere with it too much. We keep food as natural as possible, deliberately avoiding complicated cooking methods. Take our broccoli, the king of the Ottolenghi jungle. It is mightily popular (people were picketing on Ledbury Road when we tried removing it from the menu once) but it can't get any simpler. If you don't know it, you must try it (recipe on page 56); if you do, you will no doubt try it anyway.

Unfussiness and simplicity in food preparation are, for us, the only way to maintain the freshness of a dish. Each individual ingredient has a clear voice, plain characteristics that are lucid and powerful – images, tastes and aromas you remember and yearn for.

This is where we differ deeply from both complicated haute cuisine and industrial food: the fact that you can clearly taste and sense cumin or basil in our salad, that there is no room for guessing. Etti Mordo, an ex-colleague and a chef of passion, always used to say she hated dishes that you just knew had been touched a lot in the preparation.

We love real food, unadulterated and unadorned. A chocolate cake should, first and foremost, taste of chocolate. It doesn't have to involve praline, raspberries, layers of sponge, sticky liqueur and hours in the freezer. Give us a clean chocolate flavour, a muddy, fudgy texture and a plain appearance. Decorations and fancy garnishes are subject to the highs and lows of fashion. Good solid food is a source of ageless pleasure and fun.

This ability to have fun, to really enjoy food, to engage with it lightheartedly and wholeheartedly, is the key for us. After centuries of being told how bad their cuisine was, the British have started taking pride in their food in recent years, joining the European set of confident, passionate and knowledgeable devourers. Then, suddenly, they were made to feel guilty for having fun. All of a sudden it is all about diets, health, provenance, morals and food miles. Forget the food itself.

How boring, and what a mistake! This shift of focus sets us back two decades, to a time when food in the UK was just foodstuff, when it was practical instead of sensual, and so we risk once more losing our genuine pleasure in food. People will not care much about the origins of their food and how it's been grown and produced unless they first love it and are immersed in it. It is, yet again, about having fun. Don't get us wrong: supporting small farmers around the globe, treating animals humanely, making sure we don't pollute our bodies and our environment, resisting the total industrialisation of agriculture – these are all precious causes. Our wealth and the cheapness of our food give us an added responsibility to eat sensibly and ethically.

But it isn't a black-and-white choice of good versus evil when it comes to food; you can be well informed and make wise decisions about what to buy and where without turning into a fanatic. Most people's lifestyles don't allow them to grow their own vegetables or source all their meat from a local free-range farm. They must compromise without feeling guilty. So they go shopping in a supermarket during the week and visit a farmers' market at the weekend. They might choose an organic egg alongside a frozen vegetable.

This carefree but realistic approach to cooking and eating is what we try to convey with our food: the idea that cooking can be enjoyable, simple and fulfilling, yet look and taste amazing; that it mustn't be a chore or a bore but can be accessible, straightforward and frank. For us, cooking and eating are not hazy, far-off ideals but part of real life, and should be left there.

Ottolenghi

The interaction

One thing immediately evident at Ottolenghi is that you often see the chefs bringing up trays and plates heavily piled with their creations. It is a source of pride for them and for us to see a customer smile, look closely, and then gasp and give them a huge compliment. So many chefs miss out on this kind of immediate response from the diner – the reaction that leads to a leisurely chat about food.

This communication is essential to our efforts to knock down the dividing walls that characterise so many food experiences today. When was the last time you went shopping for food and actually talked to the person who made it? In a restaurant? In a supermarket? It doesn't happen very often. So at Ottolenghi we are simulating a domestic food conversation in a public, urban surrounding.

The space

When you sit down to eat, it is as close as it gets to a domestic experience. The communal dining reinforces a cosy, sharing, family atmosphere. What you get is a taste of entering your mother's or grandmother's mythical kitchen, whether real or fictitious. Chefs and waiters participate, with the customer, in an intimate moment revolving around food – like a big table in the centre of a busy kitchen.

But it's not only the way you sit, it is also what surrounds you. In Ottolenghi you will always find fresh produce, the ingredients that have gone into your food, stored somewhere where you can see them. The shelves are stacked high with fruit and vegetables from the market. A half-empty box of swede might sit next to a mother with a baby in a buggy, until one of us comes upstairs and takes the vegetable down to the kitchen to cook.

The display

Once the food is on the counter, we try to limit the distance between it and the diner. We keep refrigeration to a minimum. Of course, chilling what we eat is sometimes necessary, but chilled food isn't something we'd naturally want to eat (barring ice cream and a few other exceptions). Most dishes come into their own only at room temperature or warm. It is a chemical fact. This is especially true with cakes and pastries.

Our customers

Not many traditional hierarchies or clear-cut divisions exist in the Ottolenghi experience. You find sweet alongside savoury, hot with cold; a tray of freshly baked cakes might sit next to a scrumptious array of salads, a bowl of giant meringues or a crate of tomatoes from the market. It is an air of generosity, mild chaos and lots of culinary activity that greets customers as they come in: food being presented, replaced, sold; dishes changed, trays wiped clean, the counter rearranged; lots of other people chattering and queuing.

It is this relaxed atmosphere that we strive to maintain. Casual chats with customers allow us to cater for our clients' needs. We listen and know what they like. They bring their empty dishes in for us to make them 'the best lasagne ever' (and if it's not, we will definitely hear about it). This is what encapsulates the spirit of Ottolenghi: a unique combination of quality and familiarity.

We guess that this is what drew in our first customers. So many of them have become regulars over the years, meaning not only that they come to Ottolenghi frequently but also that we recognise them, know their names and something about their lives. And vice versa. They have a favourite sales assistant who always gets their coffee just right (probably an Italian or an Aussie), their pastry of choice (Lou's rhubarb tart), their preferred seat at the table. Our close relationship with our customers extends to all of them, whether it's the bustling city stars forever on their way somewhere; the early riser eagerly tapping his watch at five-to-opening; the chilled and chatty sales assistant from next door; the eternal party organiser with a last-minute rushed order; or a parent on the look-out for something healthy to give the children.

The Ottolenghi cookbook

The Ottolenghi cookbook came into existence through popular demand. So many customers asked for it that we simply had to do it. And we enjoyed every minute of it. We also loved devising recipes for our cooking classes at Leiths School of Food and Wine, some of which appear in this book. The idea of sharing our recipes with fans, as well as with a new audience, is hugely appealing. Revealing our 'secrets' is another way of interacting, of knocking down barriers, of communicating about food.

The recipes we chose for the book are a non-representative collection of old favourites, current hits and a few specials. Some of them have appeared in different guises in 'The New Vegetarian' column in the Guardian's Weekend magazine. They all represent different aspects of Ottolenghi's food – bread, the famous salads, hot dishes from the evening service in Islington, pâtisserie, cakes, cold meat and fish – and they are all typical Ottolenghi: vibrant, bold and honest.

We have decided not to include dishes incorporating long processes that have been described in detail in other, more specialised books – croissants, sourdough bread, stock. We want to stick to what is achievable at home (good croissants rarely are) and what our customers want from the cookbook. We would much rather give a couple of extra salad recipes than spend the same number of pages on chicken stock.

Our histories

Yotam Ottolenghi

My mother clearly remembers my first word, 'ma', short for marak ('soup' in Hebrew). Actually I was referring to little industrial soup croûtons, tiny yellowish pillows that she used to scatter over the tray of my highchair. I would say 'ma' when I finished them all, and point towards the dry-store cupboard.

As a small child, I loved eating. My dad, always full of expressive Italian terms, used to call me goloso, which means something like 'greedy glutton', or at least that's what I figured. I was obsessed with certain foods. I adored seafood: prawns, squid, oysters – not typical for a young Jewish lad from Jerusalem in the 1970s. A birthday treat would be to go to Sea Dolphin, a restaurant in the Arab part of the city and the only place that served non-kosher sea beasts. Their shrimps with butter and garlic were a building block of my childhood dreams.

Another vivid memory: me aged five, my brother, Yiftach, aged three. We are out on our patio, stark naked, squatting like two monkeys. We are holding pomegranates! Whenever my mom brought us pomegranates from the market, we were stripped and banished outside so we didn't stain the rug or our clothes. Trying to pick the sweet seeds clean, we still always ended up with plenty of the bitter white skin in our mouths, covered head to toe with juice.

My passion for food sometimes backfired. My German grandmother, Charlotte, once heard me say how much I loved one of her signature dishes. The result: boiled cauliflower, with a lovely coating of buttered breadcrumbs, served to me at 2 p.m. every Saturday for the next 15 years.

My other 'nonna', Luciana, never quite got over her forced exile from the family villa in Tuscany. When I think of it, she never really left. She and my nonno, Mario, created a Little Italy in a small suburb of Tel Aviv, where they built a house with Italian furniture and fittings; they spoke Italian to the maid and a group of relatives, and ate Italian food from crockery passed down through the family. Walking into their house felt like being teleported to a distant planet. There they were, my nonna and nonno, sitting in their refreshingly cool kitchen and sipping Italian coffee, nibbling the little savoury ciambelline biscuits. And then there was an unforgettable dish, unquestionably my desert-island food: gnocchi alla romana, flat semolina dumplings, grilled with butter and Parmesan.

But I started my professional life far away from the world of prawns, pomegranates and Parmesan. In my early twenties, I was a student of philosophy and literature at Tel Aviv University, a part-time teaching assistant and a budding journalist editing stories at the newsdesk of a national daily. My future with words and ideas was laid out for me in the chillingly clear colours of the inevitable – that is, a PhD.

I decided to take a little break first, an overdue gap year that was later extended into one of the longest 'years' in living memory. I came to London and, much to my poor parents' alarm, embarked on a cookery course at Le Cordon Bleu. 'Come on,' I told them, 'I just need to check this out, make sure it's not the right thing for me.'

And I wasn't so sure that it was. At 30, you are ancient in the world of catering. Being a commis-chef is plain weird. So I suffered a bit of abuse and had a few moments of teary doubt, but it became clear to me that this was the sort of creativity that suited me. I realised this when I was a pastry chef at Launceston Place, my first long-standing position in a restaurant, and one of the waiters shouted to me down the dumb-waiter shaft, 'That was the best chocolate brownie I've ever had!' I've heard this many times since.

Sami Tamimi

I was born to Palestinian parents in the old city of Jerusalem. It was a small and intimate closed society, literally existing within the ancient city walls. People could have lived their entire lives within these confines, where Muslims shared a minute space with Arab Christians and Armenians, where food was always plentiful on the street.

In a place where religion is central to so many, ours was a non-religious household. Although Arab culture and traditions were important at home, and are still very much part of my psyche, I did not have the identity that comes with a strong belief. I found it hard to know where I belonged and this was something I could not talk about at home.

From an early age I was interested in cooking and would spend many hours in the kitchen with my mother and grandmother. Cooking was the focus of daily life and formed the main part of most women's lives. Men did not cook, at least not like women did. My father, however, loved cooking for pleasure alone. My mother cooked to share the experience with her friends and the food with her family. I believe I have inherited both my father's love of food and my mother's love of feeding people.

Some of my earliest memories are of my father squatting on the floor, preparing food in the traditional Arab way. He took endless trouble over preparation, as did my mother. She would spend ages rolling perfect vine leaves, stuffed with lamb and rice, so thin and uniform they looked like green cigarettes. I remember my mother's kitchen before a wedding, when a group of friends and relatives gathered together to prepare for the event. It seemed as if there was enough food to feed the whole world!

My father was the food buyer. I only had to mention his name at the shop selling freshly roasted coffee beans and I got a bag of 'Hassan's mix'. Dad used to come home with boxes piled high with fresh fruit and vegetables. Once, when I was about seven, he arrived with a few watermelons. Being the youngest, I insisted on carrying one of them into the house, just like my brothers and sisters. On the doorstep, I couldn't hold it any longer and the massive fruit fell on the floor and exploded, covering us all with wet, red flesh.

I was 15 when I got my first job, as a kitchen porter at the Mount Zion Hotel. This is the lowliest and hardest job in any kitchen. You run around after everybody. I was lucky that the head chef saw my potential and encouraged me to cook. By then I was cooking at home all the time, making meals for my friends. I knew that this was what I wanted to do in life. It meant making the break from the Arab old city and entering Israeli life on the other side of the walls. I wanted to cook and explore the world outside, and Israeli culture allowed me to do this.

I made the significant move to Tel Aviv in 1989 and worked in various catering jobs before becoming assistant head chef at Lilith, one of the best restaurants in the city at the time. We served fresh produce, lightly cooked on a massive grill. I was entranced by this mix of Californian and Mediterranean cuisines, and it was there that I truly discovered my culinary identity and confidence. I moved to London in 1997 and was offered a job at Baker and Spice. During my six years there, I reshaped the traiteur section, introducing a variety of dishes with a strong Middle Eastern edge. This became my style. Recently I was in the kitchen looking at a box of cauliflower when my mother's cauliflower fritters came to mind, so that was what I cooked. Only then did I realise how much of my cooking is about re-creating the dishes of my childhood.

Our shared history

It was definitely some sort of providence that led us to meet for the first time in London in 1999. Our paths might have crossed plenty of times – we had had many more obvious opportunities to meet before – and yet it was only then, thousands of miles away from where we started, that we got to know each other.

We were both born in Jerusalem in 1968, Sami on the Arab east side and Yotam in the Jewish west. We grew up a few kilometres away from each other in two separate societies, forced together by a fateful war just a year earlier. Looking back now, we realise how extremely different our childhood experiences were and yet how often they converged – physically, when venturing out to the 'other side', and spiritually, sharing sensations of a place and a time.

As young gay adults, we both moved to Tel Aviv at the same time, looking for personal freedom and a sense of hope and normality that Jerusalem couldn't offer. There, we first formed meaningful relationships and took our first steps in our careers. Then, in 1997, we both arrived in London with an aspiration to broaden our horizons even further, possibly to escape again from a place we had grown out of.

So finally, on the doorstep of Baker and Spice in west London, we chatted for thirty minutes before realising that we shared a language and a history. And it was there, over the next two years, that we formed our bond of friendship and creativity.

A short note about ingredients

Unless otherwise stated, eggs are large and free-range, milk is full-fat, yoghurt is Greek and the tahini is one of the creamier Lebanese, Palestinian or Israeli brands available. Parsley is flat-leaf, olive oil is extra-virgin, lemon and lime pith is to be avoided when the zest is shaved, and onions and garlic and shallots are peeled. All meat and fish is organic or free-range. Two types of salt are used through the book: ordinary table salt and flaky sea salt. We refer to the first type as just 'salt' and use Maldon for the sea salt flakes. In the baking recipes, all chocolate has a cocoa solid content of between 52 and 64%.

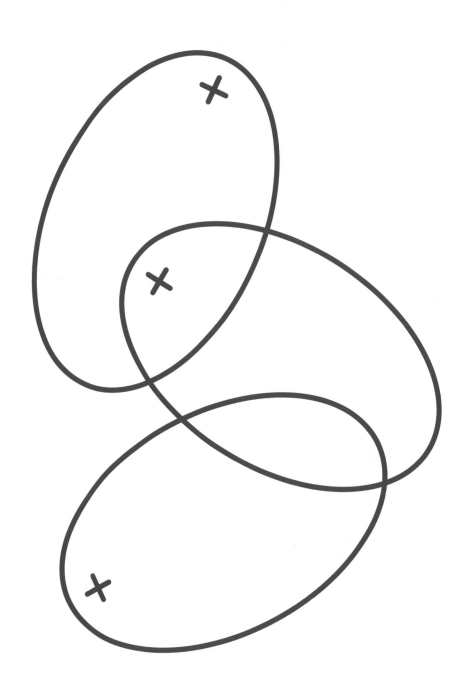

Vegetables, pulses
and grains

———

Peaches and speck with orange blossom

Serves 4–6

Simple starters are so often about the quality of the ingredients. Here, the peaches need to be sweet and juicy, the balsamic vinegar needs to be best-quality (look out for a DOP stamp) and the orange blossom water needs to be unadulterated. We like to use a Lebanese brand like Cortas for the orange blossom: it tastes sweet and perfumed, in a good way.

Get yellow-fleshed peaches, if you can: they tend to be less watery than the white variety, so will chargrill more readily. If you want to skip the grilling stage, though, you can: the salad still works without.

———

Cut the peaches in half and remove the stones. Slice each half into 3 wedges, place in a bowl and add the olive oil and some salt and pepper. Toss well to coat them.

Place a ridged griddle pan over a high heat and leave for a few minutes so it heats up well. Place the peach wedges on the pan and grill for a minute on each side. You want to get nice charcoal lines on all sides. Remove the peaches from the pan and leave to cool.

Place all the dressing ingredients apart from the oil in a bowl and whisk to combine. Trickle the oil in slowly while you whisk to get a thick dressing. Season to taste.

On a serving platter, arrange layers of peach, endive, watercress, chard and speck. Spoon over enough dressing to coat all the ingredients but not to drench them. Serve straight away.

5 ripe peaches

1 tbsp olive oil

2 red or white endives, leaves separated

50g watercress

50g baby chard leaves or other small leaves

10–12 slices speck, thinly sliced (100g)

flaky sea salt and black pepper

Dressing

3 tbsp orange blossom water

1 tbsp good-quality balsamic vinegar

1 tbsp maple syrup

3 tbsp olive oil

Figs with young pecorino and honey

2 tbsp good-quality honey

3 tbsp olive oil

600g ripe green
or black figs

300g young pecorino
(or a similar cheese)

80g rocket, preferably wild

10g basil leaves

flaky sea salt and
black pepper

The quality of the ingredients is paramount here: the figs
need to perfectly ripe, sweet and heavy, the honey needs
to be best-quality and the cheese needs to be as fresh
and young as possible.

'Pecora' means 'sheep' in Italian. Loosely applied,
'pecorino' cheese refers to any cheese made from
sheep's milk. Within this term, of course, there's a huge
range in texture and flavour: it can be young or aged,
salty or sweet, intense or mild, firm or soft. The more the
cheeses age, the drier, denser, firmer and more intense
they'll be. Young, fresh pecorinos, on the other hand –
the type we want here – have a softer texture, with a mild
and milky flavour. It's still got that unmistakably 'sheepy'
tang but is almost sweet. If you can get to a cheese shop
and they have a range, look out for a Pecorino Caciotta
Etrusca Fresca, which we like to use.

Some chunks of salty well-cured ham also work very well
against the sweet figs. For those not inclined to choosing
between one thing and another, the combination of figs,
cheese *and* ham is also rather good!

Whisk together the honey and olive oil and season with salt and
pepper to taste. Cut the figs into quarters. Use your hands to tear
the cheese into large chunks.

Arrange the rocket, basil, figs and pecorino in layers on individual
serving plates or a large platter. Drizzle over the honey dressing as
you go along, and finish with some freshly ground black pepper.

Radish and broad bean salad

Serves 4

This is an ideal brunch dish for a warm spring day. It's a little meal in itself – bulked out with the tahini sauce and bread – but also works without these hearty additions, as a refreshing and colourful salad.

Shelling broad beans is an activity that requires either outsourcing – it's a job that kids love to do – or a meditative stance. If neither are to hand and you are short on time then just leave the podded beans as they are: most – especially the ones sold frozen – are perfectly fine eaten with their skin left on. If you do this then just cook them for a minute longer. You'll lose a bit of the light 'bouncy' texture (and amazingly vibrant colour) but save yourself a lot of time.

———

Place the broad beans in a pan of boiling water and simmer for 1–2 minutes, depending on size. Drain through a large colander and rinse in plenty of cold water to refresh them. Remove the beans from their skins by gently squeezing each one with your fingertips.

Cut the radishes into 6 wedges each and mix with the broad beans, onion, coriander, preserved lemon, lemon juice, parsley, olive oil and cumin. Season with salt and pepper to taste.

To serve, pile a mound of salad in one corner of each serving plate, pour the tahini sauce into a small bowl and stand it next to the salad. Set a pita bread next to them.

500g podded broad beans, fresh or frozen

350g small radishes

½ red onion, very thinly sliced

10g coriander, finely chopped

30g preserved lemon, finely chopped

juice of 2 lemons

10g parsley, finely chopped

3 tbsp olive oil

1 tsp ground cumin

200ml Green tahini sauce (see page 284)

4 thick pita breads

salt and black pepper

Fennel and feta with pomegranate seeds and sumac

½ pomegranate

2 medium fennel heads

1½ tsp olive oil

2 tsp sumac, plus extra to garnish

juice of 1 lemon

10g picked tarragon leaves

10g parsley, roughly chopped

70g Greek feta cheese, sliced

salt and black pepper

This salad has all the little 'bursts of flavour' we look for in a dish. The little explosions of sweetness from the pomegranate seeds, for example, along with the tart astringency of the sumac. It's lovely to eat as it is, or else served alongside some grilled fish or roasted meat. If you're looking for a substitute to the pomegranate but want to keep the colour and sweetness, dried cranberries or sour cherries also work well.

___

Start by releasing the pomegranate seeds. The best way to do it is to halve the pomegranate along its 'belly' (you only need half a pomegranate here), then hold the half firmly in your hand with the seeds facing your palm. Over a large bowl, start bashing the back of the fruit with a wooden spoon. Don't hit too hard or you'll bruise the seeds and break the skin. Magically, the seeds will just fall out. Pick out any white skin that falls in.

Remove the leaves of the fennel, keeping a few to garnish later, and trim the base, making sure you leave enough of it still attached to hold the slices together. Slice very thinly lengthwise (a mandolin would come in handy here).

In a bowl, mix the olive oil, sumac, lemon juice, herbs and some salt and pepper. Add the fennel and toss well. Taste for seasoning but remember, the feta will add saltiness.

Layer the fennel, then the feta and then the pomegranate seeds in individual serving dishes. Garnish with fennel leaves, sprinkle over some sumac and serve immediately.

Cucumber and poppy seed salad

Serves 4

Get hold of the small Lebanese cucumbers for this, if you can: they're more robust, crunchy and full of earthy flavour than the larger, more water-filled varieties commonly sold. Don't worry if you can only get this larger kind, though: just slice it in half lengthways and then use a teaspoon to scoop out the seedy core, which is the part full of water.

This was put on the menu by Sami in the very early days of Ottolenghi. It works well with other salads as part of a mezze spread or served alongside some roast lamb or pork. A few little radishes, quartered, make for a colourful addition.

6 small cucumbers or 1 large cucumber (about 500g)

2 mild red chillies, thinly sliced

15g coriander, roughly chopped

60ml white wine vinegar or rice vinegar

125ml sunflower oil

2 tbsp poppy seeds

2 tbsp caster sugar

salt and black pepper

Chop off and discard the ends of the cucumbers. Slice the cucumbers at an angle, so you end up with pieces 1cm thick and 3–4cm long.

Mix together all the ingredients in a large bowl. Use your hands to massage the flavours gently into the cucumbers. Taste and adjust the amount of sugar and salt according to the quality of the cucumbers. The salad should be sharp and sweet, almost like a pickle.

If not serving immediately, you might need to drain some liquid off later. Adjust the seasoning again afterwards.

Etti's herb salad

35g picked coriander
leaves

40g picked parsley leaves

20g picked dill leaves

35g picked tarragon
leaves

30g picked basil leaves

40g rocket leaves

50g unsalted butter

150g whole unskinned
almonds

2 tbsp lemon juice

1 tbsp olive oil

flaky sea salt and
black pepper

For anyone who curses the instruction to 'pick leaves'
for an Ottolenghi salad, we have chef Etti Mordo to thank
(or blame, depending on your point of view). Etti played
a key part in putting together the menus in the early days
of our Islington restaurant and her influence is still felt
today. If you want to get ahead with picking the leaves,
you can: just keep them in a bowl in the fridge, covered
with a sheet or two of damp kitchen paper. They'll stay
fresh this way.

This is a salad that doesn't benefit from sitting around,
so get everything ready beforehand: the herbs picked
and washed, the almonds fried and chopped, the dressing
ingredients ready to go. With everything in place the salad
should then be assembled literally seconds before serving.
Don't be tempted to do it in advance as the leaves will
wilt and discolour. It's perfect as either a palate-cleansing
starter or served alongside all sorts of mains.

Gently immerse the herb leaves in plenty of cold water, being
careful not to bruise them. Drain in a colander and then dry in
a salad spinner or by spreading them over a clean kitchen cloth.
(Once dry, the herbs will keep in the fridge for up to one day. Store
them in a sealed container lined with a few layers of kitchen paper).

Heat the butter in a frying pan and add the almonds, along with
½ teaspoon each of salt and pepper. Sauté for 5–6 minutes over a
low to moderate heat, until the almonds are golden. Transfer to a
colander to drain. Make sure you keep the butter that's left in the
pan. Leave it somewhere warm so it doesn't set. Once the almonds
are cool enough to handle, chop them roughly with a large knife.

To assemble the salad, place the herbs in a large bowl. Add the
almonds, cooking butter, lemon juice and olive oil. Toss gently
and season to taste, then serve immediately.

Marinated aubergine with tahini and oregano

Serves 6 as a starter

Some combinations are just a match made in Middle Eastern heaven. With roasted wedges of aubergine and creamy tahini sauce, for example, it's hard to go wrong. The fresh oregano needs to be added with slightly more caution: it's great in marinades for roasted vegetables or substantial salads but, as with other hard herbs like rosemary or sage, it's a potent herb that can dominate if used too liberally.

Preheat the oven to 240°C/220°C fan/Gas Mark 9. Trim the stalk end off the aubergines, then cut each aubergine in two widthways. Cut the fat lower piece lengthways in half and then cut each half into 3 wedges. Do the same with the thinner piece but cut each half into 2 wedges. You should end up with 10 similar-sized pieces with skin on their curved side.

Place the aubergine pieces on a large roasting tray. Brush on all sides with plenty of olive oil and season with salt and pepper (if you want to get nice chargrill marks on the aubergines, place them on a very hot ridged griddle pan at this stage and grill for 3 minutes on each side; return them to the baking tray and continue with the next step). Place the roasting tray in the hot oven and bake the aubergines for 15–18 minutes, until they are golden brown and totally soft inside.

While the aubergines are roasting, make the marinade. Simply put all the ingredients in a bowl, along with 1 teaspoon of salt and a good grind of black pepper, and mix well.

As soon as the aubergines come out of the oven, spoon the marinade over them and leave at room temperature for up to 2 hours before serving. You can store them in the fridge for up to 2 days at this stage. Make sure you don't serve them cold, though; leave them out of the fridge for an hour at least.

To serve, arrange the aubergines on a plate. Now, you can either spoon the tahini sauce on top and garnish with a few oregano leaves, or serve the tahini in a bowl on the side, topped with oregano leaves.

3 small aubergines

olive oil, for brushing

1 quantity of Green tahini sauce (see page 284; made without the parsley)

flaky sea salt and black pepper

Marinade

1 mild red chilli, de-seeded and finely chopped

10g coriander, finely chopped

5g oregano, finely chopped, plus a few whole leaves for garnish

1 garlic clove, crushed

3 tbsp lemon juice

60ml olive oil

Burnt aubergine with yellow pepper and red onion

2 medium aubergines

2 yellow or green peppers, halved, de-seeded, core removed and cut into 1.5cm dice

1 medium red onion, roughly chopped

24 cherry tomatoes, halved

40g parsley, roughly chopped

70ml sunflower oil

90ml cider vinegar

1 tbsp ground cumin

flaky sea salt and black pepper

You want the aubergine flesh to be really smoky here. There are three ways to do this. The first – and the one we prefer, although it's the messier option! – is to burn the aubergines directly on the open flame of your gas hob. If you cover the hob surface with aluminium foil before doing so – making holes for the gas heads to come through – you'll save yourself a lot of elbow grease. Ventilating your kitchen well is also another precautionary step we'd recommend. Use long kitchen tongs to turn the aubergines around throughout the charring, so that they're burnt on all sides. The second way to do this, if you have an electric hob, is to just pop them in a chargrill pan, on a very high heat, turning again throughout. This will take longer – about 45 minutes – but the result will be the same. If you want to dispense with the hob altogether you can also pierce them with a sharp knife in a couple of places and then burn them under a very hot grill in the oven, which will take about an hour. Turn them, again, throughout the hour, so that they get grilled on all sides.

This salad – a variation on a classic Tunisian salad – is Sami's mother's recipe. Serve it with a range of other mezze salads, with some large chunks of crusty bread served alongside.

———

Place the aubergines directly on 2 separate moderate flames on the stove and roast for 12–15 minutes, turning them occasionally with metal tongs, until the flesh is soft and the skin is burnt and flaky. By this stage your kitchen will have the most magnificent charred smell. (Alternatively, place the aubergines under a hot grill for about an hour, turning them occasionally and continuing to cook even if they burst.) Leave to cool slightly.

Make a long cut through each warm aubergine. Using a spoon, scoop out the soft flesh while avoiding most of the burnt skin on the outside. If you don't like the seeds, try to avoid them as well. Leave the aubergine flesh to drain in a colander for at least 1 hour or overnight.

Chop the aubergine flesh roughly. Mix all the ingredients together, then taste and adjust the seasoning. It should be robust and pungent. Serve within 24 hours.

Aubergine-wrapped ricotta gnocchi with sage butter

1 small to medium aubergine

60ml olive oil

20g unsalted butter, melted

15g Parmesan cheese, freshly grated

Ricotta gnocchi

30g pine nuts

250g ricotta cheese

2 egg yolks

35g plain flour

40g Parmesan cheese, freshly grated

5g parsley, finely chopped

5g basil, finely shredded

¼ tsp grated nutmeg

salt and black pepper

Sage butter

90g unsalted butter

20 sage leaves

1½ tsp lemon juice (optional)

This was an early creation of Ramael Scully – Scully, as he's known – when he was evening chef in our Islington restaurant. Reflecting on where Scully's imagination has taken him over the years, this dish seems almost quaint in its simplicity. It's no less wonderful for this, though. It is also elegant, and great for a dinner party as the gnocchi can be cooked and wrapped in aubergine the day before, ready for their final sprinkle with cheese before baking.

———

Place the pine nuts in a small frying pan and dry-roast over a medium heat for 3–4 minutes, stirring them occasionally so they colour evenly. Transfer to a large bowl and add the ricotta, egg yolks, flour, grated Parmesan, herbs, nutmeg, ½ teaspoon salt and a good grind of black pepper. Stir well, then cover and refrigerate for 4 hours or overnight.

Preheat the oven to 200°C/180°C fan/Gas Mark 6. Trim the top and bottom off the aubergine and cut it lengthways into 5mm-thick slices; you will need 8–12 slices, depending on how many gnocchi you make. Lay the slices on a baking tray lined with baking parchment and brush liberally with the olive oil. Place in the oven and roast for 10–15 minutes, until tender and golden (alternatively, you could chargrill the aubergine slices over a medium heat for 2–3 minutes on each side).

To shape the gnocchi, wet your hands and scoop out 40–50g portions (about 3 tablespoons). Roll into 8 or 12 elongated barrel shapes. Meanwhile, bring plenty of salted water to the boil in a large saucepan.

Carefully add a few dumplings to the simmering water – don't cook them all at once or they will stick to each other. After about 2 minutes, they should rise to the surface. Using a slotted spoon, transfer them to a tea towel to drain. Pat dry with kitchen paper and brush them with the melted butter.

Once the gnocchi have cooled down, take a strip of aubergine and wrap it around the centre of each one, like a belt. Trim the aubergine so that the seam is at the bottom. Place the gnocchi in a greased ovenproof dish and set aside or refrigerate for up to 24 hours.

When ready to serve, sprinkle the gnocchi with the Parmesan and bake in the oven at 200°C/180°C fan/Gas Mark 6 for 8–10 minutes, until they are heated through.

Meanwhile, quickly make the sage butter sauce, as it needs to coincide with the gnocchi. Place a small saucepan over a moderate heat. Add the butter and allow it to simmer for a few minutes until it turns a golden-brown colour and has a nutty smell. Remove from the heat and carefully add the sage, a pinch of salt and lemon juice, if using. Return to the heat for a few seconds to cook the sage lightly.

Divide the gnocchi between serving plates, pour the hot butter on top with a few sage leaves and serve immediately.

Roasted aubergine with saffron yoghurt

Serves 4

Since this book was first published, this is one of a handful of recipes that readers tell us they cook most. It's a winning one to make for friends as everything can be prepared in advance – the aubergine can be roasted, the saffron yoghurt put together, all the nuts and herbs ready to go – and then just simply assembled before serving. It's also big and bold – both visually and in terms of flavour – which helps add to the 'wow'.

When dressing roasted vegetables with thick sauces like this, we tend to use a large slotted spoon in our shops. Scoop up the sauce with the spoon and then, holding the long handle in one hand (and making sure the spoon head is over the platter), use your other hand to firmly bash the handle a few times. This will, with a tiny bit of practice, help the sauce to fall through the spoon evenly and elegantly on to the vegetables.

———

For the saffron yoghurt, infuse the saffron in the hot water in a small bowl for 5 minutes. Pour the infusion into a bowl containing the yoghurt, garlic, lemon juice, olive oil and some salt. Whisk well to get a smooth, golden sauce. Taste and adjust the salt, if necessary, then chill. This sauce will keep well in the fridge for up to 3 days.

Preheat the oven to 240°C/220°C fan/Gas Mark 9. Place the aubergine slices on a roasting tray, brush with plenty of olive oil on both sides and sprinkle with salt and pepper. Roast for 20–35 minutes, until the slices take on a beautiful light brown colour. Let them cool down. The aubergines will keep in the fridge for 3 days; just let them come to room temperature before serving.

To serve, arrange the aubergine slices on a large plate, slightly overlapping. Drizzle the saffron yoghurt over them, sprinkle with the pine nuts and pomegranate seeds and lay the basil on top.

3 medium aubergines, cut into 2cm-thick round slices or long wedges

olive oil, for brushing

2 tbsp toasted pine nuts

a handful of pomegranate seeds

20 basil leaves

flaky sea salt and black pepper

Saffron yoghurt

a small pinch of saffron strands

3 tbsp hot water

180g Greek yoghurt

1 garlic clove, crushed

2½ tsp lemon juice

3 tbsp olive oil

Chargrilled asparagus, courgettes and manouri

350g cherry tomatoes, halved

140ml olive oil

24 asparagus spears

2 courgettes

200g manouri (or halloumi) cheese, sliced 2cm thick

25g rocket

flaky sea salt and black pepper

Basil oil

75ml olive oil

1 garlic clove, chopped

25g basil leaves

This salad is substantial enough to be a light meal in itself, or it works well served with some simply cooked salmon.

Manouri is a Greek, semi-soft, fresh cheese produced from the drained whey left over after making feta. It's light, creamy and subtle but also keeps its shape when fried. It's not as easy to get hold of as we'd wish, so if you can't find any, use slices of halloumi as an alternative. Another, slightly different, option, is to go for a light and creamy goat's cheese such as Rosary: it doesn't keep its shape when fried, though, so skip on this stage and just add it to the salad as it is.

With thanks to Helen Goh for creating this, in her early days with the team.

———

There is a fair amount of vegetable preparation here before making the basil oil and assembling the salad. Start with the tomatoes. Preheat the oven to 190°C/170°C fan/Gas Mark 5. Mix the tomatoes with 3 tablespoons of the olive oil and season with some salt and pepper. Spread them out on a baking tray lined with baking parchment, skin-side down. Roast in the oven for 50 minutes or until semi-dried. You can leave them there for a bit more or a bit less time, depending on how dry you like them. They will be delicious anyway. Remove from the oven and leave to cool.

Trim the woody bases of the asparagus and blanch for 4 minutes in plenty of boiling water. Drain and refresh under cold water, making sure the spears are completely cold. Drain well again, then transfer to a mixing bowl and toss with 2 tablespoons of the remaining olive oil and some salt and pepper.

Slice the courgettes very thinly lengthwise, using a mandolin (this inexpensive tool will make your kitchen life dramatically easier) or a vegetable peeler. Mix with 1 tablespoon of the olive oil and some salt and pepper.

Place a ridged griddle pan on a high heat and leave there for a few minutes. It should be very hot. Grill the courgettes and asparagus, turning them over after about a minute. You want to get nice char marks on all sides. Remove and leave to cool.

Heat the remaining 3 tablespoons of olive oil in a pan. Fry the manouri cheese for 3 minutes on each side or until it is golden.

Place on kitchen paper to soak up the excess oil. Alternatively, chargrill the cheese on the hot griddle pan for about 2 minutes on each side.

To make the basil oil, blitz all the ingredients along with a pinch of salt and ½ teaspoon black pepper in a blender until smooth. You might need to double the quantity for some blenders to be effective. Keep any extra oil for future salads.

To assemble, arrange the rocket, vegetables and cheese in layers on a flat serving plate. Try to build up the salad whilst showing all the individual components. Drizzle with as much basil oil as you like and serve.

Asparagus and samphire

Serves 4

Samphire – sometimes referred to as 'poor man's asparagus' – grows on tidal stretches of the British coast from June to September. It's salty, tender and juicy, bringing the flavour of the sea to a salad or fish dish in the way that seaweed does. It's not always easy to get hold of, but your fishmonger should be able to get you some when it's in season. Here we combine it with its richer counterpart, asparagus, to create a salad full of flavours and shades of green. The dish can either be a stand-alone starter or served alongside some pan-fried fish.

1 tbsp black sesame seeds (or white, as an alternative)

24 medium-thick asparagus spears

100g samphire, washed

2 tbsp olive oil

1 tbsp sesame oil

1 garlic clove, crushed

5g picked tarragon leaves

flaky sea salt and black pepper

———

Put the sesame seeds in a non-stick pan and place over a medium heat for 2–3 minutes, just to toast them gently. Remove from the heat and set aside.

To cook the greens, fill a large saucepan with plenty of cold water and bring to the boil. You don't need to add salt; samphire is salty enough. Trim the woody bases of the asparagus and put the spears in the boiling water. Blanch for 2–3 minutes, then add the samphire. Cook for another minute, until the asparagus is tender but still firm.

Drain the greens in a large colander and run lots of cold water over them. It's very important to get them completely cold. Leave in the colander to drain and then dry with a kitchen towel.

To finish the salad, put the asparagus and samphire in a bowl and mix with the rest of the ingredients. Toss well, then taste and adjust the seasoning. You might not need any extra salt. Serve straight away, or chill and serve within 24 hours.

French beans and mangetout with hazelnut and orange

400g French beans

400g mangetout

70g unskinned hazelnuts

1 orange

20g chives, roughly chopped

1 garlic clove, crushed

3 tbsp olive oil

2 tbsp hazelnut oil

flaky sea salt and black pepper

This is one of the most frequently cooked dishes in this book. Our customers tell us it's the salad they go back to time and again and it's also been a firm feature on our catering menus in the shops around Christmas and Thanksgiving. It's easy to see what all the fuss is about: it's totally hassle-free to make, for a start. Everything can be made well in advance (the beans can be cooked and chilled a day ahead of serving, if you like) and the recipe also doubles or trebles (or more) well, if you're feeding a crowd. It also looks great – every table needs green! – and has a flavour that is both winning and interesting without, at the same time, dominating everything else it can be served alongside.

Preheat the oven to 200°C/180°C fan/Gas Mark 6. Using a small, sharp knife, trim the stalk ends off the French beans and the mangetout, keeping the two separate. Bring plenty of unsalted water to the boil in a large saucepan – you need lots of space for the beans, as this is crucial for preserving their colour. Blanch the French beans in the water for 4 minutes, then drain into a colander and run them under plenty of tap water until cold. Leave to drain and dry. Repeat with the mangetout, but blanch for only 1 minute.

While the beans are cooking, scatter the hazelnuts over a baking tray and roast in the oven for 10 minutes. Leave until cool enough to handle, then rub them in a clean tea-towel to get rid of most of the skin. Chop the nuts with a large, sharp knife. They should be quite rough; some can even stay whole.

Using a vegetable peeler, remove the zest from the orange in strips, being careful to avoid the bitter white pith. Slice each piece of zest into very thin strips (if you have a citrus zester, you could do the whole job with that).

To assemble the dish, mix all the ingredients together in a bowl, toss gently, then taste and adjust the seasoning with some flaky sea salt and a good grind of black pepper. Serve at room temperature.

Baked artichokes and broad beans

Serves 2–4

4 lemons, plus a few thin lemon slices to finish

2 large globe artichokes

2 bay leaves

2 sprigs of thyme

2 garlic cloves, thinly sliced

1 tbsp pink peppercorns, plus extra to garnish

125ml white wine

60ml olive oil

250g podded broad beans, fresh or frozen

250g podded peas, fresh or frozen

20g parsley, roughly chopped

salt and black pepper

The clash of greens makes this a perfect dish for spring. We love to have it as a starter, with some crusty bread, but it also works well alongside some pan-fried fish. We were inspired to make this by a similar recipe from Claudia Roden, the godmother of Middle Eastern cookery and one of our all-time-great inspirations. Claudia suggests using frozen artichoke bottoms and broad beans as alternatives to fresh. What's good enough for Claudia should certainly be good enough for the rest of us, so feel free to start with frozen if you want to save a bit of time. This keeps well in the fridge for up to a day: just be sure to bring it back to room temperature before serving.

Preheat the oven to 220°C/200°C fan/Gas Mark 7. Juice the lemons and discard all but 2 of the empty lemon halves.

To clean the artichokes, cut off most of the stalk and start removing the tough outer leaves by hand. Once you reach the softer leaves, take a sharp serrated knife and trim off 1–2cm from the top of the artichoke. Cut the artichoke in half lengthways so you can reach the heart and scrape it clean. Use a small, sharp knife to remove all the 'hairs'. Immediately rub the heart with a little lemon juice to prevent it discolouring. Cut each artichoke half into slices 5mm thick. Place in cold water and stir in half the remaining lemon juice.

Drain the artichoke slices and spread them out on a baking tray. Add the remaining lemon juice, the 2 reserved lemon halves and all the rest of the ingredients except the broad beans, peas and parsley. Cover with foil and bake for 45–60 minutes or until the artichokes are tender. Remove from the oven, take off the foil and let the artichokes cool down.

Fill a large saucepan with plenty of cold water and bring to the boil. Add the broad beans and peas and blanch for 2 minutes, then drain in a colander and run under cold water to refresh. Leave in the colander to dry. If the broad beans are large and have tough skins, you may want to remove them. Simply press each one gently with your fingertips until the bean pops out.

Remove the lemon halves from the artichokes. Mix the artichokes with the beans, peas and parsley, and stir in the lemon slices. Taste for salt and pepper, plate, sprinkle with peppercorns and serve.

Sweet broccolini with tofu, sesame and coriander

Serves 4

It now seems very normal for us to bring Asian brushstrokes to an otherwise Middle Eastern canvas when we're thinking about a dish. When Helen Goh first brought this to us, though, it all seemed very novel. This is great served at room temperature, either by itself or alongside some roast chicken or beef.

Kecap manis is a thick, sweet Indonesian soy sauce made from fermented soy beans, palm sugar and spices. It's like the ultimate ketchup, in the best possible sense. You can get it from specialist shops as well as larger supermarkets.

———

First, marinate the tofu. In a bowl, whisk the kecap manis, chilli sauce and sesame oil together. Cut the tofu into strips about 1cm thick, mix gently (so it doesn't break) with the marinade and leave in the fridge for half an hour.

Trim any hard leaves off the broccolini and discard. Place the broccolini in a large saucepan full of boiling water and blanch for 2 minutes. Drain in a colander and run under a cold tap at once to stop further cooking. Leave to dry.

Scatter the sesame seeds in a non-stick pan and place it over a medium heat for about 5 minutes. Jiggle them around so they toast evenly and then remove from the heat.

Place a wok or a thick iron pan over a high heat and allow it to heat up well. Add the groundnut oil. Reduce the heat to medium to prevent the oil spitting (it may spit a little), then carefully add the tofu strips and leave for 2–3 minutes, until they colour underneath. Using tongs, gently turn them over to colour the other side. (If you are making a large quantity, you may need to fry the tofu in 2 or 3 batches, otherwise it will 'stew' rather than fry.)

Add any remaining marinade to the pan, plus the cooked broccolini. Add the coriander and half the sesame seeds and stir together gently. Remove from the heat and let everything come to room temperature in the pan. Taste and add more sesame oil, soy sauce or salt if necessary. Divide between serving plates and sprinkle with the remaining sesame seeds.

3 tbsp kecap manis (sweet soy sauce)

60ml Sriracha (or another savoury chilli sauce)

2 tbsp sesame oil

250g firm tofu (tau kwa)

450g broccolini

1 tbsp sesame seeds

1 tbsp groundnut oil

10g picked coriander leaves

Chargrilled broccoli with chilli and garlic

2 heads of broccoli
(about 500g)

115ml olive oil

4 garlic cloves,
thinly sliced

2 mild red chillies,
thinly sliced

toasted flaked almonds
or very thin slices of lemon
(with skin), to garnish
(optional)

flaky sea salt and
black pepper

If there's one dish our customers won't let us take off the menu, it's this. It's been with us since the day Ottolenghi first opened its doors. Sami started to cook it in Lilith, a restaurant he worked at in Tel Aviv before moving to the UK. He took it to the Baker and Spice kitchens where we first met and then kept it in his suitcase when making the move to set up the Ottolenghi shop. As with so many green vegetables, the secret is to 'blanch, refresh and dry' the florets well so that they keep their bite and colour. Keep an eye, also, on the garlic and chilli: there's a fine line between the golden-brown you want and the overdone you don't.

If you want to add a little extra oomph to the salad, put four chopped anchovy fillets in with the chilli and garlic before they're cooked in the oil.

Prepare the broccoli by separating it into florets (leave on the individual small stems on which the florets grow). Fill a large saucepan with plenty of water and bring to the boil. It should be big enough to accommodate the broccoli easily. Throw in the broccoli and blanch for 2 minutes only. Don't be tempted to cook it any longer! Using a large slotted spoon, quickly transfer the broccoli to a bowl full of ice-cold water – you need to stop the cooking at once. Drain in a colander and allow to dry completely. It is important that the broccoli isn't wet at all. In a mixing bowl, toss the broccoli with 45ml of the olive oil and a generous amount of salt and pepper.

Place a ridged griddle pan over a high heat and leave it there for at least 5 minutes, until it is extremely hot. Depending on the size of your pan, grill the broccoli in several batches. The florets mustn't be cramped. Turn them around as they grill so they get char marks all over. Transfer to a heatproof bowl and continue with another batch.

While grilling the broccoli, place the rest of the oil in a small saucepan with the garlic and chillies. Cook them over a medium heat until the garlic just begins to turn golden brown. Be careful not to let the garlic and chilli burn – remember, they will keep on cooking even when off the heat. Pour the oil, garlic and chilli over the hot broccoli and toss together well. Taste and adjust the seasoning.

Serve warm or at room temperature. You can garnish the broccoli with almonds or lemon just before serving, if you like.

Purple sprouting broccoli and salsify with caper butter

juice of 2½ lemons

4 salsify (or scorzonera) roots

600g purple sprouting broccoli, trimmed (or broccolini, as an alternative)

100g unsalted butter

2 tbsp baby capers, drained

10g chives, finely chopped

10g parsley, finely chopped

10g tarragon, finely chopped

10g dill, roughly chopped

salt and black pepper

There are a lot of white root vegetables that need, well, a bit more rooting for. Turnip, kohlrabi, swede: it's easy for these to quite literally pale in comparison with the vibrant colours of their orange and purple root relatives. Salsify is another example: its long, pale white root can look positively unprepossessing compared to, say, a bright orange carrot. It's very much worth seeking out, though: the stem has a delicate, earthy – almost 'oystery' – flavour when cooked.

You can prepare the salsify and broccoli in advance, but the dish needs to be put together at the last minute and served warm. It makes for an impressive starter.

———

Bring a pan of salted water to the boil with 2 tablespoons of the lemon juice. Peel the salsify and cut each one into 3 batons. Add to the boiling water and simmer for 10 minutes or until al dente. Remove from the water with a slotted spoon and allow to cool a little. Cut each baton in half lengthwise and then the same way again.

Simmer the broccoli in the same water for 3 minutes, until slightly tenderised, then drain and keep warm. (You can stop at this stage and do the rest just before serving; if you choose to do this, you will need to refresh the broccoli under cold water after draining and then reheat it before serving by quickly tossing it with a little oil in a small pan).

Heat half the butter in a frying pan over a medium heat. When it is foaming, add the salsify and fry until golden brown. Season with salt and pepper, then remove from the pan and arrange on serving plates with the broccoli. Give it height by shaping it like a pyramid. Keep in a warm place.

To make the caper butter sauce, reheat the frying pan until nearly smoking. Throw in the remaining butter and cook it from gold to a nut brown. Be brave! When you reach the right colour, take the pan off the heat and gently pour in the remaining lemon juice. Be careful, it will spit. Throw in the capers and herbs and season well.

Immediately pour the caper butter over the arranged vegetables and serve.

Baked okra with tomato and ginger

Serves 2–4

This is one of our go-to easy supper recipes at the end of a day's work. It's easy, comforting and full of fresh flavour. You can eat it either as it is or served alongside some plain rice. For anyone who associates okra with the 'sliminess' that can result from the pods being sliced open, do try this. Baking the pods whole – just lightly trimmed at the top – means that all the 'slimy' seeds are kept contained within the pods.

———

Preheat the oven to 220°C/200°C fan/Gas Mark 7. To prepare the okra, take a small, sharp knife and carefully remove the stalk end. Try not to cut very low; leave the end of the stalk to seal the main body of the fruit, so the seeds are not exposed.

Mix the okra with 3 tablespoons of the olive oil and some salt and pepper. Scatter in a roasting tray in a single layer, then place in the oven and bake for 15–20 minutes, until just tender.

Meanwhile, prepare the sauce. Heat the remaining oil in a large saucepan, add the garlic, ginger and chilli flakes and fry for about a minute. Add the tomatoes, sugar and some salt and pepper and cook, uncovered, over a medium heat for 10 minutes, until the mixture thickens slightly.

When the okra is ready, stir it gently into the sauce and cook for 2 minutes. To serve warm, spoon the okra on to serving plates and scatter the coriander on top. If serving at room temperature, adjust the seasoning again before serving and garnish with the coriander.

500g okra

75ml olive oil

2 garlic cloves, crushed

3cm piece of ginger, finely chopped

¼ tsp dried chilli flakes

3 large ripe tomatoes, finely chopped

2 tsp caster sugar

5g picked coriander leaves

salt and black pepper

Roasted butternut squash with burnt aubergine and pomegranate molasses

Serves 2–4

Roasted wedges of butternut squash are a staple in the Ottolenghi kitchen. We've paired them with all sorts of flavours over the years but return often to the pumpkin's old friends: burnt aubergine and pomegranate molasses. Don't be tempted to peel the squash: the skin is much softer than with other pumpkins so it's lovely to eat as it is. It also helps the wedges stay together when roasting.

———

Preheat the oven to 240°C/220°C fan/Gas Mark 9. Trim the top and bottom off the butternut squash and cut it in half lengthways. Remove the seeds using a small knife or a spoon. Cut each half into wedges 2–3cm thick. Arrange the wedges in a roasting tray, standing them up with the skin underneath if possible. Brush with half the olive oil and season generously with salt and pepper. Place in the oven for 25–30 minutes, by which time the wedges should be tender and slightly browned. Leave to cool.

Reduce the oven temperature to 200°C/180°C fan/Gas Mark 6. Scatter the seeds and almonds on a roasting tray and toast for 8–10 minutes, until lightly browned. Leave to cool.

For the sauce, place the aubergine directly on a moderate flame on a gas hob (see page 42). Burn the aubergine for 12–15 minutes, until the skin dries and cracks and smoky aromas are released. Turn it around occasionally, using metal tongs. Remove from the heat and leave to cool slightly. (Alternatively, you can place the aubergine under a very hot grill for about an hour, turning it around occasionally; continue until burnt on the outside, even if it bursts.)

Make a long cut through the aubergine. Using a spoon, scoop out the soft flesh while avoiding most of the burnt skin. Drain in a colander for 10 minutes, then transfer to a board and chop roughly.

In a mixing bowl stir together the aubergine flesh, yoghurt, oil, pomegranate molasses, lemon juice, parsley and garlic. Taste and season with salt and pepper. It should be sweetly sharp and highly flavoursome.

Arrange the squash wedges on a serving platter, piling them up on top of each other. Drizzle with the remaining olive oil, sprinkle the nuts and seeds over and garnish with the basil. Serve the sauce on the side.

1 large butternut squash

60ml olive oil

1 tbsp pumpkin seeds

1 tbsp sunflower seeds

1 tbsp black sesame seeds (or white, as an alternative)

1 tsp nigella seeds

10g flaked almonds

10g basil leaves

flaky sea salt and black pepper

Sauce

1 medium aubergine

150g Greek yoghurt, at room temperature

2 tbsp olive oil

1½ tsp pomegranate molasses

3 tbsp lemon juice

5g parsley, roughly chopped

1 garlic clove, crushed

Serves 6

Caramelised endive with Serrano ham

6 endives, cut in half
lengthways

40g unsalted butter

4 tsp caster sugar

50g sourdough
breadcrumbs

70g Parmesan cheese,
freshly grated

10g picked thyme leaves

120ml whipping cream

12 thin slices of
Serrano ham

olive oil, for drizzling

5g parsley, roughly
chopped (optional)

flaky sea salt and
black pepper

These are the ultimate starter, perfect with a glass of sherry or red wine on a cold winter's night. They're salty, sweet, crunchy, creamy and very decidedly moreish. Serrano ham is a mild and salty dry-cured ham from Spain. If you can't get hold of any then Italian Prosciutto also works well.

Thanks to Nir Feller, who developed the recipe whilst running our kitchen in Notting Hill.

———

Preheat the oven to 220°C/200°C fan/Gas Mark 7. Begin by caramelising the endive. You will probably have to do it in 2–3 batches, depending on the size of your largest frying pan; the endive halves need to fit lying flat without overlapping. If working in 2 batches, put half the butter and half the sugar in the pan and place over a high heat. Stir to mix. As soon as the butter starts to bubble, place 6 endive halves facing down in the pan and fry for 2–3 minutes, until golden. You might need to press them down slightly. Don't worry if the butter goes slightly brown. Remove and repeat the process with the remaining butter, sugar and 6 endive halves.

Line a baking tray with baking parchment and arrange the endives on it, caramelised side facing up. Sprinkle with a little salt and pepper.

Mix the breadcrumbs, Parmesan, thyme, cream, ¼ teaspoon salt and a good grind of black pepper. Spoon this mixture over the endives and top each one with a slice of ham. Roast in the oven for 15–20 minutes, until the endives feel soft when poked with a knife. Serve hot or warm, drizzled with some olive oil and sprinkled with the chopped parsley, if using.

Cauliflower and cumin fritters with lime yoghurt

Serves 4

These addictive fritters are Sami's mother's recipe. She used to make them once a week and give them to the kids in a pita to take to school for lunch. They're as good today for grown-up kids, keeping well for those who still like their lunch in a Tupperware, either at work or on a picnic. Don't forget the pita, of course, along with some hummus and tomato.

———

Put all the sauce ingredients in a bowl and whisk well. Taste – looking for a vibrant, tart, citrusy flavour – and adjust the seasoning. Chill or leave out for up to an hour.

To prepare the cauliflower, trim off any leaves and use a small knife to divide the cauliflower into little florets. Add them to a large pan of boiling salted water and simmer for 15 minutes or until very soft. Drain into a colander.

While the cauliflower is cooking, put the flour, chopped parsley, garlic, shallots, eggs, spices, 1½ teaspoons of salt and 1 teaspoon of black pepper in a bowl and whisk together well to make a batter. When the mixture is smooth and homogenous, add the warm cauliflower. Mix to break down the cauliflower into the batter.

Pour the sunflower oil into a wide pan to a depth of 1.5cm and heat up. When it is very hot, carefully spoon in generous portions of the cauliflower mixture, 3 tablespoons per fritter. Take care with the hot oil! Space the fritters apart with a fish slice, making sure they are not overcrowded. Fry in small batches, controlling the oil temperature so the fritters cook but don't burn. They should take 3–4 minutes on each side.

Remove from the pan and drain well on a few layers of kitchen paper. Serve scattered with parsley leaves and with the sauce on the side.

1 small cauliflower (about 320g)

120g plain flour

15g parsley, roughly chopped, plus a few extra leaves to garnish

1 garlic clove, crushed

2 shallots, finely chopped

4 eggs

1½ tsp ground cumin

1 tsp ground cinnamon

½ tsp ground turmeric

500ml sunflower oil, for frying

salt and black pepper

Lime sauce

300g Greek yoghurt

10g coriander, finely chopped

finely grated zest of 1 lime

2 tbsp lime juice

2 tbsp olive oil

Serves 2–4

Chargrilled cauliflower with tomato, dill and capers

2 tbsp capers, drained and roughly chopped

1 tbsp French wholegrain mustard

2 garlic cloves, crushed

2 tbsp cider vinegar

120ml olive oil

1 small cauliflower, divided into florets

5g dill, roughly chopped, plus extra to garnish

50g baby spinach leaves

20 cherry tomatoes, halved

flaky sea salt and black pepper

It's not just broccoli florets that benefit from being blanched, refreshed, dried and then chargrilled. Doing this also allows cauliflower to retain its bite, colour and flavour, as well as preparing it for getting the black stripes we like to think of as our trademark. Although it all sounds like a bit of an effort, it's really not. Particularly given how un-time-sensitive it all is. Do the blanching and refreshing in the morning, if you like (or even the day before) and then chargrill later, after the cauliflower has been set aside to dry. The whole salad can also be put together well in advance of serving. The end result is lovely as it is or served with a roasted chicken, or alongside a selection of other salads.

———

First make the dressing, either by hand or in a food processor. Mix together the capers, mustard, garlic, vinegar and some salt and pepper. Whisk vigorously or run the machine while adding half the oil in a slow trickle. You should get a thick, creamy dressing. Taste and adjust the seasoning.

Add the cauliflower florets to a large pan of boiling salted water and simmer for 3 minutes only. Drain in a colander and immediately run under a cold tap to stop the cooking. Leave in the colander to dry well. Once dry, place in a mixing bowl with the remaining olive oil and some salt and pepper. Toss well.

Place a ridged griddle pan over the highest possible heat and leave it for 5 minutes or until very hot. Grill the cauliflower in a few batches – make sure the florets are not cramped. Turn them around as they grill, then once nicely charred, transfer to a bowl. While the cauliflower is still hot, add the dressing, dill, spinach and tomatoes. Stir together well, then taste and adjust the seasoning.

Serve warm or at room temperature, adjusting the seasoning again at the last minute.

Fennel, cherry tomato and crumble gratin

Serves 6–8

Given the huge amounts of food coming out of our Notting Hill kitchen, visitors are always amazed to see how small it is. Its size has both disadvantages and advantages. On the one hand, sharing such small quarters can sometimes lead to extraordinary kinds of personal interaction. The occasional tense moment has been had over the years between the savoury chefs on one 'side' of the kitchen and the pastry department on the other.

On a culinary level, however, working so closely together can be an advantage, leading to the creation of some unusual hybrids. Using the pastry department's crumble mix for this gratin, for example, was originally Sami's 'revenge' for some freshly squeezed lemon juice that was 'stolen' by a pastry chef to make curd. It turned out that the creamy sweetness of the crumble offsets the dominant savoury tones of the fennel and the acidity of the tomato to create a most comforting experience. Inspiration for recipes comes from all sorts of places.

You can make this up well in advance, sitting ready to put in the oven at the last minute.

1kg fennel bulbs

3 tbsp olive oil

5g picked thyme leaves, plus a few whole sprigs

3 garlic cloves, crushed

200ml whipping cream

⅓ quantity of Crumble (see page 291)

100g Parmesan cheese, freshly grated

300g cherry tomatoes, on the vine

5g parsley, finely chopped

flaky sea salt and black pepper

Preheat the oven to 220°C/200°C fan/Gas Mark 7. Trim off the fennel stalks and cut each bulb in half lengthways. Cut each half into slices 1.5cm thick. Place in a large bowl with the olive oil, thyme leaves, garlic, 1 tablespoon of salt and 1 teaspoon of black pepper and toss together. Transfer to an ovenproof dish and pour the cream over the fennel. Mix the crumble with the grated Parmesan and scatter evenly on top.

Cover the dish with foil and bake for 45 minutes. Remove the foil and arrange the tomatoes on top. You can leave some on the vine and scatter some loose. Scatter a few thyme sprigs on top. Return to the oven and bake for another 15 minutes. By now the fennel should feel soft when poked with a knife and the gratin should have a nice golden colour. Remove from the oven and allow to rest for a few minutes. Sprinkle chopped parsley over and serve hot or warm.

Marinated romano peppers with buffalo mozzarella

6 romano peppers

120ml olive oil

5g coriander, finely chopped

5g parsley, finely chopped, plus extra to garnish

1 garlic clove, crushed

3 tbsp cider vinegar

100g rocket

200g buffalo mozzarella

flaky sea salt and black pepper

This is a really versatile dish: lovely for either a stand-alone starter, as part of a mezze selection or else made into a vegetarian main served with some nutty brown rice.

We like to maintain the long pointy shape of the romano peppers, so don't peel them when they're roasted. It means you'll have a bit of skin and some seeds on the plate, though, so if you don't want these, just roast the peppers for an extra 10 minutes and then place them in a bowl – sealed with cling film – to cool down before peeling them and removing the seeds. The peppers will disintegrate slightly but the skin and seeds won't be there.

Use the best-quality mozzarella you can for this, so that it can hold its own against the other ingredients. Feta or small pieces of Parmesan also work well, if you're looking for an alternative.

If you want to get ahead, the peppers can be marinated well ahead of time – even the day before, if you like – and the dish assembled just before serving.

———

Preheat the oven to 220°C/200°C fan/Gas Mark 7. Spread the peppers out on a roasting tray, drizzle with 2 tablespoons of the olive oil and sprinkle with salt and pepper. Mix well and roast for 12–15 minutes, until the peppers become tender and their skin begins to colour.

Meanwhile, mix together the coriander, parsley, garlic, vinegar and 80ml of the olive oil. Season liberally and taste to make sure the flavours are robust. Put the warm peppers in a bowl, pour the marinade over them, then cover and leave at room temperature for at least 2 hours.

To serve, lay out the peppers and rocket on a serving plate and spoon the marinade over them. Break the mozzarella into large chunks with your hands and dot it over the peppers. Drizzle with the remaining oil and garnish with parsley.

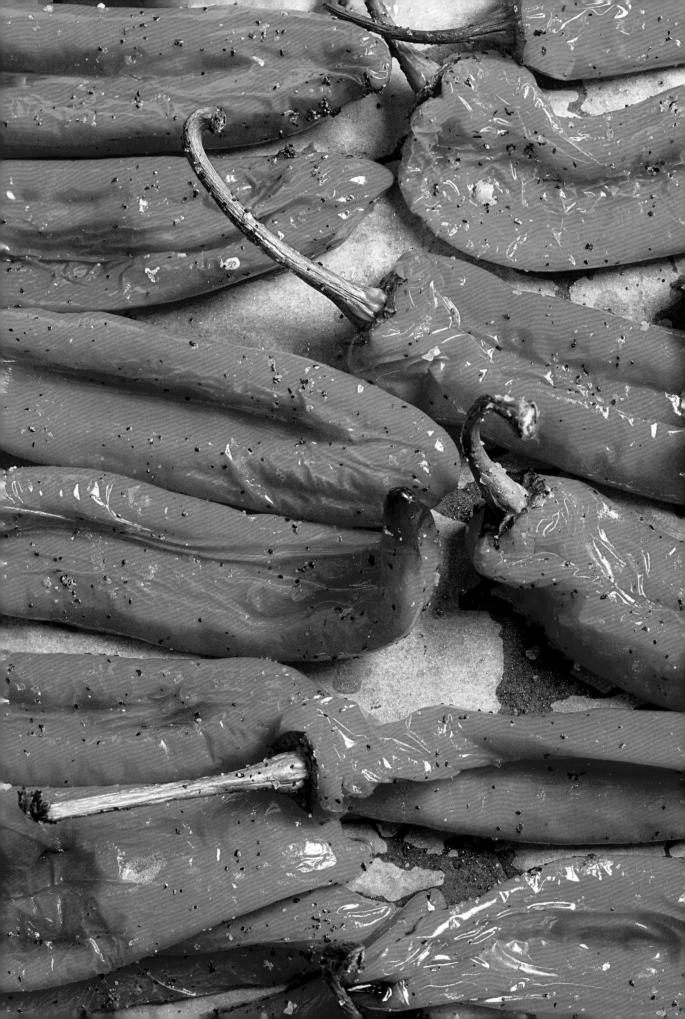

Mixed mushrooms with cinnamon and lemon

Serves 6–8

This bold treatment for mushrooms, with its sharp intensity of flavours, makes for a hearty starter. Some chunks of crusty bread are needed alongside, to soak up the juices. Any leftovers, if you have them, can be warmed through over the next couple of days and served alongside scrambled eggs. Don't restrict yourself to the types of mushrooms specified – mix and match to suit your taste. Don't be alarmed by the amount of salt needed, either: there are a lot of mushrooms in the pan, all thirsty for the seasoning.

———

First you will need to pick through the mushrooms, paring away dirt from the feet of the mushrooms and using a stiff pastry brush to clear any dirt from the caps and gills (don't be tempted to clean them in a bucket of water, as they will absorb the water and go soggy).

Put a large sauté pan over a medium heat and add the olive oil to heat it slightly. Sprinkle in the thyme, garlic, parsley and cinnamon sticks, salt and pepper. Lay the button, chestnut and shiitake mushrooms on top. Do not stir. Turn the heat up high and cook for 5 minutes. Only then give the pan a good shake and add the oyster mushrooms. Give a little stir and leave to cook for another 3 minutes. Turn off the heat and add the enoki mushrooms, followed by the lemon juice. Give the pan another good shake around, taste and add more salt and pepper if necessary. Serve warm or at room temperature.

400g button mushrooms
400g chestnut mushrooms
300g shiitake mushrooms
400g oyster mushrooms
200g enoki mushrooms
160ml olive oil
30g chopped thyme
10 garlic cloves, crushed
100g parsley, chopped
6 cinnamon sticks
25g flaky sea salt
1 tbsp black pepper
60ml lemon juice

Portobello mushrooms with pearl barley and preserved lemon

100g unsalted butter

15g thyme sprigs

6 large Portobello mushrooms

180ml dry white wine

250ml vegetable stock

2 garlic cloves, finely sliced

flaky sea salt and black pepper

Pearl barley

1 tbsp sunflower oil

1 medium onion, finely chopped

1 garlic clove, finely chopped

750ml vegetable or chicken stock

110g pearl barley

1 quarter of preserved lemon, flesh removed and skin finely chopped

50g feta cheese, crumbled

5g parsley, roughly chopped

5g picked thyme leaves

10g purple basil sprouts, radish sprouts, or purple basil leaves, shredded

1 tbsp olive oil

Scully's been cooking in the Ottolenghi and NOPI kitchens for a long time. He brings a great deal to the stove, including butter. Butter has gone in and out of fashion through the years; for Scully, it never went away. Here, what seems like a lot of butter is put to good work, helping the mushrooms absorb a ton of flavour. They are then served with our favourite sort of topping: one that is both comforting, soothing and surprising all at once.

If you are buying preserved lemons, you'll have a choice between the larger kind with thicker skin or else the smaller variety (more widely on sale) with a soft, thin skin. We tend to prefer the boldness of the thick-skinned type but either will work well: if you go for the smaller lemons you'll need the finely chopped skin of one whole lemon, rather than the quarter listed. Preserving a batch of your own lemons (see page 286) is also easy and rewarding, if you're planning ahead.

First cook the barley. Heat the sunflower oil in a heavy-based saucepan and sauté the onion and garlic until translucent. Add the stock and bring to the boil. Stir in the barley, reduce the heat, then cover and simmer for 1 hour, until all the liquid has been absorbed and the barley is tender.

Meanwhile, preheat the oven to 200°C/180°C fan/Gas Mark 6. Take a large baking tray and grease it heavily with two-thirds of the butter. Scatter the sprigs of thyme over it and place the mushrooms on top, stem-side up. Pour over the wine and stock and scatter the sliced garlic over. Dot each mushroom with a couple of knobs of the remaining butter, then season with salt and pepper. Cover the tray with foil and place in the oven for 15–20 minutes, until the mushrooms are tender. Leave them in their cooking juices until you are ready to serve.

When the barley is done, remove the pan from the heat and stir in the preserved lemon, feta, parsley and thyme. Taste and add salt and pepper. To serve, reheat the mushrooms in the oven for a few minutes, if necessary. Place each mushroom on a serving plate, stem-side up. Scoop the barley on top and spoon some of the mushroom cooking juices over. Garnish with the basil and drizzle over the olive oil.

Roasted red and golden beetroot

500g golden beetroot

500g red beetroot

80g sunflower seeds

90ml maple syrup

60ml sherry vinegar

60ml olive oil

2 garlic cloves, crushed

20g chervil leaves,
plus more to garnish

60g baby chard leaves,
baby spinach or rocket

flaky sea salt and
black pepper

Whenever we can, we love to clash colours. A riot of tomatoes, carrots or, as here, beetroot is just such an effective way to make a simple dish sing. We've suggested a mix of golden and red beetroot but add some pink candied to the mix as well, if you can: with their pink-and-white pinwheels, they are the rock candy of the vegetable world. On the other hand, the dish also works well if you can only get hold of one colour of beetroot.

This salad (which keeps well in the fridge for up to 2 days) is perfect served alongside some oily fish. You can also bulk it up into a stand-alone meal, if you like, by dotting through some ricotta or soft goat's cheese just before serving.

———

Preheat the oven to 220°C/200°C fan/Gas Mark 7. Wash the beetroot well and wrap them in foil individually. Bake in the oven for anything from 40 to 90 minutes, depending on their size (baby beetroot might take even less). Check each one, as cooking times can vary a lot: the beetroot should be tender when pierced with a sharp knife.

Spread the sunflower seeds out in an ovenproof dish and toast in the oven alongside the beetroot for 8 minutes, just until lightly coloured.

Once the beetroot are ready, unwrap them and peel with a small knife while still warm. Cut each into halves, quarters or 2–3cm dice. Mix the beetroot with the rest of the ingredients in a bowl. Toss well and then taste: there should be a clear sweetness balanced by enough salt. Adjust the seasoning if necessary, plate, sprinkle with more chervil and serve.

Serves 6

Crushed new potatoes
with horseradish and sorrel

1kg new potatoes

300g Greek yoghurt

100ml olive oil,
plus extra for drizzling

2 garlic cloves, crushed

25g fresh horseradish
root, grated

20g sorrel leaves, roughly
chopped

25g garden cress
(or another small
sprouting leaf)

2 spring onions, sliced

flaky sea salt and
black pepper

This sits somewhere between a mash and a potato salad and benefits from being more interesting than either. It can either be eaten warm or – if you want to make it ahead for big gatherings – at room temperature. It's a great one to add to a big spread of food, working alongside all sorts of other dishes: baked salmon or roast beef, for example.

Sorrel is a leaf with a really lemony kick. We love it, but even when it's in season through the summer months it's not always that easy to find. If you're looking for an alternative, rocket leaves can be used instead, with a squeeze of lemon to give the dish that kick. Similarly, if you can't get hold of fresh horseradish then use horseradish (or even wasabi) paste instead, adjusting the amount to a level of heat that you like.

—

Wash the potatoes well but don't peel them. Put them in a pan with plenty of salted water, bring to the boil and simmer for 25–30 minutes, until tender. Drain well, transfer to a large mixing bowl and, while they are still hot, crush them well with a fork or a potato masher. Make sure most of the hard lumps are crushed.

In another bowl, mix together the yoghurt, olive oil, garlic, horseradish and salt and pepper to taste. Pour this dressing over the hot potatoes, add the sorrel and mix well. Taste and adjust the seasoning.

Just before serving, garnish with the cress, spring onions and a drizzle of olive oil.

Sweet and sour celeriac and swede

Serves 4–6

We've gone for two white root vegetables here – the celeriac and the swede – but feel free to play around with colour, depending on what vegetables you have. Beetroots, carrots, turnips, cabbage, kohlrabi: these all – separately or in combination – work very well. This wintery slaw is exactly what's needed to enliven all sorts of hearty dishes. It's got a savoury tang from the capers and lemon but also a soft sweetness from the herbs and cherries. It's the perfect way to cut through any rich oily fish or roast meat.

Use a mandolin, if you have one, to help slice the vegetables as thinly as you want them to be. Once they've been thinly sliced, it's then easy to turn them into matchsticks using a large sharp knife.

———

Place the julienned celeriac and swede in a mixing bowl. Add all the rest of the ingredients and use your hands to mix everything together thoroughly. 'Massaging' the vegetables a little will help them absorb the flavours. Taste and add salt and pepper to your liking. You might also want to add some extra sugar and vinegar.

Allow the salad to sit for an hour so the flavours can evolve. It will keep for up to 2 days in the fridge. Add more herbs just before serving, for a fresher look.

250g celeriac, peeled and julienned

250g swede, peeled and julienned

20g parsley, roughly chopped

20g dill, roughly chopped

50g capers, drained and roughly chopped

60ml lemon juice

1 tsp cider vinegar

60ml olive oil

60ml sunflower oil

1 tbsp Dijon mustard

2 garlic cloves, crushed

2 tsp caster sugar

100g dried sour cherries

salt and black pepper

Parsnip and pumpkin mash

1 large pumpkin or
butternut squash, cut
into 2–3cm dice (600g)

3 tbsp olive oil,
plus extra for drizzling

1 head of garlic

5 medium parsnips,
peeled and cut into
large chunks

200ml sunflower oil

2 onions, sliced into
pinwheels

80g unsalted butter

1 tsp ground nutmeg

300g crème fraîche,
at room temperature

15g chives, roughly
chopped

salt and black pepper

There's a lovely contrast in textures, flavours and colours here, from the sweet creamy mash on the one hand to the darkly crisp onion on the other. Root vegetables are often interchangeable, depending on what you have, so feel free to use turnip, celeriac, potato, carrot or sweet potato instead of the parsnip or pumpkin. It's nice to keep the clash of colours, though, if you can. This is a dish made for the Thanksgiving or Christmas table but it is just as great throughout the year, served alongside any roasted bird.

———

Preheat the oven to 220°C/200°C fan/Gas Mark 7. Toss the pumpkin or squash with the olive oil and a little salt and pepper and spread out in a roasting tray. Roast for 30–45 minutes, until soft and mashable. Once out of the oven, keep somewhere warm. Meanwhile, using a good serrated knife, cut about 1cm off the top of the garlic head and place the bottom part in the oven next to the roasting pumpkin. Bake it for approximately 30 minutes, until the cloves are completely tender.

While the pumpkin is roasting, cook the parsnips in boiling salted water for 30 minutes, until they are completely soft. Drain and keep warm. Pour the sunflower oil into a medium saucepan, heat well and fry the onion rings in it in 2–3 batches. They should turn brown, almost burnt. Transfer to a colander and sprinkle with salt.

Take a large bowl that can accommodate the whole mixture. Hold the bottom of the head of garlic and gently press upwards to release the cooked flesh into the bowl. Add the butter, nutmeg, some seasoning and then the parsnips. Crush well, using a potato masher. Add the cooked pumpkin and mash very lightly (use a fork). Don't over-mix; the mash should remain chunky and the pumpkin and parsnip distinct.

Gently fold in the crème fraîche and chives to form a ripple in the mash. Spoon a mound on to each serving plate, garnish with the fried onions and a drizzle of olive oil and serve at once.

Roasted sweet potato with pecan and maple

Serves 4

We know there's a lot of sweetness going on in this dish: the potatoes are sweet enough as they are, before the maple syrup and sultanas have even been added. Trust us, though (and all the Americans who put a version of this on their table at Thanksgiving): there's enough of a kick being given by all the other ingredients for the dish to retain its balance. This is most at home alongside a roast turkey but also works well as the main feature of a dish, served alongside some couscous or quinoa.

———

Preheat the oven to 210°C/190°C fan/Gas Mark 6. Start with the sweet potatoes. Don't peel them! Cut them into 2cm cubes, spread them out on a baking tray and drizzle with the olive oil. Sprinkle with some salt and pepper, mix well with your hands and then roast in the oven for about 30 minutes, until just tender. Turn them over gently half way through cooking.

In a separate baking tray, toast the pecans for 5 minutes. Remove from the oven and chop roughly.

To make the dressing, whisk together all the ingredients in a small bowl with some salt and pepper. Taste and adjust the seasoning, if necessary.

When the potatoes are ready, transfer them to a large bowl while still hot. Add the spring onions, parsley, coriander, chilli, pecans and sultanas. Pour the dressing over and toss gently to blend, then season to taste. Serve at once or at room temperature.

2 sweet potatoes (about 850g)

3 tbsp olive oil

35g pecan halves

4 spring onions, roughly chopped

20g parsley, roughly chopped

20g coriander, roughly chopped

¼ tsp dried chilli flakes

35g sultanas

salt and black pepper

Dressing

60ml olive oil

2 tbsp maple syrup

1 tbsp sherry vinegar

1 tbsp lemon juice

2 tbsp orange juice

2 tsp grated ginger

½ tsp ground cinnamon

VEGETABLES, PULSES AND GRAINS

Carrot and peas

Serves 6

When we first started cooking in the UK, a dish we called 'carrot and peas' had to work hard to get over the association it carried of 'soggy' carrots and 'mushy' peas. All these years on, the secret to cooking young fresh vegetables is not so secret anymore. It's all about just *undercooking* them so that they maintain their bite and vibrant colour. This dish – singing in natural sweetness, bright in all its colour – is at home served either with a hot festive meal or as a light spring salad.

Start by making the sweet sauce for roasting the carrots. Pour the orange juice, wine and honey into a saucepan, add the cinnamon and star anise and bring to a simmer. Cook gently, uncovered, for 20–40 minutes (depending on the size of your pan and the heat level), until reduced to about a third. Set aside.

Preheat the oven to 250°C/230°C fan/Gas Mark 9. Heat a small frying pan, add the coriander seeds and dry toast them over a high heat for about 3 minutes. Put the seeds in a bowl and mix with the carrots, olive oil, garlic and some salt and pepper. Spread the mixture out on a large baking tray and put in the oven. After about 15 minutes (the carrots should have taken on some serious colour by now), remove the tray carefully, add the sweet sauce (including the cinnamon and star anise), stir well and return to the oven for about 7 minutes, until the carrots are cooked through but still have a bit of bite. Remove from the oven and allow them to cool down.

Throw the peas into a pot containing plenty of boiling salted water and simmer for a minute. Drain at once into a colander, run under a cold tap to stop the cooking and then leave to drain thoroughly.

Before serving, gently stir together the carrots and peas. Taste and add more salt and pepper if you like. Dot with the pea shoots as you pile the vegetables on to a serving plate.

130ml orange juice

60ml red wine

50g honey

2 cinnamon sticks

4 star anise

1½ tsp coriander seeds

1kg carrots, peeled and cut on an angle into 1cm-thick slices

90ml olive oil

3 garlic cloves, crushed

450g podded peas, fresh or frozen

75g pea shoots (or lamb's lettuce, as an alternative)

salt and black pepper

Danielle's sweet potato gratin

6 medium sweet potatoes (about 1.5kg)

25g sage, roughly chopped, plus extra to garnish

6 garlic cloves, crushed

250ml whipping cream

flaky sea salt and black pepper

This is both a hugely comforting and really elegant dish: a great addition to the table for a leisurely weekend lunch. Everything can be prepared the day before serving, if you like: just keep it in the fridge and then it's all ready to go in the oven. Use a mandolin, if you have one: it'll make slicing the potatoes into neat round discs much easier.

With thanks to Danielle Postma for developing this in the early years of Ottolenghi. It continues to make us smile, as she always did.

———

Preheat the oven to 220°C/200°C fan/Gas Mark 7. Wash the sweet potatoes (do not peel them) and cut them into discs 5mm thick. A mandolin is best for this job but you could use a sharp knife.

In a bowl, mix together the sweet potatoes, sage, garlic, 2 teaspoons of salt and a good grind of black pepper. Arrange the slices of sweet potato in a deep, medium-sized ovenproof dish by taking tight packs of them and standing them up next to each other. They should fit together quite tightly so you get parallel lines of sweet potato slices (skins showing) along the length or width of the dish. Throw any remaining bits of garlic or sage from the bowl over the potatoes. Cover the dish with foil, place in the oven and roast for 45 minutes. Remove the foil and pour the cream evenly over the potatoes. Roast, uncovered, for a further 25 minutes. The cream should have thickened by now. Stick a sharp knife in different places in the dish to make sure the potatoes are cooked. They should be totally soft.

Serve immediately, garnished with sage, or leave to cool down. In any case, bringing the potatoes to the table in the baking dish, after scraping the outside clean, will make a strong impact.

Roast potatoes and Jerusalem artichokes with lemon and sage

500g Jersey Royals
or other small potatoes

500g Jerusalem artichokes

4 garlic cloves, crushed

50ml olive oil

10g sage, roughly
chopped

1 lemon

250g cherry tomatoes

170g Kalamata olives,
pitted

10g parsley, roughly
chopped

salt and black pepper

The appeal here is in the complementary flavours of earth (artichokes and potatoes) and acid (lemon and tomato), with the dominant background note of the oily black olives. It goes well with most light, simply cooked main courses – fish, meat or vegetarian – served warm or at room temperature.

Jerusalem artichokes are a bit of a con – neither artichokes nor (unlike us) from Jerusalem. Still, they have a superb deep flavour – sweet, nutty and earthy – that spreads throughout a whole dish. Some varieties, the tough-skinned ones resembling ginger roots, require peeling. Others are fine unpeeled so long as you slice them thinly.

———

Preheat the oven to 220°C/200°C fan/Gas Mark 7. Wash the potatoes well, put them in a large saucepan and cover with plenty of salted water. Bring to the boil and simmer for 20 minutes, until semi-cooked. Drain, cool slightly and then cut each potato in half lengthways. Put them in a large roasting tray.

Wash the Jerusalem artichokes, cut them into slices 5mm thick and add to the potatoes. Add the garlic, olive oil, sage, 1 teaspoon of salt and ½ teaspoon of black pepper. Mix everything well with your hands and put in the oven.

Meanwhile, thinly slice the lemon and remove the pips. After the vegetables have been roasting for about 30 minutes, add the sliced lemon, stir with a wooden spoon and return to the oven for 20 minutes. Now add the cherry tomatoes and olives, stir well again and cook for a further 15 minutes.

Remove from the oven and stir in some of the chopped parsley. Transfer to a serving dish and garnish with the remaining parsley.

Butterbeans with sweet chilli sauce and fresh herbs

Serves 6

Every recipe book has one or two 'cheat' ingredients – ingredients that are a fast-track to everything tasting good. Chorizo, for example, or – for a creamy and nutty cheat – tahini paste. Sweet chilli sauce is the happy culprit here. It brings just the right sweet-yet-spicy kick to a dish that is very low on fuss and very high on praise. We used to be sticklers for the need to start with dried butterbeans here. Over the years however, we've been told by many readers that starting with tinned works just fine. If you do this then you'll need to start with 800g cooked butterbeans. Ingredients that cheat, methods that fast-track: this pretty much constitutes 'fast food' in the world of the Ottolenghi salad!

——

If starting with dried butterbeans, put them in a large bowl and fill with enough water to cover them by twice their volume. Leave to soak overnight at room temperature.

The next day, drain the beans and place in a large saucepan. Cover with plenty of cold water and bring to a simmer. Cook for 35–55 minutes, skimming froth from the surface and topping up with boiling water if necessary, until tender. The cooking time will vary according to the bean size and freshness, so try them a few times during cooking to make sure they don't turn to a mush. In case they begin to overcook, remove from the heat and add plenty of cold water to the pan to stop the cooking. When they are done, drain in a colander and leave to one side.

While the beans are cooking, make the sauce. Place the crushed garlic in a bowl large enough to hold the beans. Add the sweet chilli sauce, sesame oil, soy sauce and lemon juice and mix well with a small whisk. Add the red peppers, season the mixture with salt and pepper and set aside.

Once the beans have cooled down slightly but are still warm, add them to the sauce, together with the spring onions, herbs and plenty of seasoning. Mix gently with your hands. Taste and adjust the seasoning. Eat warm or cold – just remember to readjust the seasoning before serving.

400g dried butterbeans (or 800g cooked butterbeans)

6 garlic cloves, crushed

70ml sweet chilli sauce

2 tbsp sesame oil

3 tbsp soy sauce

3 tbsp lemon juice

2 red peppers, halved, de-seeded, core removed and cut into 2cm squares

4 spring onions, white and green bits, chopped

35g coriander, roughly chopped

30g mint leaves, chopped

flaky sea salt and black pepper

Camargue red rice and quinoa with orange and pistachios

Serves 4

This is a great dish to make for parties as all the elements can be prepared well in advance – the day before, if you like – and then just kept separate until the dish is ready to be assembled.

We love the contrast in textures, between the nutty wholegrain Camargue rice and the springy light quinoa. If you want to go all-out on the colour front, red or black quinoa can also be added to the mix, in addition to the more regular white variety. With thanks to Tricia Jadoonanan for introducing us to Camargue red rice, back in the day.

Preheat the oven to 190°C/170°C fan/Gas Mark 5. Spread the pistachios out on a baking tray and toast for 8 minutes, until lightly coloured. Remove from the oven, allow to cool slightly and then chop roughly. Set aside.

Fill 2 saucepans with salted water and bring to the boil. Simmer the quinoa in one for 12–14 minutes and the rice in the other for 20 minutes. Both should be tender but still have a bite. Drain in a sieve and spread out the two grains separately on flat trays to hasten the cooling down.

While the grains are cooking, sauté the onion in 60ml of the olive oil for 10–12 minutes, stirring occasionally, until golden brown. Leave to cool completely.

In a large mixing bowl combine the rice, quinoa, cooked onion and the remaining oil. Add all the rest of the ingredients, then taste and adjust the seasoning. Serve at room temperature.

60g shelled pistachio kernels

200g quinoa

200g Camargue red rice

1 medium onion, sliced

150ml olive oil

finely grated zest and juice of 1 orange

2 tsp lemon juice

1 garlic clove, crushed

4 spring onions, thinly sliced

100g dried apricots, roughly chopped

40g rocket

salt and black pepper

Couscous and mograbiah with oven-dried tomatoes

16 large, ripe plum tomatoes, halved lengthways

2 tbsp muscovado sugar

150ml olive oil

2 tbsp balsamic vinegar

2 onions, thinly sliced

250g mograbiah

400ml chicken or vegetable stock

a pinch of saffron strands

250g couscous

5g picked tarragon leaves

1 tbsp nigella seeds

100g labneh

flaky sea salt and black pepper

Mograbiah is a large variety of couscous. It's often sold outside of the Arab world as 'giant couscous' or 'pearl couscous'. It's fairly widely available but if you're looking for a substitute then fregola – the Sardinian equivalent – also works well. You can also make do with using just regular couscous: the dish won't be as texturally interesting but it will still taste great. If you are just using regular couscous then you'll need to up the quantity to 500 grams and double the amount of stock and oil added.

Make a batch of the oven-dried tomatoes, when you have time, to keep at the ready for future dishes. They keep well, covered with a thin layer of oil, and do wonders for elevating the simplest of dishes: the cauliflower and cumin fritters (see page 67), for example, or just some plain scrambled eggs. If you're in the mood for batch cooking, a jar of caramelised onion (see page 189) is also very handy to have in the fridge. Again, it will keep well (for at least 5 days) and makes a great addition to egg dishes or spooned on top of bruschetta or pasta: anything, really!

_____

Preheat the oven to 170°C/150°C fan/Gas Mark 3. Arrange the tomato halves on a baking tray, skin-side down, and sprinkle with the sugar, 2 tablespoons of the olive oil, plus the balsamic vinegar and some salt and pepper. Place in the oven and bake for 2 hours or until the tomatoes have lost most of their moisture.

Meanwhile, put the onions in a large pan with 4 tablespoons of the olive oil and sauté over a high heat for 10–12 minutes, stirring occasionally, until they are a dark golden colour.

Throw the mograbiah into a large pan of boiling salted water (as for cooking pasta). Simmer for 15 minutes, until it is soft but still retains a bite; some varieties might take less time, so check the instructions on the packet. Drain well and rinse under cold water.

In a separate pot, bring the stock to the boil with the saffron and a little salt. Place the couscous in a large bowl and add 3 tablespoons of the olive oil and the boiling stock. Cover with cling film and leave for 10 minutes.

Once ready, mix the couscous with a fork or a whisk to get rid of any lumps and to fluff it up. Add the cooked mograbiah, the tomatoes and their juices, the onions and their oil, plus the tarragon and half the nigella seeds. Taste and adjust the seasoning and oil. It is likely that it will need a fair amount of salt. Allow the dish to come to room temperature. To serve, arrange it gently on a serving plate, place the labneh on top (in balls or spoonfuls), drizzle with the remaining oil and finish with the rest of the nigella seeds.

Couscous with dried apricots and butternut squash

1 large onion, thinly sliced

90ml olive oil

50g dried apricots

1 small butternut squash (about 450g), peeled, de-seeded and cut into 2cm dice

250g couscous

400ml chicken or vegetable stock

a pinch of saffron strands

15g tarragon, roughly chopped

15g mint, roughly chopped

15g parsley, roughly chopped

1½ tsp ground cinnamon

finely grated zest of ½ lemon

flaky sea salt and black pepper

Quinoa can also be used here, instead of the couscous, if you are looking for a gluten-free dish. If you do this then just cook the quinoa in regular (rather than saffron) water. Soak the saffron threads separately in a tablespoon of boiling water for a good 30 minutes and then pour the threads and water evenly over the quinoa when it's cooked.

All the orange going on here makes this perfectly apt for a light autumn lunch or as a side to a more hearty meal. It works particularly well served alongside some end-of-year quail or roasted poussins.

———

Preheat the oven to 200°C/180°C fan/Gas Mark 6. Place the onion in a large frying pan with 2 tablespoons of the oil and a pinch of salt. Sauté over a high heat, stirring frequently, for about 10 minutes, until golden brown. Set aside.

Meanwhile, pour enough hot water from the tap over the apricots just to cover them. Soak for 5 minutes, then drain and cut into 5mm dice.

Mix the diced squash with 1 tablespoon of the olive oil and some salt and pepper. Spread the squash out on a baking tray, place in the oven and bake for about 25 minutes, until lightly coloured and quite soft.

While waiting for the butternut squash, cook the couscous. Bring the stock to the boil with the saffron. Place the couscous in a large heatproof bowl and pour the boiling stock over it, plus the remaining olive oil. Cover with cling film and leave for about 10 minutes; all the liquid should have been absorbed.

Use a fork or a whisk to fluff up the couscous, then add the onion, butternut squash, apricots, herbs, cinnamon and lemon zest. Mix well with your hands, trying not mash the butternut squash. Taste and add salt and pepper if necessary. Serve warmish or cold.

Puy lentils with sour cherries, bacon and Gorgonzola

Serves 2–4

These lentils keep well in the fridge for a good few days, so double or treble the recipe here, if you want to. That way you'll have a good many grab-and-go lunches at the ready, all set to be accessorised as you like. Leave out the salty bacon, if you like, to keep it vegetarian. You can play around with more herbs, if you want to lighten the load for lunch. A big handful of chopped parsley or quickly fried kale leaves work well instead of (or along with) the spinach.

———

Wash the lentils under cold running water and then drain. Transfer to a saucepan and add enough water to cover them by 3 times their height. Add the bay leaves, bring to the boil and then simmer for about 20 minutes, until the lentils are al dente.

Meanwhile, make the sauce. Place the shallots in a pan with 2 tablespoons of the olive oil and sauté over a medium heat for about 10 minutes, until golden. Add the sugar, cherries, vinegar and 3 tablespoons of water and continue simmering over a low heat for 8–10 minutes, until you get a thick sauce. Taste and season with salt and pepper.

Drain the lentils well and immediately add them to the sauce so they can soak up all the flavours. Stir together, taste and adjust the salt again. It will need quite a lot, but remember you are adding bacon and Gorgonzola later, which are salty. Set aside to cool down.

Heat the remaining olive oil in a saucepan and fry the bacon in it for 3 minutes on each side, until it turns quite crisp. Transfer to a piece of kitchen paper to cool. Tear the bacon into large pieces and add to the lentils, then add the spinach and stir well. Taste and see if the salad needs any more oil, salt or pepper.

Transfer to serving plates and dot with broken chunks of Gorgonzola.

125g Puy lentils

2 bay leaves

2–3 shallots, finely chopped

3 tbsp olive oil

1 tsp caster sugar

60g dried sour cherries

70ml red wine vinegar

8 streaky bacon rashers

80g baby spinach

120g creamy Gorgonzola cheese

salt and black pepper

Whole wheat and mushrooms with celery and shallots

200g whole wheat grains

3 tbsp soft brown sugar

50ml good-quality
sherry vinegar

2–3 shallots,
finely chopped

3 celery stalks,
finely chopped

200g button mushrooms,
sliced ½cm thick

40g picked parsley leaves

10g picked tarragon
leaves

50ml olive oil

flaky sea salt and
black pepper

Whole wheat grains are just that: grains where the whole kernel has been left intact, rather than stripped of its outer bran and germ. As a result, the grains have a really nutty bite and chew. It also means that there's a lot more work for the water to do in terms of getting through to the grain to cook it. That's why you need to soak the wheat overnight: to help the cooking on its way. If you want to skip this soaking stage, substitute with pearl barley instead, following the cooking instructions on the packet. This is lovely either on its own or served along with some grilled meat or fish. If you want to bulk it out then gently mix through some oven-dried tomatoes (see page 189) before serving.

———

Wash the wheat in plenty of cold water, then transfer to a large bowl and cover with fresh water. Leave to soak overnight.

The next day, drain the wheat, put it in a large pan with plenty of fresh water to cover and simmer for 45–60 minutes. The grains should have now softened up but still have a bite. Drain in a colander and leave to cool.

You need to make the dressing at least an hour before serving the salad. Whisk together the sugar and vinegar until the sugar has completely dissolved. Add the shallots and celery and leave to marinate.

To assemble the salad, put the mushrooms in a mixing bowl and toss with the dressing. Add the wheat and then tear in the parsley leaves. Add the whole tarragon leaves, plus the olive oil and some salt and pepper. Taste, adjust the seasoning accordingly and serve.

Chickpeas and spinach with honeyed sweet potato

Serves 6–8

We prefer to start with dried chickpeas, which need soaking overnight, but tinned chickpeas are also fine – you'll need about 500 grams. Just increase the amount of cooking time from 5 to 10 minutes when the chickpeas are added to the tomato sauce.

Start the night before by putting the chickpeas in a large bowl. Fill with enough cold water to cover the chickpeas by twice their height. Add the bicarbonate of soda and leave to soak overnight at room temperature.

The next day, drain and rinse the chickpeas, place them in a large saucepan and cover with plenty of fresh water. Bring to the boil, then reduce the heat and simmer for 1–1½ hours (they could take much longer in extreme cases). They should be totally tender but retain their shape. Occasionally you will need to skim the froth off the surface. You might also need to top up the pan with boiling water so the chickpeas remain submerged. When they are ready, drain them in a colander and set aside.

Put the sweet potatoes in a wide saucepan with the water, butter, honey and ½ teaspoon of salt. Bring to the boil, then reduce the heat and simmer for 35–40 minutes, until the potatoes are tender and most of the liquid has been absorbed. Turn them over half way through the cooking to colour evenly. Remove from the heat and keep warm.

Meanwhile, prepare the sauce for the chickpeas. Heat the olive oil in a large frying pan and add the onion, cumin seeds and coriander seeds. Fry for 8 minutes, while stirring, until golden brown. Add the tomato purée, cook for a minute while you stir and then add the tomatoes, sugar and ground cumin. Continue cooking for about 5 minutes over a medium heat. Taste and season with salt and pepper.

Stir the spinach into the tomato sauce, then add the cooked chickpeas. Mix together and cook for another 5 minutes. Taste again and adjust the seasoning.

Make the yoghurt sauce by whisking together all the ingredients. Season with salt and pepper to taste.

To serve, spoon the warm chickpeas into a serving dish, arrange the sweet potato slices on top and garnish with the coriander leaves. Spoon the yoghurt sauce on top or serve on the side.

200g dried chickpeas

1 tsp bicarbonate of soda

2 tbsp olive oil

1 onion, finely chopped

1 tsp cumin seeds

1 tsp coriander seeds

1 tbsp tomato purée

400g Italian tinned chopped tomatoes

1 tsp caster sugar

1½ tsp ground cumin

100g baby spinach leaves

10g coriander leaves, to garnish

salt and black pepper

Honeyed sweet potato

500g sweet potatoes, peeled and cut into 2.5cm-thick slices

700ml water

50g unsalted butter

4 tbsp honey

Yoghurt sauce

100g Greek yoghurt

1 garlic clove, crushed

finely grated zest and juice of 1 lemon

3 tbsp olive oil

1 tsp dried mint

Serves 4

Kosheri

300g green lentils

200g basmati rice

40g unsalted butter

50g vermicelli noodles,
broken into 4cm pieces

400ml chicken stock
or water

½ tsp grated nutmeg

1½ tsp ground cinnamon

60ml olive oil

2 onions, halved
and thinly sliced

salt and black pepper

Spicy tomato sauce

60ml olive oil

2 garlic cloves, crushed

2 hot red chillies,
de-seeded and
finely diced

8 ripe tomatoes, chopped
(tinned are also fine)

370ml water

60ml cider vinegar

2 tsp ground cumin

20g coriander leaves,
chopped

Very popular in Egypt, this dish is not too far removed from the Indian *kitchari*, ancestor to the British kedgeree.

The chances are you'll have everything you need already sitting in your cupboards. Don't go out just to get the thin rice vermicelli noodles: the dish still works well without them. Try serving with the beef and lamb meatballs (see page 120), or with a cucumber, tomato and yoghurt salad.

———

Start with the sauce. Heat the olive oil in a saucepan, add the garlic and chillies and fry for 2 minutes. Add the chopped tomatoes, water, vinegar, 1 tablespoon of salt and cumin. Bring to the boil, then reduce the heat and simmer for 20 minutes, until slightly thickened. Remove the sauce from the heat, stir in the coriander and then taste. See if you want to add any salt, pepper or extra coriander. Keep hot or leave to cool; both ways will work with the hot kosheri. Just remember to adjust the seasoning again when cold.

To make the kosheri, place the lentils in a large sieve and wash them under a cold running tap. Transfer to a large saucepan, cover with plenty of cold water and bring to the boil. Reduce the heat and simmer for 25 minutes. The lentils should be tender but far from mushy. Drain in a colander and leave to one side.

In a large bowl, cover the rice with cold water, wash and then drain well. Melt the butter in a large saucepan over a medium heat. Add the raw vermicelli, stir, and continue frying and stirring until the vermicelli turns golden brown. Add the drained rice and mix well until it is coated in the butter. Now add the stock or water, nutmeg, cinnamon, 1½ teaspoons of salt and a good grind of black pepper. Bring to the boil, cover and then reduce the heat and simmer for 12 minutes. Turn off the heat, remove the lid, cover the pan with a clean tea towel and put the lid back on. Leave for about 5 minutes; this helps make the rice light and fluffy.

Heat the olive oil in a large frying pan, add the onions and sauté over a medium heat for about 20 minutes, until dark brown. Transfer to kitchen paper to drain.

To serve, lightly break up the rice with a fork and then add the lentils and most of the onions, reserving a few for garnish. Taste for seasoning and adjust accordingly. Pile the rice on a serving platter and top with the remaining onions. Serve hot, with the tomato sauce.

Tamara's stuffed vine leaves

20–25 pickled vine leaves,
plus extra for lining
the pan

1½ tsp olive oil

1 tbsp lemon juice

150g full-fat yoghurt
or goat's milk yoghurt
(optional)

Filling

1 tbsp olive oil

1 onion, finely chopped

110g short grain rice
(pudding rice is best)

1½ tsp lemon juice

2½ tsp currants

2 tbsp pine nuts

10g parsley, roughly
chopped

½ tsp ground allspice
(pimento)

¼ tsp ground cinnamon

¼ tsp ground cloves

½ tsp dried mint

salt and black pepper

There's something disproportionately satisfying and rewarding about rolling your own vine leaves. Whatever else you produce on the night, these are the guaranteed 'wow'-bringers for any gathering and they are great for pre-dinner snacks. Everything can be done well in advance – the rolled and cooked vine leaves keep well, in the fridge, for a couple of days – so there needn't be any last-minute work.

With thanks to Tamara Meitlis for showing us how to make these.

———

First prepare the filling. Heat the olive oil in a medium saucepan, add the onion and sauté over a medium heat for 8 minutes or until softened but not coloured. Add the rice and cook for 2 minutes, stirring to coat it in the oil. Add all the remaining filling ingredients, along with ½ teaspoon of salt and a good grind of black pepper, and cook over a medium heat for 10 minutes, stirring from time to time (the mixture should be sweet and sour, the rice still hard). Remove from the heat and leave to cool.

Pour boiling water over the vine leaves and leave to soak for 10 minutes. Remove the vine leaves from the water and pat dry. Using a pair of kitchen scissors, cut the stalks from the leaves. Put any torn or unusable leaves in the bottom of a medium heavy-based saucepan, making sure it is covered with a layer of leaves a few millimetres thick. This will prevent the stuffed leaves from burning later.

To fill and roll the vine leaves, choose medium leaves, roughly 13cm wide (you can cut them to this size with scissors, if necessary). If possible, use fine, pale leaves, not dark, thick ones. Place a leaf on a work surface, the beautiful veiny side down, and spoon about ¾ teaspoon of the filling in the centre-bottom of the leaf, steering clear of the edges. Take the 2 sides and fold them tightly over the rice. Now roll neatly towards the top of the leaf, ending with a tight, short cigar. They should be small – roughly 3 x 1cm.

Repeat with all the leaves and arrange inside the lined saucepan
in neat layers. They should fit quite tightly. Pour in enough water just
to cover, then add the olive oil, lemon juice and ¼ teaspoon of salt.
Place a small plate or saucer on top to prevent the leaves moving
during cooking. Bring to a gentle boil, cover and cook on the lowest
possible heat for 50–60 minutes, until the leaves are tender and
almost no cooking liquid is left. You may need to add a little more
boiling water during cooking.

Transfer the stuffed vine leaves to a serving platter and set aside
to cool down. Serve cold, with the yoghurt if you like.

Chilled red pepper soup
with soured cream

Serves 4

This soup – a great alternative to gazpacho – is the perfect way to open a summery meal. It's a beauty to look at – bright red, piled high with green herbs, with a spoon of white soured cream swirled through – and will excite and delight everyone without overfilling them for what is to come. You can make it a day or two before serving: just hold back on the herbs and soured cream.

———

Peel the onion and chop it roughly. Heat up the oil in a large saucepan. Add the onion and sage and sauté on medium heat for 5 minutes or until the onion is translucent.

While the onion is cooking, halve the peppers lengthways. Take a half of one pepper, remove the seeds and white flesh and cut it into 1.5cm dice. Keep it for later.

Remove the seeds from the rest of the peppers, roughly chop them and stir into the saucepan with the onions. Add ¾ teaspoon of salt, bay leaves, ground cumin, sugar and chilli.

Sauté for another 5 minutes. Add the stock and bring to a light simmer. Cover the pot and cook on a very low heat for 15 minutes.

Once the peppers are soft, remove the bay leaves from the soup. While still hot, use a liquidiser or a hand stick blender to pulverise the soup until it is totally smooth. This may take a few minutes. Leave to cool down a little.

Once the soup is just warm, stir in the celery, diced red pepper, lemon zest and garlic. Leave until it comes to room temperature and then refrigerate for a few hours or overnight.

Remove the soup from the fridge half an hour before serving. Stir well, taste and adjust the seasoning. Divide into serving bowls, sprinkle over a generous amount of chopped basil and parsley, add a spoonful of soured cream per portion and finish with a drizzle of olive oil.

1 large onion

3 tbsp olive oil, plus extra to finish

8 sage leaves, finely chopped

4 large red peppers

2 bay leaves

2 tsp ground cumin

1 tsp caster sugar

pinch of dried chilli flakes

500ml chicken or vegetable stock

1 celery stick, cut into 1.5cm dice

finely grated zest of ½ lemon

1 garlic clove, crushed

25g basil leaves, roughly chopped

10g parsley, roughly chopped

100g soured cream

salt

Clockwise from top left: chilled red pepper soup; grilled aubergine and lemon soup; Jerusalem artichoke and rocket soup; harira.

Red lentil and chard soup

500g split red lentils

2.5 litres cold water

2 medium red onions

2 tbsp olive oil

200g Swiss chard

50g coriander leaves

2 tsp ground cumin

1 tsp ground cinnamon

1 tbsp coriander seeds

3 garlic cloves, crushed

50g unsalted butter

finely grated zest
of ½ lemon

sourdough bread, to serve

6 lemon wedges,
to serve

salt and black pepper

Chard is in season throughout the year but this soup is one we like to make in late summer, when the leaves are in abundance. They have an earthy, lemony flavour that we love to pull out with the final squeeze of lemon that every bowl gets. This is super simple, totally comforting and utterly delicious.

Wash the lentils in plenty of cold water. Place in a large saucepan with the water, bring to the boil and simmer for 35 minutes or until soft. Skim off any scum that rises to the surface during cooking.

Using a slotted spoon, remove about half the lentils from the cooking liquid and set aside in a bowl. Add a generous pinch of salt to the lentils and water in the pan and liquidise using a stick blender or in a food processor. Return the reserved lentils to the soup.

Now comes the arduous chopping part of the recipe. Peel the red onions, halve and thinly slice them. Place a frying pan over a medium heat, add the olive oil and onions and cook, stirring occasionally, for 4–5 minutes, until the onions soften and become translucent. Meanwhile, remove and discard the large stems from the Swiss chard. Wash and rinse the leaves thoroughly, then chop them roughly. Do the same with the coriander, leaving a few whole leaves for garnish later, and that's all the chopping done.

Mix the cooked onions, chard leaves and chopped coriander into the lentil soup and season with the cumin, cinnamon and some salt and pepper to taste. Reheat the soup and simmer gently for 5 minutes.

In a pestle and mortar, or using the heel of a large knife, crush the coriander seeds and garlic together. Melt the butter gently in a small saucepan over a medium heat, add the garlic and coriander seeds and fry for 2 minutes, until the garlic starts to colour slightly. Stir this into the soup, remove the pot from the stove and cover with a lid. Leave the soup to infuse for 5 minutes before serving.

Serve garnished with lemon zest and coriander leaves and pass round some sourdough bread and lemon wedges. Make sure everybody squeezes the lemon into their soup.

Harira (lamb, chickpeas and spinach)

Serves 4–6

This is a variation on the traditional Moroccan soup, harira. It's flavoured in the same way but without the extra carbs that are often added to the original in the form of rice or pasta. Feel free to add these back in, if you like, to make the soup into a substantial meal. Traditionally, harira is a dish with which to break the Ramadan fast. Regardless of where your hunger comes from, it's certainly a good way to keep it at bay for a while. Tinned chickpeas – roughly 500 grams – are also fine here, if you haven't had time to soak your own overnight.

Start preparing the soup the night before by putting the dried chickpeas in a large bowl with the bicarbonate of soda and covering them with plenty of cold water – it should cover the chickpeas by at least twice their height. Leave at room temperature to soak overnight.

The next day, drain the soaked chickpeas, place in a large saucepan and cover with plenty of fresh water. Bring to the boil and simmer for about 1–1½ hours, until the chickpeas are tender. Drain through a colander and leave to one side.

Place a large saucepan over a medium heat and add the olive oil. Add the onion and fry until soft and translucent. Increase the heat, add the diced lamb and cook for 2–3 minutes, until the lamb is sealed on all sides and has taken on a bit of colour. Add the tomato purée and sugar and mix well. Cook for 2 minutes, then add the chopped tomatoes, drained chickpeas, stock or water and some salt and pepper.

Bring the soup to the boil and reduce the heat to a simmer. Use a large spoon to skim off any scum that forms on the surface, then cook for about 35 minutes, until the meat is tender.

Squeeze the lemon juice into the soup. Season the soup with the ground cumin, ginger and saffron. Taste and adjust the salt and pepper.

When ready to serve, bring the soup back to the boil. Wash and drain the spinach leaves and chop them roughly. Add the spinach and coriander to the soup just before you bring it to the table. Serve with a wedge of lemon.

200g dried chickpeas (or 500g cooked chickpeas)

1 tsp bicarbonate of soda

3 tbsp olive oil

1 large onion, cut into 1cm dice

200g lamb neck fillet, cut into 1cm dice

2 tbsp tomato purée

1 tbsp caster sugar

1kg tinned chopped tomatoes

1.2 litres chicken stock or water

juice of 1 lemon

1 tsp ground cumin

1 tsp ground ginger

a pinch of saffron strands

100g baby spinach

20g coriander, roughly chopped

4–6 lemon wedges, to serve

salt and black pepper

Grilled aubergine and lemon soup

3 large aubergines
(about 1.4kg in total)

120ml sunflower oil

1 litre chicken or
vegetable stock

2 tbsp lemon juice

70ml double cream

10 basil leaves

salt and black pepper

Whenever we have an aubergine or two lying around, we find ourselves burning it on the stove top and adding the smoky flesh to whatever is on the go. Tomato soups or sauces, braised minced beef, a bean-filled stew: the smoky flavour of the burnt aubergine flesh rarely fails to improve a dish. For instructions of how to burn your aubergine, see page 42. Making a soup based on this smoky wonder is, therefore, a joy in itself. Covering your stove top with aluminium foil (with holes for the gas rings to pop through) is a helpful precaution if you want to save yourself work when cleaning down. Ventilating your kitchen well is also a must.

First you need to grill 2 of the aubergines to impart the smoky flavour necessary for this soup. If you have a gas hob, cover your stove top with foil and place the whole aubergines directly on 2 separate open flames. Using a pair of metal tongs, turn the aubergines regularly until the skin becomes crisp and the aubergines are very soft – about 15 minutes. Remove to a bowl and leave to cool. (If you don't have a gas hob, place the aubergines under a hot grill for roughly an hour, turning them occasionally. Don't worry if they burst slightly during the cooking.)

Cut the remaining aubergine into 2cm cubes. Put a large frying pan over a moderate heat and pour in half the oil. When it is hot, add half the aubergine cubes and fry, turning with a wooden spoon, until brown on all sides. Drain on kitchen paper and sprinkle with a little salt. Repeat the process with the rest of the aubergine cubes and the remaining oil.

When the grilled aubergines have cooled down a little, make an incision along each one and spoon out the cooked flesh, avoiding any black bits of skin. Chop the flesh roughly with a large knife and place in a saucepan with the stock, lemon juice and roughly 1½ teaspoons of salt and 1 teaspoon of pepper. Bring to the boil, then reduce the heat and simmer for 30 minutes. Add the fried aubergine cubes and cook for a further 5 minutes. Taste the soup and adjust the seasoning if needed.

To serve, mix the cream into the hot soup and ladle into warm bowls. Tear the basil leaves and scatter them on top.

Jerusalem artichoke and rocket soup

This is hearty enough to be a meal in itself, if you like, served with some fresh crusty bread. Be sure to follow the instructions for adding the soup to the yoghurt (rather than the other way round), to prevent it splitting. It's not complicated: it just needs to be done a ladle at a time.

———

Peel the artichokes with a potato peeler, wash them thoroughly and cut into 1cm dice, not too perfect. Put them in a large saucepan with the rocket, stock, garlic and a couple of pinches of salt. Bring to the boil and then simmer lightly for 25 minutes, until the artichokes are tender; insert a small knife in one to make sure they are totally soft.

While the soup is cooking, cut the spring onions in half lengthways and then cut across these lengths into small dice. Set aside. Break the egg into a large mixing bowl and whisk well with the yoghurt.

When you are ready to serve the soup, reheat it to boiling point. Take a ladleful of hot soup and whisk it into the yoghurt mix, stirring constantly. Repeat a few times, using about half the soup. You need to bring up the temperature of the yoghurt. Now pour the warm yoghurt into the soup pan, whisking constantly. Bring back to a very(!) gentle boil and leave there for a minute or two.

Taste the soup and season with plenty of salt and pepper. Stir in the spring onions and serve garnished with rocket.

400g Jerusalem artichokes

45g rocket, roughly chopped, plus extra to garnish

1 litre chicken or vegetable stock

10 garlic cloves, crushed

6 spring onions

1 egg

350g Greek yoghurt

salt and black pepper

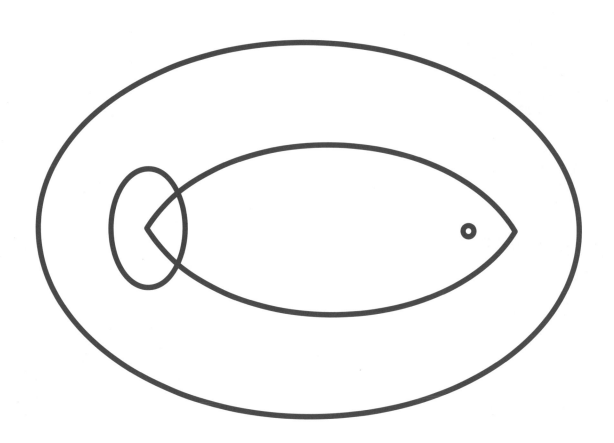

Meat and fish

———

Marinated rack of lamb with coriander and honey

1kg rack of lamb, French trimmed (you can ask your butcher to do this)

20g parsley, leaves and stalks

30g mint, leaves and stalks

30g coriander, leaves and stalks

4 garlic cloves, peeled

3cm piece of ginger, peeled and sliced

3 chillies, de-seeded

50ml lemon juice

60ml soy sauce

120ml sunflower oil

3 tbsp honey

2 tbsp red wine vinegar

salt

All the work for this is done the day before – the meat just sits marinating overnight – and the dish can then be ready on the table within 20 minutes. It's our kind of fast food for friends. The lamb is great either hot from the oven or else at room temperature, if you want to cook it in advance. It is really versatile, as good as a centrepiece main as it is simply piled in a sandwich with some mayonnaise or taken on a picnic, with the sauce in a little pot to dip in alongside.

———

Make sure most of the fat is trimmed off the lamb, leaving a uniform thin layer that will keep the meat moist and add to the flavour. Use a very sharp knife to separate the rack into portions of 2 or 3 cutlets. Place in a non-metal container.

Blitz together all the remaining ingredients in a blender or food processor, along with 60ml water and ½ teaspoon of salt. Pour them over the lamb and make sure it is well covered for a night in the marinade. Refrigerate overnight.

Preheat the oven to 220°C/200°C fan/Gas Mark 7. Heat up a heavy cast-iron pan, preferably a griddle pan. Remove the meat from the marinade and shake off the excess. Sear well on all sides, about 5 minutes in total. Transfer to a baking tray and cook in the oven for about 15 minutes, depending on the size of the racks and how well you want them cooked.

Meanwhile, heat the marinade in a small saucepan and simmer for 5 minutes. Put the cutlets on serving plates and serve the sauce in a separate bowl. Both cutlets and sauce can be served hot or at room temperature.

Lamb cutlets with walnut, fig and goat's cheese salad

This is another dish where much of the work is done beforehand – the meat gets marinated, the sauce can be made and all the elements for the salad can be prepared, ready to be mixed gently before serving. It's everything you want from a dinner party main: high on 'wow', very low on stress and needing very little else alongside. Splash out on your salad ingredients here, with some really good soft goat's cheese – we like English Perroche or a good Italian Caprino Frescho – and super-ripe, dark-skinned, fresh figs.

———

First you need to marinate the lamb. Take the cutlets, throw the marinade ingredients on and massage them lightly into the meat. Place in a sealed container and refrigerate for at least 4 hours or overnight.

Now prepare the sauce. Place all the ingredients in a heavy-based saucepan, stir and put over a medium heat. Bring to the boil, reduce the heat and simmer for 30–40 minutes, until reduced by two-thirds. Remove from the heat and keep somewhere warm.

Place the walnuts in a non-stick frying pan and toast over a medium heat for 5 minutes, stirring occasionally. Set aside to cool.

To finish the dish, heat up a barbecue or griddle pan until piping hot. Season both sides of the lamb cutlets with salt and pepper. Place on the heat for 3–4 minutes on each side; this will give rare to medium meat. Cook longer if you prefer. Remove the lamb from the grill and leave to rest in a warm place for 2 minutes. While you wait, gently toss together all the salad ingredients, apart from the figs, seasoning with salt and pepper. Make sure the components stay separate and that the cheese doesn't smear the leaves.

To serve, put the cutlets on serving plates, pile the salad next to them and the figs alongside. Spoon a scant tablespoon of sauce over each portion of lamb and drizzle a small amount of it over the figs and salad. Serve at once.

12 lamb cutlets, French trimmed (you can ask your butcher to do this)

flaky sea salt and black pepper

Marinade

leaves from 6 thyme sprigs, roughly chopped

leaves from 1 rosemary sprig, roughly chopped

2 garlic cloves, crushed

90ml olive oil

Sauce

125ml freshly squeezed orange juice

60ml red wine vinegar

50g honey

1 star anise

1 cinnamon stick

Salad

50g walnut halves, broken

100g soft goat's cheese, crumbled

20g picked mint leaves

25g picked parsley leaves

2 tbsp olive oil

4 fresh figs, halved or quartered

Courgette-wrapped lamb kebabs

2 tbsp pine nuts

50g stale white bread, crusts removed

300g minced lamb

55g feta cheese, crumbled

1½ tsp ground allspice (pimento)

1 tsp ground cinnamon

¼ tsp ground nutmeg

1 garlic clove, crushed

1 egg

15g parsley, finely chopped

light olive oil for frying, plus a little extra for brushing

2 medium courgettes

salt and black pepper

Sauce

2 tbsp olive oil

2 garlic cloves, crushed

400g Italian tinned chopped tomatoes

a pinch of dried chilli flakes

10 basil leaves

These can either be a main course – served with some rice or bulgur – or else pared down to a starter or nibble. The courgette wrapping is impressive but not necessary and the kebabs also work well as finger food, with a squeeze of lemon, if you want to do without the sauce. Either way, the recipe is wonderfully versatile, depending on what you have in your cupboards. Leftover cooked potato or couscous can be used instead of the bread, for example, if you have some lying around. The herbs and spices can also be adapted: some ground or fresh coriander or mint are both nice additions or substitutions. The sauce can also be substituted for the tahini sauce on page 120, for example, or the Green tahini sauce on page 284.

Start by making the sauce. Place the olive oil and crushed garlic in a saucepan and stir over a medium heat for 1–2 minutes, just until the garlic cooks lightly. Add the tinned tomatoes and season with the chilli flakes and some salt. Bring to the boil, then reduce to a gentle heat and simmer for 25 minutes, until slightly thickened. Remove from the heat, taste and adjust the seasoning. Set aside.

Toast the pine nuts in a small, dry frying pan for 4–5 minutes, shaking the pan occasionally, just until they get a little colour. Remove from the heat and leave to cool.

Soak the bread in cold water for 2 minutes, then drain and squeeze to remove most of the water. Crumble the bread into a large mixing bowl and add the lamb, crumbled feta, pine nuts, spices, garlic, egg, chopped parsley, ½ teaspoon of salt and a good grind of black pepper. Time to roll up your sleeves and get your hands dirty. Mix all of the ingredients together with your hands until well combined; do not overwork the mixture. Shape it into fingers, roughly 10cm by 5cm. There should be 12.

Pour a 5mm depth of olive oil into a large frying pan and shallow-fry the kebabs for 1 minute on each side or until they have taken on a nice brown colour. Remove from the pan and set aside on a baking tray.

Preheat the oven to 220°C/200°C fan/Gas Mark 7. To prepare the courgettes, use a small knife to slice off both ends and then cut long, thin slices down the length of each courgette (a mandolin will make this job much easier). You will need 12 slices. Brush each slice with a little olive oil and season with salt and pepper. Place a ridged griddle pan over a high heat and leave it there for a few minutes to heat up well. Lay the courgette slices on the hot pan and cook for 2 minutes on each side, so that they get distinctive char marks. Remove to a tray and leave to cool.

Wrap each meat finger in a slice of courgette and arrange them in a single layer in a baking dish, seam-side down. Bake in the preheated oven for 8–10 minutes, until cooked through.

To serve, bring the sauce back to the boil, tear the basil leaves roughly and stir them in. Arrange the kebabs on serving plates and spoon the sauce over. Drizzle with a little olive oil to finish.

Serves 6–8

Roasted beef fillet
(plus three sauces)

1 whole beef fillet,
trimmed (around 1.5kg)

3 tbsp olive oil

flaky sea salt and
black pepper

For all the changes our restaurant menus go through, 'roasted fillet of beef with daily changing sauces' remains an absolute staple. It's a tender cut, receptive to all sorts of flavours, and happy to be served either warm or at room temperature along with one or two of the three sauces we've suggested here. They're all big on flavour but they won't overpower the beef.

When choosing a fillet, look for some fat marbling through the meat and ask the butcher to trim off any sinewy bits. If you need less than a whole fillet, ask for a piece cut from the centre: you'll get more even cooking this way.

———

Preheat the oven to 240°C/220°C fan/Gas Mark 9. To get the strong, meaty flavours from the fillet, we start by chargrilling it. Depending on the size of your griddle pan, divide the whole fillet into 2 or 3 pieces that will easily fit in the pan. The head-end piece will be the thickest and therefore will need to cook the longest when it is later put in the oven.

After dividing the fillet, place the pieces in a bowl with the oil, 1½ teaspoons of salt and some black pepper and massage, rubbing the seasoning into the meat. Place a heavy ridged griddle pan over the highest possible heat and leave for a few minutes, until very hot. Now sear each piece individually, turning it around to get nice dark char marks on all sides; it should take 2–3 minutes in total.

Transfer the seared pieces to a roasting tray and put them in the oven to roast. This should take 10–14 minutes for medium-rare, 15–18 minutes for medium or longer for well done. Remember, these are just guidelines. Not all ovens are the same, and neither are fillets, so you should check the meat at different stages. Pressing it with your finger is one option. The more the meat tends to bounce back, the clearer the indication that it is cooked through. If it doesn't, it is still rare. Another option is to stick a sharp knife into the fillet and try to look inside. This is safer but not as elegant. If the knife comes out cold, the meat is definitely not cooked. But keep in mind that the meat will carry on cooking in its own heat after it comes out of the oven.

When ready, remove from the oven and leave the fillet in the tray to rest for 10 minutes, then cut it into slices 1–2cm thick. You can also serve at room temperature. Serve with sauce on the side (opposite).

MEAT AND FISH

Choka (smoky tomato sauce)

Place a large, heavy-based frying pan over a high heat and allow it to heat up well. Put the whole tomatoes in it and cook for about 15 minutes, turning them occasionally. The burnt skin will give the sauce its smoky flavour (beware, though; it will take a bit of scrubbing to clean the pan once you're done). Place the hot tomatoes in a bowl and crush them roughly with a wooden spoon. Pick out most of the skin.

In a saucepan, heat up the oil well. Remove the pan from the heat while you add the onion so it doesn't spit all over. Return to the heat and cook for 3 minutes on a medium heat, just to soften slightly. Add the onion and oil to the crushed tomatoes, together with the chilli, garlic, coriander, paprika and chilli flakes. Taste and season liberally with salt and pepper. Serve warm or at room temperature.

450g plum tomatoes

3 tbsp sunflower oil

1 small onion, thinly sliced

1 red chilli, de-seeded and chopped

2 garlic cloves, crushed

10g coriander, roughly chopped

1 tbsp paprika

a pinch of dried chilli flakes

salt and black pepper

Rocket and horseradish sauce

Put all the ingredients except the yoghurt in a blender or food processor and pulse until smooth. Transfer to a bowl, add the yoghurt and mix well. This sauce will keep for a few days in the fridge in a sealed container.

50g rocket

2 tbsp freshly grated horseradish root

2 garlic cloves, crushed

2 tbsp olive oil

1 tbsp milk

125g Greek yoghurt

salt and black pepper

Watercress and mustard sauce

Put all the ingredients except the soured cream in a blender or food processor and pulse until smooth. Transfer to a bowl, add the soured cream and mix well. This sauce will keep for a few days in the fridge in a sealed container.

40g watercress

20g wholegrain mustard

1 tbsp Dijon mustard

2 garlic cloves, crushed

2 tbsp olive oil

2 tbsp milk

110ml soured cream

salt and black pepper

Beef and lamb meatballs baked in tahini

35g stale white bread, crusts removed

300g minced beef

300g minced lamb

3 garlic cloves, crushed

35g parsley, finely chopped

2½ tsp ground allspice (pimento)

1½ tsp ground cinnamon

1 egg

light olive oil, for frying

5g parsley, roughly chopped, to garnish

finely grated zest of ½ lemon, to garnish

salt and black pepper

Tahini sauce

150ml tahini paste

150ml water

70ml white wine vinegar

1 garlic clove, crushed

It's pretty much impossible for things not to taste great when they are baked in (or drizzled or spread with) tahini. It's a thick and creamy sesame paste that makes everything taste nutty and rich. Get hold of one of the many Lebanese, Palestinian or Israeli brands available, if you can: they don't have the clagginess that those from other regions can have. Serve these with Kosheri (see page 100) or some plain steamed rice or bulgur.

———

First make the tahini sauce. In a bowl, mix together the tahini paste, water, vinegar, garlic and a pinch of salt. Whisk well until it turns smooth and creamy, with a thick, sauce-like consistency. You might need to add some more water. Set the sauce aside while you make the meatballs.

Preheat the oven to 220°C/200°C fan/Gas Mark 7. Soak the bread in cold water for 2–3 minutes until it goes soft. Squeeze out most of the water and crumble the bread into a mixing bowl. Add the beef, lamb, garlic, parsley, spices, egg, 1 teaspoon of salt and a good grind of black pepper, and mix well with your hands.

Shape the meat mixture into balls, roughly the size of golf balls. Pour a 5mm depth of light olive oil into a large frying pan. Heat it up, being careful it doesn't get too hot or it will spit all over when frying. Shallow-fry the meatballs in small batches for about 2 minutes, turning them around as you go, until they are uniformly brown on the outside.

Put the meatballs on kitchen paper to soak up the oil and then arrange them in a single layer in an ovenproof serving dish. Place in the oven for 5 minutes. Carefully remove from the oven, pour the tahini sauce over and around the meatballs and return to the oven for another 10 minutes. The tahini will take on just a little bit of colour and thicken up; the meatballs should be just cooked through. Transfer to individual plates, garnish liberally with the parsley and lemon zest and serve at once.

Roast pork belly (plus two relishes)

Serves 6–8

When this recipe was first published, Scully – master of the details of cooking, not so much master of the details of writing it up – scribbled '1 bunch of thyme, 1 bunch of rosemary, 1 head of garlic, 150ml olive oil, 1 piece of pork belly, a bottle of wine and some salt and pepper'. Our way of writing recipes has become more precise over the years – whether or not people follow our measures to the letter, we feel more relaxed putting all the information there – so we've now added precise amounts for the herbs. The recipe has not changed, though, and nor has Scully's skill in achieving the crispiest of pork bellies. It's all about starting with a very hot oven, the very even layer of salt being applied and then the wine not touching the skin (so that it can remain dry) as it's poured into the tray.

We've offered two seasonal relishes here – the gooseberries for the summer and the plums for early autumn – but all sorts of relishes work well.

30g thyme, roughly chopped

30g rosemary, roughly chopped

1 whole head of garlic, cloves peeled and crushed

150ml olive oil

1 piece of pork belly, weighing 2–3kg

1 x 750ml bottle of white wine

flaky sea salt and black pepper

Heat the oven to 260°C/250°C fan/Gas Mark 10 or its highest setting. Place the herbs, garlic and olive oil in a heavy-duty blender or food processor and purée them roughly.

Lay the pork belly in an oven tray, skin-side down, and sprinkle lightly with salt and pepper. Use your hands to spread the herb mixture evenly all over the top, pressing it on so it sticks to the meat.

Turn the belly skin-side up, wipe the skin dry with kitchen paper and sprinkle sea salt evenly all over the skin (but don't put too much on, as it might create a crust and prevent the crackling forming). Put the tray in the oven and roast for 1 hour, turning the tray around every 20 minutes. Once the skin has formed some crackling, turn the oven down to 190°C/170°C fan/Gas Mark 5, pour the white wine into the tray (avoiding the pork skin) and continue roasting for another hour. If the belly starts turning black, cover it with foil.

For the last cooking stage, turn the oven down to 130°C/110°C fan/Gas Mark ¾ and continue roasting for another hour, until the skin has crackled completely and thoroughly dried.

Remove the pork from the oven. Use a sharp knife to divide it into segments of a few ribs, cutting between the rib bones. Give as many ribs per portion as the appetite demands. Serve with relish (see overleaf) on the side.

Gooseberry, ginger and elderflower relish

3cm piece of ginger,
peeled and julienned

1 tsp mustard seeds

330g gooseberries,
trimmed

80g caster sugar

70ml elderflower cordial

Put the ginger and mustard seeds into a square of muslin, tie it up tightly and put in a heavy-based saucepan. Add the gooseberries, sugar and cordial, stir and place over a very low heat. Simmer gently for an hour, stirring occasionally. You might need to skim off the froth that accumulates on the surface.

When ready, the relish should have the consistency of a runny jam. To check this, chill a saucer, put a teaspoonful of the relish on it, then run your finger through it; it should just stay separated but still be slightly runny.

Remove the muslin bag, decant the relish into a jar and leave to cool. Either serve straight away with the pork or store in the fridge. It will keep for a week or two.

Spiced red plum, ginger and rhubarb relish

5 red plums (about 240g),
pitted and cut into quarters

1 red chilli, halved
lengthways and
de-seeded

2 cinnamon sticks

1 star anise

100ml red wine vinegar

200g caster sugar

4 stalks of champagne
rhubarb (about 200g),
cut into 3cm lengths

3cm piece of ginger,
peeled and julienned

Heat the oven to 170°C/150°C fan/Gas Mark 3. Place the plums and chilli in a heavy-based saucepan and add the cinnamon, star anise, vinegar and half the sugar. Stir well, bring to a light boil and simmer for 20–25 minutes, stirring occasionally and skimming any froth from the surface if necessary. The plums should have a jam-like consistency. To check this, chill a saucer, put a teaspoonful of the relish on it, then run your finger through it; it should stay separated. Remove from the heat and leave to cool.

While the plums are simmering away, place the rhubarb, ginger and remaining sugar in an ovenproof dish. Rub them together with your hands and place in the oven. Cook for 20–30 minutes, stirring from time to time, until the rhubarb is tender. Remove from the oven and leave to cool.

Combine the plums and rhubarb and mix well, remove the chilli, then transfer to a jar and leave to cool. Either serve the relish straight away with the pork or store in the fridge, where it will keep for a week or two.

Oxtail stew with pumpkin and cinnamon

olive oil, for frying

2kg oxtail pieces

200g shallots, roughly chopped

3 large carrots, roughly chopped

2 garlic cloves, crushed

400ml red wine

650g Italian tinned chopped tomatoes

10g thyme sprigs

5g rosemary sprigs

zest of ½ orange, peeled off in long strips

2 bay leaves

2 cinnamon sticks

2 star anise

500g pumpkin or butternut squash, peeled, de-seeded and cut into 2.5cm dice

300ml water

salt and black pepper

Gremolata

10g parsley, roughly chopped

finely grated zest of 1 large lemon

2 garlic cloves, crushed

This is one for the weekend, when there is time to casually make a meal over the course of the day, tending to it every hour or so whilst you get on with something else. There's not a lot of meat on an oxtail but we love how rich it becomes with all the long, slow cooking on the bone. Thanks to Nir Feller for inspiring this dish.

———

Preheat the oven to 200°C/180°C fan/Gas Mark 6. Place a large, heavy-based pan (large enough to accommodate the whole stew later; there will be a lot!) over a high heat and add 2 tablespoons of olive oil. When this is smoking hot, add some of the oxtail pieces and fry on all sides for about 4 minutes, browning the meat well. Make sure you don't sear too many pieces at once or they will boil in their own liquid rather than fry. Transfer the oxtail to a colander and leave to drain off excess fat while you brown the remaining pieces.

Remove most of the fat from the pan and add the shallots, carrots and garlic. Return to a medium-high heat and sauté, stirring occasionally, for about 10 minutes, until the vegetables are golden brown.

Add the wine to the pan and scrape the base with a wooden spoon to mix in any flavoursome bits left there. Bring to the boil and simmer until it has almost evaporated. Now add the tomatoes. Tie together the thyme and rosemary sprigs with string and drop them in as well, then add the orange zest, bay leaves, cinnamon, star anise, some salt and a good grind of black pepper. Decant the simmering mixture into a deep baking dish and lay the oxtail pieces on top of the sauce in one layer (keep the pan for later). Cover first with a sheet of baking parchment, placed directly on the oxtail, and then with a tight-fitting lid or a couple of layers of aluminium foil, then place in the oven and bake for 2–3 hours. The meat is ready when it comes easily away from the bone.

Lift the oxtail from the sauce, place in a large bowl and leave to cool slightly. If a lot of fat accumulates at the bottom of the bowl, decant some of it using a slotted spoon but keep the rest.

When the oxtail is cool enough to handle, pick all the meat from the bones and place back in the large pan. Add the sauce the meat was cooked in, along with the pumpkin cubes and the water. Bring to the boil, then reduce the heat to a gentle simmer and cook for 30 minutes or until the pumpkin is soft. Taste and season the sauce with salt and more black pepper.

To make the gremolata garnish for the stew, simply mix the parsley, lemon zest and garlic together. Transfer the stew to a serving bowl and sprinkle the gremolata on top. Serve at once.

Harissa-marinated chicken with red grapefruit salad

800g chicken thigh meat (about 8–10 thighs)

Harissa marinade

1 red pepper

¼ tsp coriander seeds

¼ tsp cumin seeds

¼ tsp caraway seeds

1½ tsp olive oil

1 small red onion, roughly chopped

3 garlic cloves, roughly chopped

2 mild fresh red chillies, de-seeded and roughly chopped

1 dried red chilli, de-seeded and roughly chopped

1½ tsp tomato purée

2 tbsp lemon juice

1 tbsp Greek yoghurt

salt

Red grapefruit salad

2 red grapefruit

120g peppery wild rocket

1 tsp olive oil

flaky sea salt and black pepper

Sauce

150ml pink grapefruit juice

130ml lemon juice

150ml maple syrup

a pinch of ground cinnamon

1 star anise

This version of harissa – the Tunisian chilli paste – is slightly fruitier than others due to the addition of a whole roasted pepper and some lemon juice. We love to make a batch to keep in the fridge. It's then at hand whenever you're looking for a fast-track way to spice things up. Try stirring a teaspoon or two through some yoghurt to serve alongside a simple rice dish or roast chicken, or add as it is to some sliced onions sautéing in the pan. Whisked into an omelette mix or stirred through a stew, it's a really useful flavour-bomb to have around.

There are lots of good commercial brands available, though, if you don't want to make your own. The difference between rose harissa and regular harissa, (if both are on offer), is the addition of rose petals to the former. They have a slight sweetness that softens the chillies' kick.

There is a lot of big and bold colour going on here. If you want to run with the theme, serve this with some black rice or quinoa: it looks fantasticly dramatic.

——

First make the marinade for the chicken. Over a gas ring or under a very hot grill, toast the red pepper until blackened on the outside. This should typically take about 8 minutes on an open flame, 15–20 minutes under a very hot grill. Place the pepper in a bowl, cover with cling film and leave to cool. Peel the pepper and discard the seeds.

Place a dry frying pan on a low heat and lightly toast the coriander, cumin and caraway seeds for 2 minutes. You should be able to smell the aromas of the spices. Transfer them to a pestle and mortar and grind to a powder.

Heat the olive oil in a frying pan, add the onion, garlic and fresh and dried chillies and fry over a medium heat for 6–8 minutes, until they turn a dark, smoky colour. Now blitz together all the marinade ingredients except the yoghurt in a food processor or blender along with ½ teaspoon of salt; you will have a pure harissa paste.

To marinate the chicken, mix the paste with the yoghurt and use your hands to rub it all over the chicken thighs. Layer them in a plastic container, seal and refrigerate overnight.

The next day, take each grapefruit and use a small, sharp knife to slice off the top and tail. Now cut down its sides, following its natural lines, to remove the skin and white pith. Over a small bowl, cut in between the membranes to remove the individual segments. Squeeze any remaining juice into a bowl and keep to make up the 150ml juice required for the sauce.

Preheat the oven to 240°C/220°C fan/Gas Mark 9. Lay out the marinated chicken pieces, spaced well apart, on a large baking tray and place in the hot oven. After 5 minutes, reduce the oven temperature to 200°C/180°C fan/Gas Mark 6 and cook for another 12–15 minutes, until the chicken is almost cooked through. Now place the chicken under a hot grill for 2–3 minutes to give it extra colour and cook it through completely.

Meanwhile, place all the sauce ingredients in a small pan with ¼ teaspoon of salt and bring to a light simmer. Simmer for about 20 minutes, or until reduced to a third.

To serve, toss the rocket and grapefruit segments with the olive oil, salt and pepper. Pile in the centre of 4 serving plates, put the warm chicken on top and drizzle about a tablespoonful of the sauce over each portion.

Roast chicken with sumac, za'atar and lemon

1 large chicken, divided into quarters: breast and wing, leg and thigh

2 red onions, thinly sliced

2 garlic cloves, crushed

60ml olive oil, plus extra for drizzling

1½ tsp ground allspice (pimento)

1 tsp ground cinnamon

1 tbsp sumac

1 lemon, thinly sliced

200ml chicken stock or water

2 tbsp za'atar

20g unsalted butter

50g pine nuts

20g parsley, roughly chopped parsley

salt and black pepper

So popular are these two recipes that we could, in tribute to Simon Hopkinson's classic book, re-title our book 'Roast Chicken and Other Recipes'. They are so loved for many a good reason: they're both super simple to make, packed full of juicy flavour and completely free of fuss, bother and even effort, really, as all the work is being done by the marinade as the chicken sits in it overnight. They're the ultimate dish to make for friends and can then be served with whatever sides you fancy: the sumac chicken is particularly good with just some rice, fresh pita or roasted potatoes and then a garlicky yoghurt or simple tahini sauce (see page 284 for the Green tahini sauce, and just make it without the parsley). The chicken with saffron and hazelnuts overleaf is good with all sorts of things: from just simple couscous or rice to roasted aubergine with saffron yoghurt, for example, or a good root vegetable mash. If you wanted to pair either up with one of this book's other favourite recipes, the French beans and mangetout (see page 52) or the Chargrilled broccoli (see page 56) both also work very well.

In a large bowl, mix the chicken with the onions, garlic, olive oil, spices, lemon, stock or water, 1½ teaspoons of salt and a good grind of black pepper. Leave in the fridge to marinate for a few hours or overnight.

Preheat the oven to 220°C/200°C fan/Gas Mark 7. Transfer the chicken and its marinade to a baking tray large enough to accommodate all the chicken pieces lying flat and spaced apart. They should be skin-side up. Sprinkle the za'atar over the chicken and onions and put the tray in the oven. Roast for 30–40 minutes, until the chicken is coloured and just cooked through.

Meanwhile, melt the butter in a small frying pan, add the pine nuts and a pinch of salt and cook over a moderate heat, stirring constantly, until they turn golden. Transfer to a plate lined with kitchen paper to absorb the fat.

Transfer the hot chicken and onions to a serving plate and finish with the chopped parsley, pine nuts and a drizzle of olive oil. You can sprinkle on more za'atar and sumac, if you like.

Serves 4

Roast chicken with saffron, hazelnuts and honey

1 large chicken, divided into quarters: breast and wing, leg and thigh

2 onions, roughly chopped

60ml olive oil

1 tsp ground ginger

1 tsp ground cinnamon

a generous pinch of saffron strands

juice of 1 lemon

60ml cold water

100g unskinned hazelnuts

70g honey

2 tbsp rosewater

2 spring onions, roughly chopped

flaky sea salt and black pepper

In a large bowl, mix the chicken pieces with the onions, olive oil, ginger, cinnamon, saffron, lemon juice, water, 2 teaspoons of salt and a good grind of black pepper. Leave to marinate for at least an hour, or overnight in the fridge.

Preheat the oven to 210°C/190°C fan/Gas Mark 6. Spread the hazelnuts out on an oven tray and roast for 10 minutes, until lightly browned. Chop roughly and set aside.

Transfer the chicken and marinade to a roasting tray large enough to accommodate everything comfortably. Arrange the chicken pieces skin-side up and put the tray in the oven for about 35 minutes.

While the chicken is roasting, mix the honey, rosewater and nuts together to make a rough paste. Remove the chicken from the oven, spoon a generous amount of nut paste on to each piece and spread it to cover. Return to the oven for 5–10 minutes, until the chicken is cooked through and the nuts are golden brown.

Transfer the chicken to a serving dish and garnish with the chopped spring onions.

Roast chicken and three-rice salad

1 whole chicken,
weighing about 1.5kg

70ml olive oil

200g basmati rice

50g wild rice

50g brown rice

1 onion, thinly sliced

6 spring onions, thinly
sliced

4 mild red chillies,
de-seeded and julienned

50g coriander, roughly
chopped

20g mint leaves, roughly
chopped

20 shiso leaves, shredded
(or rocket)

salt and black pepper

Dressing

65ml lemon juice

2 tbsp sesame oil

2 tbsp Thai fish sauce

2½ tsp olive oil

This follows hot on the heels of the previous two recipes
for chicken in terms of being a readers' favourite. It's a
great one to make for a lunch party as everything can
be made well in advance. The rice can even be cooked
the day before serving, if you like: just make sure it cools
completely before keeping it in the fridge overnight and
bringing it back to room temperature before serving.
As is often the case with fresh herbs, hold back on the
chopping and mixing through of these until the last minute.
Mint, in particular, does not benefit from sitting around.
You can still get ahead, though, by picking the leaves off
the stalk all ready to be chopped. If you do this, just keep
them in a bowl covered with a damp bit of kitchen paper:
this will help keep them fresh and then they are ready
to be chopped when you want.

Shiso leaves are an East Asian leaf that we love –
they bring a savoury freshness to a dish – but don't
worry if you can't get hold of any: rocket works well
as an alternative.

If you're looking to bulk out any leftovers the next day,
chunks of ripe avocado are a very nice addition here.

———

Preheat the oven to 240°C/220°C fan/Gas Mark 9. Rub the chicken
with 40ml of the olive oil and season liberally with salt and pepper.
Place in a roasting tin and put in the oven for 10 minutes. Reduce
the temperature to 210°C/190°C fan/Gas Mark 6 and continue to
roast for 50–60 minutes, basting with the juices occasionally, until
the chicken is thoroughly cooked. Remove from the oven and leave
to cool to room temperature. Do not get rid of the cooking juices.

While the chicken is roasting, cook the rice. Place the basmati in a saucepan with 400ml of water and a pinch of salt. Bring to the boil, then reduce the heat to minimum, cover and simmer for 20 minutes. Remove from the heat and leave, covered, for 10 minutes. Uncover and leave to cool completely.

Place the wild and brown rice in a saucepan and pour in enough cold water to cover the rice by at least 3 times its volume. Bring to the boil and simmer gently, uncovered, for 40–45 minutes, until the rice is tender but still retains a little firmness. If the water runs low, top up with extra boiling water. Drain through a sieve and run under plenty of cold water to stop the cooking. Leave there to drain.

Carve the meat from the chicken or simply tear it off in largish chunks. Put it in a bowl large enough to hold the whole salad. In a separate bowl, whisk all the dressing ingredients together with the cooking juices from the chicken. Pour the dressing over the chicken and set aside.

Heat the remaining olive oil in a pan, add the onion and a pinch of salt and fry over a medium heat until golden. Remove from the heat and leave to cool.

Add the 3 rices, the fried onion and spring onions, chillies and chopped herbs to the chicken. Mix well, then taste and adjust the seasoning.

Turkey and sweetcorn meatballs with roasted pepper sauce

Serves 4

We like to double or treble the red pepper sauce here and freeze for future use. It's great with fried tofu, pan-fried salmon, roasted florets of cauliflower or grilled meat. These meatballs are a hit with all ages and can even be served as a canapé. Just shape the mixture into bite-sized portions and cook for less time. You can make these ahead of time, and then just warm through before serving.

The breadcrumbs in the mix can be replaced with some coarsely grated courgette, for a gluten-free alternative. Start with 1 large courgette, weighing about 200g.

———

Preheat the oven to 220°C/200°C fan/Gas Mark 7. To prepare the peppers for the sauce, quarter them with a sharp knife and shave off the white parts and the seeds. Put them in a roasting tray and toss with 2 tablespoons of the olive oil and ½ teaspoon of salt, then roast in the oven for 35 minutes or until soft. Transfer the hot peppers to a bowl and cover it with cling film. Once they have cooled down a little, you can peel them, although it isn't essential for this sauce. In any case, place them in a blender or food processor with their roasting juices and add the rest of the sauce ingredients plus ½ teaspoon of salt. Process until smooth and set aside.

For the meatballs, place a heavy, non-stick frying pan over a high heat and throw in the corn kernels. Toss them in the hot pan for 2–3 minutes, until lightly blackened. Remove and leave to cool.

Soak the bread in cold water for a minute, then squeeze well and crumble it into a large bowl. Add all the rest of the ingredients except the sunflower oil and mix well with your hands.

Pour a 5mm depth of sunflower oil into your heavy frying pan. Allow it to heat up well and then fry about a teaspoonful of the mince mix in it. Remove, let cool a little and then taste. Adjust the amount of salt and pepper in the uncooked mixture to your liking.

With wet hands, shape the mince mix into balls, about the size of golf balls. Cook in small batches in the hot oil, turning them around in the pan until golden brown all over. Transfer to an oven tray, place in the oven at 220°C/200°C fan/Gas Mark 7 and cook for about 5 minutes. When you press one with your finger, the meat should bounce back. If unsure, break one open to check that it is cooked inside. Serve hot or warm, with the pepper sauce on the side.

100g sweetcorn kernels (fresh or frozen)

3 slices of stale white bread, crusts removed

500g minced turkey breast

1 egg

4 spring onions, finely chopped

10g parsley, finely chopped

2½ tsp ground cumin

1 garlic clove, crushed

sunflower oil, for frying

salt and black pepper

Roasted pepper sauce

4 red peppers

3 tbsp olive oil

25g coriander, leaves and stalks

1 garlic clove, peeled

1 small mild chilli, de-seeded

2 tbsp sweet chilli sauce

2 tbsp cider vinegar or white wine vinegar

Marinated turkey breast with cumin, coriander and white wine

20g mint leaves

20g parsley leaves

20g coriander leaves

1 garlic clove, peeled

60ml lemon juice

60ml olive oil

125ml white wine

½ tsp ground cumin

½ small turkey breast (about 1kg)

salt and black pepper

The run-up to Thanksgiving and Christmas is always a really fun time in our bakery, with the ovens taken up overnight with turkeys roasting for our catering clients. However much we try to ring the changes with the flavours in the sauce, we always return to this no-nonsense classic. It allows the turkey to shine at the same time as not completely dominating all the other dishes it will be served alongside. This can either be served warm or at room temperature. If you do want to try something different, though, serve this sauce with lamb, which also works very well.

———

Put all the ingredients except the turkey breast in a food processor or blender with ½ teaspoon of salt and a good grind of black pepper and process for 1–2 minutes to get a smooth marinade. Put the turkey in a non-metallic container and pour the marinade over it. Massage the marinade into the meat, cover the container and leave in the fridge for 24 hours. Make sure the turkey is immersed in the sauce.

Preheat the oven to 240°C/220°C fan/Gas Mark 9. Remove the turkey from the marinade (keep the marinade for later) and put it on a roasting tray. Place in the oven and roast for 15 minutes, then reduce the temperature to 220°C/200°C fan/Gas Mark 7. Continue to cook for 15 minutes, then reduce the temperature again to 200°C/180°C fan/Gas Mark 6. Cook until the turkey is done – another 30–45 minutes. To check, stick a small knife all the way into the centre; it should come out hot. If the meat goes dark before it is ready, cover it with foil.

To prepare the sauce, heat up the turkey marinade in a small saucepan and simmer for 15 minutes, until reduced by about half. Taste and season with some more salt and pepper.

Remove the turkey from the oven and let it rest for 10 minutes. Slice it thinly and serve with the warm sauce.

To serve cold, leave the turkey to cool completely and then slice. Taste and adjust the seasoning of the sauce once it is cold and serve on the side.

Seared duck breasts with blood orange and star anise

4 duck breasts, weighing 180–200g each

2 tbsp fennel seeds

a pinch of dried chilli flakes

2 tsp ground cumin

240ml blood orange juice (from about 4 oranges), plus 4 whole blood oranges

180ml red wine

2 tbsp sherry vinegar

16 star anise

6 dried chillies

flaky sea salt and black pepper

The ruby red of the blood oranges looks great here but don't worry if you can't get any: they are only in season for the first few months of the year and regular oranges work just as well. Start with nice large, succulent duck breasts, if you can: either the English Gressingham or the French Barbary ducks are good choices. This is lovely served with either the Parsnip and pumpkin mash (see page 84) or some simply roasted chicory. The combination of all three is also great.

———

Score the skin of each duck breast in 3 or 4 parallel incisions, without cutting into the meat. Repeat at a 90° angle to the other cuts to get square-shaped incisions. Mix the fennel seeds, chilli flakes and cumin with 1 teaspoon of salt and a very good grind of black pepper, then rub them thoroughly all over the duck breasts with your hands. Place in a bowl, cover with cling film and leave to marinate for a few hours or in the fridge overnight.

Using a small, sharp knife, trim off 1cm from the top and bottom of each orange. Standing them up, neatly follow the natural curves of each one with the knife to cut off the skin and white pith. Cut each orange horizontally into roughly 6 slices. Remove the pips, place the slices in a small bowl and set aside.

To sear the duck, thoroughly heat a large, heavy frying pan (one for which you have a lid). Place the duck breasts in it, skin-side down, and cook for 3 minutes, until the skin is golden brown and crisp. Turn and cook the other side for 3 minutes, then remove the duck from the pan and keep in a warm place.

Discard most of the fat from the frying pan and add the wine, vinegar, orange juice and star anise. Bring to the boil and simmer for 5–6 minutes, until reduced by about half. Taste and add salt and pepper if necessary. Return the duck breasts to the pan and stir to coat them in the sauce. Cover with a lid and simmer gently for 7 minutes.

Take the dried chillies, orange slices, plus any extra juice in their bowl, and place carefully next to the duck breasts. Cover again and simmer for another 3 minutes. By this time the meat should be medium-rare.

Remove the duck breasts from the sauce, place on a cutting board and leave to rest for 3–4 minutes. While you wait, check the sauce. It may need to be simmered a little longer to thicken it slightly. Taste again and adjust the seasoning if necessary.

Slice each breast at an angle into pieces 1cm thick and place on serving plates. Pick the oranges from the sauce and arrange them on the plates with the duck. Pour some of the sauce on top and serve the rest on the side.

Barbecued quail
with mograbiah salad

8 large quails (or
chicken legs or thighs),
spatchcocked

Marinade

1 tbsp ground cinnamon

2 tbsp ground cumin

10 whole cardamom pods

4 allspice berries (pimento)

1 tbsp ground turmeric

1½ tsp paprika

4 garlic cloves, peeled

6cm piece of ginger,
peeled and coarsely
chopped

2 tbsp honey

180ml olive oil

salt

Salad

125g mograbiah or fregola

10g unsalted butter

1 tbsp olive oil

1 mild red chilli

1 spring onion

1 lemon

15g parsley, roughly
chopped

15g coriander, roughly
chopped

15g mint, roughly
chopped

flaky sea salt and
black pepper

This is a dish that looks complicated – a little intimidating,
even – with all the various components, but is, in fact,
nothing of the sort. All the work on the meat, for example,
is done overnight when it gets marinating and the salad
can also be made well ahead, taken up to the point just
before the fresh herbs are added. Plenty of substitutions
can also be made, if you're looking for alternatives:
chicken legs or thighs, for example, instead of the quail;
or Sardinian fregola, regular couscous or even quinoa
instead of the mograbiah. If you stick with the quail,
ask your butcher to remove the backbone and ribs
and spatchcock (butterfly or flatten) the birds for you:
trying to do so yourself is very fiddly.

Start with the marinade. Put all the spices and a pinch of salt in
a small food processor bowl or a spice grinder and work them to
get a fine, homogenous powder (you could use a pestle and mortar
instead, although the mixture won't become as fine). Add the garlic
and ginger and continue working to a paste. Transfer the mixture
to a large bowl and whisk in the honey and oil until you get a light,
uniform mixture. Add the prepared quails, fold back your sleeves
and massage the birds intensively with the marinade. Transfer the
birds and marinade to a smaller container, then cover and chill for
at least 4 hours, preferably overnight.

The next day, start by cooking the mograbiah. Bring a litre of water
to the boil with a pinch of salt and add the mograbiah. Simmer
for 15–18 minutes, until tender but with quite a substantial bite
(the cooking time will vary according to the brand, so check the
instructions on the packet). Strain into a colander, leave to drain
well and then transfer to a bowl. Add the butter and oil, stir well
and season with plenty of salt and pepper. Set aside to cool.
While you wait, cut the chilli in half lengthways, get rid of the seeds
and chop it finely. Finely slice the spring onion. Add them to the
cooling mograbiah.

To segment the lemon, use a small, sharp knife to trim off 1cm
from the top and bottom. Stand it up on a board and neatly follow
its natural curves with the knife to take off the skin and all the white
pith. Holding the lemon over the bowl of mograbiah, cut along the
white membranes encasing the segments to release the segments
into the bowl. Squeeze in any remaining juice.

To cook the quail, place a griddle pan over a medium heat and leave for a few minutes so it heats up well. Lay the quails on it, spaced well apart, and grill for 10–14 minutes, turning them over half way through. The birds should be just cooked through. Make sure the heat is not too fierce or the birds will darken before they cook through; if this does happen, you could finish them off in a hot oven.

When the quail are almost ready, stir the herbs into the mograbiah. Taste and see if you need any more salt, pepper or olive oil.

Pile the salad on to serving dishes and place the quail on top, 2 per portion. Serve at once.

Seafood, fennel and lime salad

Serves 4

Fennel, herbs and seafood go together like sun, sea and sandcastles. You can almost smell the Mediterranean here in this dish, which needs little more than a glass of white wine alongside. It can be either a stand-alone starter or light lunch, with some fresh crusty bread to mop up the juices, or else served as part of a mezze selection. This can be made up to a day before serving, up to the point before the sumac and coriander are added.

—

Trim the bases and tops of the fennel bulbs, then slice widthwise as thinly as you can. A mandolin would be useful here. In a large bowl, mix the fennel and red onion with the lime juice and zest, garlic, dill, parsley, chilli, 2 tablespoons of the olive oil and ½ teaspoon of salt. Set aside.

Place a heavy cast-iron pan, preferably a griddle pan, over a high heat and leave for a few minutes until piping hot. Meanwhile, mix the prawns and squid with the rest of the oil and a pinch of salt. Grill them in small batches, turning them over after 1 minute and continuing until just done (roughly 1 more minute for the squid and 2–3 for the prawns). Transfer to a chopping board and slice the squid into thick rings. You can leave the prawns whole or cut them in half.

Add the seafood to the salad bowl and toss together. You can serve immediately or leave it in the fridge for up to 24 hours. To serve, stir in the sumac and coriander, then taste and adjust the seasoning. When pomegranate is available, it makes a beautiful garnish.

2 small fennel bulbs

½ red onion, very thinly sliced

finely grated zest and juice of 1 lime

2 garlic cloves, crushed

10g dill, roughly chopped

10g parsley, roughly chopped

1 mild chilli, de-seeded and finely chopped

60ml olive oil

8 tiger prawns, peeled and de-veined

350g cleaned baby squid

1 tbsp sumac

10g coriander, roughly chopped

pomegranate seeds, to garnish (optional)

flaky sea salt

Grilled mackerel with green olive, celery and raisin salsa

8 mackerel fillets, pin bones removed

2 tbsp olive oil

flaky sea salt and black pepper

Salsa

125g celery stalks, thinly sliced

60g good-quality green olives, pitted and thinly sliced

3 tbsp capers, rinsed

70g good-quality plump raisins

1½ tsp sherry vinegar

60ml olive oil

3 tbsp honey

15g parsley, roughly chopped

It seems as though there are lots of contradictions in this salsa – the salty capers, the sweet raisins – but the combination is one that works very well against an oily fish like mackerel. Just make sure you get the absolute freshest mackerel to let this simple dish shine. The salsa can be made the day before serving, if you like. If you do this then lunch can be on the table in less than 5 minutes.

———

Stir together all the salsa ingredients. Taste it; it should be sweet, sour and salty. Season with salt and pepper and leave to sit for at least 15 minutes for the flavours to evolve. (At this point, the salsa can be refrigerated for up to 24 hours, if necessary. Before serving, allow it to come to room temperature, refresh with extra chopped parsley and adjust the seasoning.)

Set an oven grill to its highest setting. Toss the mackerel fillets gently with the oil and some salt and pepper. Lay the fillets on a flat oven tray, skin-side up, and place under the hot grill for 3–4 minutes, or until just cooked.

Serve the fish hot or at room temperature, with a spoonful of salsa on top.

Grilled mackerel with sweet potato pickle and mint yoghurt

8 mackerel fillets,
pin bones removed

2 tbsp olive oil

salt and black pepper

Spice paste

1½ tsp cumin seeds

1½ tsp coriander seeds

1½ tsp caraway seeds

1½ tsp fennel seeds

½ cinnamon stick

1 star anise

3 garlic cloves, crushed

½ red chilli, de-seeded
and roughly chopped

6cm piece of ginger,
peeled and roughly
chopped

150g tamarind paste

100ml vegetable oil

flaky sea salt and
black peppercorns

Sweet potato pickle

5 limes

50g caster sugar

½ red chilli, de-seeded
and finely diced

2g coriander, finely
chopped

500g sweet potato,
peeled and cut into 1cm
dice

Mint yoghurt

1 mini cucumber

225g Greek yoghurt

¾ tsp paprika

juice of ½ lemon

2g mint leaves, finely
chopped

1½ tsp olive oil

As with the Barbecued quail with mograbiah salad (see page 142) this is another dish that tracks the progress of Scully as a chef (and also gives away the secret as to how he can produce such involved dishes and yet still remain completely chilled). Again, it's a recipe with all sorts of diverse components and elements but one which, when broken down, does not need to overwhelm: the spice paste can be made and ready weeks in advance, the pickle can be made days before serving and the mint yoghurt can be prepared the day before (hold back on the mint leaves, stirring these through just before serving). With these elements all made up and ready, you just have the quick and easy job of grilling the mackerel fillets for under 5 minutes just before serving and then assembling the dish.

Tamarind is an ingredient we've used more and more of as the years have gone by. It's a sour fruit originating from Asia that either comes as a sticky, dark brown pulp (which you soak and then strain to make your own paste or water) or else you can buy ready-made tamarind pastes. Start with the pulp, if you can, and make your own: the result has a depth that is sweet and sour – at once sharp and acidic but also fruity and soothing – and balanced in a way that some of the ready-made versions are not.

DAY 1

First make the spice paste. Place a thick-bottomed frying pan over a low heat and spread all the spice paste ingredients out in it apart from the oil. Cook gently for a few minutes, shaking the pan occasionally, until the spices start to release their aroma (do not let them brown or they will taste bitter). Tip everything into a pestle and mortar and pound to a uniform paste. Continue working the spices whilst slowly adding the oil to get a smooth consistency. (You will only need 1 tablespoon of the spice paste for this recipe but the rest can be stored in a clean jar in the fridge for a few months.)

Now for the sweet potato pickle. Take the limes and use a small, sharp knife to trim off their tops and tails. Now cut down the sides of the limes, following their natural curves, to remove the skin and all the white pith. Over a small bowl, remove the segments from each lime by slicing between the membranes. Squeeze out any remaining juice over the segments, then discard the membrane.

Add the sugar and 1 tablespoon of the spice paste to the lime segments. Stir well to dissolve the sugar, then add the chilli and coriander.

Put the sweet potato dice in a pan of boiling salted water and simmer for 3–5 minutes, until they are just cooked but still hold their shape. Drain thoroughly and transfer to a non-metallic bowl. Dress with the lime mixture, leave to cool and then cover with cling film and chill overnight. Remove from the fridge an hour before using.

DAY 2

Start by making the mint yoghurt. Peel the cucumber, cut it in half lengthways and scoop out the seeds with a spoon. Cut the cucumber into 1cm dice and place in a bowl. Add the yoghurt, paprika, lemon juice, mint and oil. Stir well, try a bit and add salt and pepper to taste. Refrigerate until ready to serve.

To cook the fish, preheat the grill to its highest setting. Brush the mackerel fillets with the oil and season with salt and pepper. Place the fillets on a baking tray, skin-side up, and put under the grill for 3–4 minutes or until they are cooked through.

To serve, place a large spoonful of the pickle on each plate and top with the hot fish. Finish with a little of the mint yoghurt over the fish and serve the rest in a bowl on the side.

Seared tuna with pistachio crust and papaya salsa

150g shelled pistachio kernels

finely grated zest of 1 lemon

1kg tuna loin

2 tbsp olive oil

5 tbsp Dijon mustard

flaky sea salt and black pepper

Papaya salsa

1 mini cucumber or ¼ of a large cucumber, watery core removed

1 large, ripe papaya, peeled, de-seeded and cut into 1cm dice

1 large, ripe mango, peeled, pitted and cut into 1cm dice

2 red chillies, de-seeded and finely chopped

2cm piece of ginger, peeled and grated

1 small red onion, finely chopped

finely grated zest and juice of 2 limes

2 tbsp lemon juice

2 tbsp Thai fish sauce

60ml olive oil

2 tbsp caster sugar

Both the tuna and the salsa can be prepared the day before serving and kept in the fridge. The flavours of the salsa actually improve and intensify with time, so getting ahead has lots of advantages. Just make sure you start with papaya and mango that are beautifully ripe and sweet. Once made, the salsa will keep in a sealed container in the fridge for up to 5 days. Bring both the salsa and the tuna back to room temperature and then slice the tuna just before serving.

If you like, you can roast the pistachios before coating the fish with them. Doing so will help draw out their flavour, but it does result in a slight loss of their vibrant green colour. Either way, the dish is an absolute corker.

We know, by the way, that cooked fish should not go near a blue chopping board according to the rules of a restaurant kitchen. Rest assured that after our photographer made his aesthetic (rather than hygienic) decision, the board was confined to the annuls of history, by way of the recycling bin.

Start with the salsa. Peel the cucumber, halve it lengthways, then scoop out and discard the seeds. Cut it into 1cm dice and put it in a bowl. Add all the rest of the salsa ingredients, stir well and season with salt and pepper. Taste and adjust the seasoning, then chill. It is advisable to allow it to rest for at least an hour for all the flavours to combine.

Now for the tuna. Preheat the oven to 260°C/250°C fan/Gas Mark 10, or as high as it will go. Chop the pistachios, preferably in a food processor, until you get fine crumbs. Scatter them on a baking tray and mix with the lemon zest, then set aside.

Take the tuna loin and use a sharp knife to divide it along its length into 2 or 3 cylindrical pieces. They should be 6–7cm thick and show the layers of the loin at their ends. Brush the tuna with the olive oil and season with salt and pepper. Place a griddle pan or a heavy cast-iron pan over a high heat and leave for a few minutes to heat up. Place the tuna pieces in the pan and sear lightly for 3–4 minutes in total, turning them around as you go. Remove from the pan and leave to cool down a little.

Now brush the tuna generously with the mustard and then roll it
in the chopped pistachio mixture, using your fingers to cover any
bare patches. Place the tuna in a baking tray, transfer to the oven
and roast for 5–6 minutes. Check carefully (stick a knife in; it should
come out cold), as it might not take that long. What you want is
a slightly raw centre with a 1–2cm ring of cooked meat around it.
Remove and allow to cool down completely.

To serve, cut the tuna into slices 2cm thick. Serve with the salsa
on the side or poured on top.

Pan-fried sea bass on pita with labneh, tomato and preserved lemon

½ preserved lemon, if starting with large, or 2 if starting with small

4 sea bass fillets (about 600g in total), scaled and pin bones removed, cut in half at an angle

3 tbsp olive oil

2 large pita breads, quartered

120g labneh, bought or homemade, at room temperature

2 tbsp pomegranate seeds (optional)

flaky sea salt and black pepper

Salsa

3 sweet and ripe tomatoes (about 350g in total)

1 mild red chilli, de-seeded and finely chopped

½ tsp dried chilli flakes

5g parsley, roughly chopped

10g coriander, roughly chopped

50ml lemon juice

When asked to describe our food, we often talk about wanting 'bursts of flavour' or 'surprise' in otherwise comforting food. There are certain ingredients that are a fast-track to these sorts of bursts, preserved lemon being one. We tend to make our own (see page 286) in our shops and at home but they are now also widely available to buy, if you like. You can either get the larger kind with the thick skin or else the smaller variety, which have a much thinner and softer skin. Preserved lemon works with (or against, in the best possible sense) all sorts of foods but particularly well with very fresh fish.

The labneh can either be bought or made (see page 285) or else replaced with some thick Greek yoghurt mixed through with a little bit of olive oil.

First make the salsa. Score a little shallow cross at the bottom of each tomato and then drop them into boiling water for about 30 seconds. Remove, refresh under plenty of cold water and then peel. Grate them coarsely on a cheese grater and mix with the fresh and dried chilli, herbs and lemon juice. Add salt to taste, then set aside.

Remove the flesh of the preserved lemon, discard and slice the skin very finely. Set aside.

Now prepare the fish. First, heat the oven to 200°C/180°C fan/Gas Mark 6. Then season the fillets with plenty of salt and pepper. Heat the oil in a non-stick frying pan, large enough to hold all the fillets at once. Add the sea bass and fry, skin-side down, over a medium heat for 3 minutes, until the skin is crisp. Turn the fish over and continue to fry for about 2 minutes, until it is cooked through.

While the fish is frying, place the pitas in the oven for 2 minutes, just to warm them up slightly. Put 2 pita quarters on each serving plate and spread a rough, thick layer of labneh over them.

Place the hot fish on top of the pitas and spoon some of the salsa over and around the fish. Finish with a few slices of preserved lemon and the pomegranate seeds, if using.

Pan-fried sea bream with green tahini and pomegranate seeds

Serves 4

Our use of pomegranate seeds is certainly more liberal in this book than any of our others. We've learnt to rein in on these jewels but they're just such a lovely addition to all sorts of dishes. Here, for example, they bring both their flash of bright colour – the pinky-red against the white fish and green sauce backdrop – as well as a little pop of juicy sweetness when you crunch down on a seed.

The rise of pre-prepared pomegranate seeds means they are now there for all to buy in the chilled section of many large supermarkets but, for those who want the satisfaction of extracting their own, the best way is as follows. Slice the pomegranate in half, widthways, and then hold it in the palm of one hand, cut side down. Splay your fingers apart so that the seeds can fall through. Do this in your kitchen sink (the juice can spray everywhere otherwise), with a large bowl sitting in the basin to catch the seeds. Hold a long-handed heavy wooden spoon or rolling pin with the other hand, and bash down on the outside of the pomegranate half. All the seeds should fall through your fingers – either separately or in small clumps – into the bowl. And if you've gone to all the trouble of extracting the seeds from the pomegranate, why would you not want to sprinkle them over everything you can?

Make the tahini sauce and get your seeds all ready and then this dish can, as with so many fish dishes, be on the table within 10 minutes of getting into the kitchen.

---

4 sea bream fillets, scaled and pin bones removed

60ml olive oil

½ quantity of Green tahini sauce (see page 284) at room temperature

10g parsley, roughly chopped

finely grated zest of 1 lemon

100g pomegranate seeds (about ½ pomegranate)

4 lemon wedges, to serve (optional)

flaky sea salt and black pepper

Preheat the oven to 220°C/200°C fan/Gas Mark 7. Line a baking tray with greaseproof paper. Season the fish with plenty of salt and pepper and lay it in the tray, skin-side down. Drizzle with the olive oil and then bake for 6–7 minutes. The fish should be firm and 'bounce' back when you poke it with a finger.

Place the fish on serving plates and spoon the tahini sauce generously on top. Garnish with the chopped parsley, lemon zest and pomegranate seeds. Place a lemon wedge next to the fish, if you like, and serve at once.

Sardines stuffed with bulgar, currants and pistachios

Serves 4

This also works well with mackerel fillets, but do give the sardines a try: people are often predisposed against them after a lifetime of little bony things in a tin but this is a far cry from how they should be. Ask your fishmonger to scale, bone and butterfly the sardines: trying to do this yourself is not the way to endear yourself back to them.

If you can get hold of some, barberries are a good alternative to the currants. You can get them at many Middle Eastern shops, or online.

This is the lunch for when you want to be on holiday by the sea but aren't. It's a staycation on a plate.

––––

Put the bulgar in a bowl, cover it with cold water and leave to soak for 15–20 minutes, until soft. Drain in a fine sieve and squeeze to remove excess moisture. Return to the bowl.

In a separate bowl, cover the currants with a little warm water and leave to soak for 5 minutes, then drain.

Heat the oven to 170°C/150°C fan/Gas Mark 3. Sprinkle the pistachios over a baking tray and roast in the oven for 10 minutes, until lightly coloured. Leave to cool and then chop roughly.

Now add the drained currants and the pistachios to the bulgar, with the lemon zest, juice and chopped parsley (reserving a little parsley to garnish). Stir in the spices, mint, garlic, molasses, sugar and 5 tablespoons of olive oil, then season with salt and pepper to taste.

In a separate bowl, mix the prepared sardines with the remaining olive oil and season with a little salt and pepper.

Heat the oven to 200°C/180°C fan/Gas Mark 6. To stuff the sardines, lay them on a chopping board, skin-side down, with the tail facing away from you. Spoon a little bit of the bulgar stuffing in the middle of each fish and fold first the head end over the stuffing and then the tail to form a roll. Carefully push a wooden cocktail stick down through the fish, catching both sides of the fillets. The tail should slightly stick up in the air. Gently press back any mix that is escaping from the sides.

Arrange the sardines on a baking tray lined with baking parchment, place in the oven and roast for 5–6 minutes, until just cooked through. Serve hot or at room temperature, accompanied by the lemon wedges and garnished with a little chopped parsley.

100g medium bulgar wheat

30g currants

30g shelled pistachio kernels

finely grated zest of 1 lemon

40ml lemon juice

10g parsley, roughly chopped

½ tsp ground cinnamon

1 tsp ground allspice (pimento)

3 tbsp dried mint

2 garlic cloves, crushed

2 tbsp pomegranate molasses

1 tsp caster sugar

90ml olive oil

8 fresh sardines, scaled, boned and butterflied

4 lemon wedges, to serve

salt and black pepper

Serves 4

Chargrilled salmon with red pepper and hazelnut salsa

4 salmon fillets, weighing 200g each

2 tbsp olive oil

salt and black pepper

Red pepper and hazelnut salsa

2 red peppers

90ml olive oil

15g hazelnuts

15g chives, chopped

1 garlic clove, crushed

finely grated zest and juice of 1 lemon

2 tbsp cider vinegar

Fish is such a good option for a fast-food meal. If you make the salsa the day before, it's then just a case of cooking the fish briefly before serving. The meal is on the table less than 10 minutes after you've started. The fish is lovely warm from the oven but also works well at room temperature, if you want to make it ahead of time. We've peeled the red peppers here to get a smooth salsa but feel free to skip this stage, if you like. The resulting salsa won't be as smooth, but it will stll work well. If you want to add a nice visual twist, try a mix of yellow or orange peppers with or instead of the red: the clash of colours, as always, looks fantastic.

———

First make the salsa. Preheat the oven to 220°C/200°C fan/Gas Mark 7. Quarter the peppers and remove the seeds. Put them in a baking tray and toss with 2 tablespoons of the olive oil and a generous pinch of salt. Roast them in the oven for about 20 minutes, until they are cooked through and slightly charred. Transfer to a bowl, cover with cling film and leave to cool. Keep any of the roasting juices.

Roast the hazelnuts on a separate baking tray for 10 minutes, until lightly coloured (you can do this while the peppers are in the oven). Allow them to cool down and then rub with your hands to remove the skins. Chop them roughly.

When the peppers are cool, peel them and cut into 5mm dice. Mix with the hazelnuts, the remaining olive oil and all the rest of the salsa ingredients. Taste and add salt and pepper.

Put a ridged griddle pan on the highest possible heat and leave for a few minutes. It needs to be very hot! Have an oven tray lined with baking parchment ready. Brush the salmon fillets with the olive oil and sprinkle with salt and pepper. Put them on the hot griddle, skin-side up, and cook for about 3 minutes. Using a fish slice, carefully but briskly remove the fish from the griddle and place them on the lined tray, skin-side down. Be careful not to scrape off the nice char marks when you handle the fish. Bake in the oven for 5–8 minutes, until the fish is just done and very light pink inside. Serve warm, with a generous spoonful of salsa on top.

Fried scallops with saffron potatoes, asparagus and samphire

Serves 4 as a starter

The samphire adds a salty note to the dish but don't worry if you can't get hold of any: just increase the number of asparagus spears to about 12.

First make the aioli. Preheat the oven to 170°C/150°C fan/Gas Mark 3. Place the garlic cloves on a sheet of aluminium foil, drizzle with a little olive oil and sprinkle with a pinch of salt. Wrap in the foil to seal and then roast in the oven for 25–35 minutes, until very tender. Remove from the oven and leave to cool, then mash with a fork.

Mix together the olive oil and sunflower oil. In a mixing bowl, combine the egg yolk, vinegar, mustard, garlic, salt and a good grind of black pepper. Whisk constantly by hand or in a food processor while slowly trickling in the oils until thick, like mayonnaise.

Put the potatoes in a medium saucepan, cover with cold water, then add the saffron and a generous pinch of salt. Bring to the boil, reduce the heat and simmer for 6–8 minutes; the potatoes should still be slightly firm. Drain and leave in a cool place.

Wash the samphire in plenty of water and then throw it into a pan of boiling water. Leave for just 1 minute, then use a slotted spoon to lift it from the pan and into a colander. Refresh under cold running water and set aside.

Trim the woody ends of the asparagus and cut each spear into 3cm lengths. Drop into the pan of boiling water the samphire was cooked in, simmer for 2–3 minutes, then drain at once into a colander and run under plenty of cold water. Set aside to dry.

To serve, heat up 2 large frying pans with half the olive oil in each. When piping hot, add the potatoes to one of the pans. Toss them for a minute or two to get some colour and then add the asparagus and samphire just to warm them up. Taste and season.

At the same time, season the scallops liberally with salt and pepper and put them into the other pan. Sear them for 30–50 seconds on each side or until just cooked (this will depend on their size).

Straight away, divide the warm scallops and vegetables between small serving plates or the scallop shells and spoon about a teaspoon of the aioli on top of each portion (the leftover aioli will keep in the fridge for 2 days). Garnish with the diced tomato and a drizzle of olive oil and serve at once.

400g Desiree potatoes, peeled and cut into 1cm dice

a large pinch of saffron strands

1 small tomato, quartered, seeds removed, and cut into 5mm dice

40g samphire

8 medium asparagus spears

60ml olive oil

8 medium-large fresh hand-dived scallops, trimmed

4 scallop shells, washed (optional)

flaky sea salt and black pepper

Aioli

7 garlic cloves, peeled

100ml olive oil, plus a little extra for roasting the garlic

50ml sunflower oil

1 egg yolk

1½ tsp white wine vinegar

¼ tsp Dijon mustard

salt

Buttered prawns with tomato, olives and Arak

Serves 4 as a starter

For all that our recipes evolve and develop through our collection of books, there are certain threads – or combinations of ingredients – holding things together. Prawns, tomatoes and Arak are one of these combinations. New ingredients share the stage – chunks of feta, the addition of more fish, bringing in a new herb or a different vegetable – but the trilogy still holds tight. This – the simplest and quickest version – remains the classic, the template against which all others are measured. It needs to be eaten as soon as it's made, served with fresh crusty bread to mop up the juices.

———

Start by preparing the tomatoes. Make a tiny shallow cross with a sharp knife at the bottom of each one and put them in boiling water for 30 seconds. Remove, refresh under plenty of cold water, then drain. Now peel the skin away and cut each tomato into 4–6 wedges. Set aside.

To prepare the prawns, peel the shells away from the bodies, keeping the tail segment of the shell on. Cut a shallow slit along the back of each prawn and remove the dark vein using the tip of a small knife.

Place a frying pan over a high heat. When very hot, add 20g of the butter and sauté the prawns quickly for 2 minutes, shaking the pan as you go. Add the tomatoes, chilli and olives and cook for another 2–3 minutes, until the prawns are nearly cooked through. Add the Arak carefully (it tends to catch fire!). Let the alcohol evaporate for a minute before quickly adding the remaining butter plus the garlic, parsley and some salt. Toss for a second for everything to come together in a runny sauce, then serve immediately, with bread.

4 plum tomatoes

12 tiger or king prawns, shell on

50g softened unsalted butter

½ tsp dried chilli flakes

50g Kalamata olives, pitted

20ml Arak (or Pernod)

3 garlic cloves, very thinly sliced

10g parsley, roughly chopped

flaky sea salt

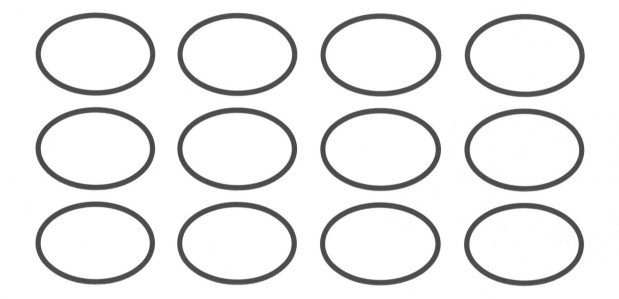

Baking and pâtisserie

———

Don't be scared of baking!

If you can read, you can cook; if you can cook, you can bake; if you can bake, you'll always make your kitchen smell amazing and you'll always make people happy. These are all very good reasons, in short, not to be scared.

As well as being able to read and cook, baking is often just about getting organised before you start. Read through the recipe in full – you don't want to find out that something needs to be chilled for four hours when you were planning to serve it for lunch that day – and have all your ingredients weighed out and ready. It might feel a bit wannabe-TV-show-presenter but you'll be able to enjoy making something far more if you know you can just add the flour when needed, for example, rather than having to stop the whisk, weigh it out and then add it in. Baking is not complicated but it's often important to keep up momentum once you've started a recipe: having carefully whisked lots of air into a batter, for example, delaying proceedings whilst you go off to find the baking powder or crack the eggs is not going to help produce the magically light result you're after. Getting everything organised and into little bowls in the first place will help you no end.

As with all recipes, there's a balance to be struck between following the instructions and using your initiative. If you are told to rest some dough in the fridge for 30 minutes then don't be tempted to skip this – if you don't want your pastry to shrink once its cooked, it needs resting, it needs chilling – but, on the other hand, have the confidence to leave something in the oven if you think it needs five minutes more than the recipe states. If your dough for the crusty white Italian loaf needs a bit more flour then you should add it; if your brownies want more toffee shards than we've suggested, that's fine. Recipes are there to be cooked, cooked again and then cooked so many times that you start to tweak and tailor them. A recipe succeeds when it becomes something different: it becomes yours.

A few short notes on kit, methods and ingredients

Kit

Electric mixer – if you want to make brioche, breads and show-stopping meringues then you need a freestanding electric mixer with all the attachments: a whisk, a paddle and a dough hook. They come in all sorts of lovely bright colours so will make your kitchen look the part as well. For lots of other recipes, though – where simply creaming the butter and sugar is called for, whisking eggs or whipping up creams – a handheld electric whisk will also do the job.

Blender – Whether you have a handheld stick blender or a freestanding blender, these are really useful for making fruit purees and liquidising sauces.

Tins and moulds – Having the right sized baking tin or mould is really important. There is more scope for flexibility on the shape of the tin – so long as you don't mind, a square cake will work just as well as a round one – but the size will make a difference to cooking time and quantities so do try and keep these as accurate as you can.

Palette knife and pastry brush – if the garlic press and lemon squeezer are our savoury desert-island kitchen must-haves then these are what we'd need to keep things sweet: they are a must, for us, when baking.

Methods

Creaming – This is the starting point for many cakes and biscuits, where a paste of butter and sugar is mixed together before eggs and flour are added. The more the paste gets mixed, the whiter and puffier it will become and the more aerated it becomes. It's important to note how long this paste should get mixed: brownies, for example, don't need a lot of air in them, while the very life of meringues depends on it. When you've worked really hard to get air into a batter, don't then bash it all out by adding all the eggs at once. Instead, add them a little at a time, waiting for the previous addition to be incorporated before adding the next bit. The dry ingredients (check if they require sifting or not) should all be added at once and the mix worked just until everything is incorporated, no longer. Doing all this with a free standing electric mixer takes the ache out of the arm and converts the whole process to one of easy joy.

Greasing and lining tins – Whether you prefer to use melted butter or vegetable oil (either wiped on or from a spray can), always brush your tins and moulds thoroughly and then line them with non-stick baking parchment that has been cut to the right size. It's such a shame for that 'ta da' moment to be ruined by everything getting stuck to places it shouldn't.

Baking times – Two seemingly contrary bits of advice here. On the one hand it's really important to follow oven temperatures and baking times but also to follow your instincts. If you think a pastry shell needs 4 or 5 more minutes in the oven to become nice and golden-brown, then that is what it needs; if a knife inserted into a cake does not come out as clean as you're told it should be, then keep it in the oven for longer. Our experience, though, is that people tend to underbake biscuits, tarts and breads and overbake chocolate cakes and brownies. Again, cook these recipes again and again, write notes in the margins and perfect them according to your oven, your kitchen, your palate.

Ingredients

Unless otherwise stated, the chocolate used contains 53–64% cocoa solids. The yeast used is dried: if you want to use fresh instead then you'll need to start with double the amount, weight-wise.
Flour is either plain or strong: they have different gluten levels and will produce really different results: they're not interchangeable so don't be tempted to substitute one with the other. As with the recipes in the rest of the book, all salt is regular table, unless flaky sea salt flakes are specified. Unless otherwise stated (for example when butter should be fridge-cold), ingredients should be at room temperature for baking.

Crusty white Italian loaf

25g Italian '00' flour, plus extra for dusting

2½ tsp polenta, plus extra for dusting

2 tsp dark spray malt powder

110ml tepid water

1 tsp salt

olive oil, for keeping your hands moist

Biga

200g Italian '00' flour

175g strong white bread flour

170ml tepid water

1 tsp active dried yeast or 1½ tsp (tightly packed) fresh yeast

When thinking about what to serve alongside any given dish, it's all too easy to revert to the suggestion of some 'crusty white bread'. So often, though, it *is* exactly what we want to soak up the juices or bulk out a meal. The smell of fresh bread makes a house become home, and its presence on the table makes a meal complete.

You need to get going two days before you want this out of the oven. You also need a good electric mixer with a dough hook. The dough for this bread is incredibly wet – wetter than you'll be expecting and far too wet to work by hand. Trust in the recipe, though, and trust in the ingredients listed: the 25 grams of flour is not a typo!

Dark spray malt powder adds real character and depth to the bread. It's widely available online (thanks to the rise in the number of home-brewing sites) but you can substitute it, if you need to, with some soft dark brown sugar.

___

DAY 1

The day before you want to make your bread, you will need to make the biga starter. Using an electric mixer with the dough hook attached, knead together all the ingredients for the biga. Run the machine on low speed for about 7 minutes. This should create a very tight dough with no lumps. Place it in a bowl large enough to allow it to at least double in size, then cover the bowl with cling film and leave at room temperature overnight – anything from 15 to 20 hours.

DAY 2

The starter should now have doubled in volume. Take it in your hands and cut it into small pieces with a pair of scissors. Put the pieces in the mixer bowl and add the flour, polenta, malt powder and water. Run the mixer on a low speed for 5 minutes, then increase to a fast speed and knead for another 5 minutes. At this point the dough will look very wet and sticky – much wetter than you might expect from a bread dough – but trust in the recipe here. Add the salt and continue mixing on a fast speed for a further 15–20 minutes. The dough should now come together as a ball and appear shiny.

Take a large bowl and dust it generously with flour. Oil your hands and lift the dough from the mixer to the bowl. Cover with a damp cloth and leave in a warm place for 30 minutes.

Wet your hands with a little olive oil. Whilst it is still in the bowl, pick the dough up from one edge and stretch it. Fold the stretched edge on top. Repeat this, stretching and folding the dough from all sides of the bowl. In the end you will get a few 'flaps' gathered together on top of the dough. Now turn the dough over and place it back in the bowl, flaps on the bottom. Cover with the damp cloth and leave for another 30 minutes.

Repeat the same turning process once more and then leave to rest, covered, for about 10 minutes.

Now turn the dough out on to a floured work surface and gather the edges together on top of the dough to form a rustic ball shape. Lay out a clean tea towel on the work surface and dust it liberally with flour. Lift the ball gently and place it in the centre of the towel, seam-side down. Gather gently the edges of the towel and place them on top of the ball to cover it totally. Transfer the entire parcel to a bowl large enough to support its sides and leave to rise for about 30 minutes.

Place a small ovenproof dish with water in it in the bottom of your oven and heat it to 250°C/230°C fan/Gas Mark 9. Make sure it reaches this temperature! Take a heavy baking tray and dust it with a little polenta. Very gently turn the dough out on to the tray and remove the cloth. Try not to lose much air.

Bake the loaf in the oven for about 25 minutes or until a good dark brown colour forms. When you tap it on its bottom, the bread should sound hollow. Leave upside down on a wire rack to cool.

Green olive loaf

ingredients as for Crusty
white Italian loaf (see
page 170)

200g good-quality
green olives, pitted

Once you've cracked the crust on the master recipe,
variations abound for all sorts of additions you can make
to the dough. We've suggested green olives here but
black olives also work well, if you prefer. Shredded sage
leaves, lightly sautéed in olive oil, are also good. This is
perfect served with any salty cheese: goat's and ewes'
milk cheese in particular.

Make the dough as described on page 170. Drain the olives and dry
them well on a kitchen cloth. Add them to the dough at the end
of the final mixing stage and mix on medium speed for 2 minutes.

For a distinctive elongated shape, stretch the dough gently
as you transfer it to the baking tray to create a thick stick form.
Bake as on page 171.

Sour cherry and walnut stick

160ml lukewarm water (not more than 30°C)

1½ tsp active dried yeast or 2¼ tsp (tightly packed) fresh yeast

40ml orange juice

250g country brown flour (Allinson's country grain brown bread flour or Hovis granary flour), plus extra for dusting

65g buckwheat flour

1 tsp salt

50g dried sour cherries

50g walnut halves, roughly broken into pieces

This sweet and nutty bread sits very well on a cheeseboard or alongside cured meats. The buckwheat flour in the dough also gives it a nice earthy depth, perfect for a picnic. Thanks to Jim Webb for this recipe.

Put the water and yeast in the bowl of an electric mixer, stir together and leave to stand for 10 minutes. Add the orange juice, mix again and then add both types of flour. Set the machine on a low speed and knead for 5 minutes with the dough hook until everything comes together in a rough ball.

Stop the machine and scrape the dough from the bottom of the bowl. Add the salt, turn up to a high speed and work for 4 minutes, by which time the dough should be smoother and have a silky texture. Stop the mixer, add the cherries and walnuts and mix on a medium speed for another minute.

Turn the dough out on to a lightly floured work surface and knead by hand, turning it as you do so, until all the cherries and walnuts are inside the dough and it appears smooth. Shape the dough into a ball and put it in a large bowl. Cover with a damp cloth and leave in a warm place for 1½ hours or until the dough has doubled in volume.

Turn the risen dough out on to a floured surface. Trying not to beat too much air out of it, pull the edges of the dough so that they all meet at the centre top to form a puffed, round cushion shape. Use a long object such as the handle of a wooden spoon to divide the dough into 2 equal spheres. Press down a little and then fold one half over the other. Crimp the round edges together with your fingers to seal them as if you were making a Cornish pasty. Now roll this on the floured surface to create a torpedo-like baguette shape. Lay it gently on a floured tea towel, cover loosely with cling film and leave to rise in a warm place for another 45 minutes.

Heat the oven to 240°C/220°C fan/Gas Mark 9 and put a small, shallow pan of hot water in the bottom. Once the dough has risen by about 50 per cent, roll it off the cloth and on to a baking sheet. Be careful not to shake it too much or to press hard, so as not to lose air. Use a very sharp non-serrated knife to make 3 diagonal slashes, 1cm deep, on top of the bread (an old-fashioned razor blade is best).

Place the tray in the oven and bake for 20–25 minutes. Check if the bread is ready by tapping on its base; it should sound hollow. Leave to cool on a wire rack.

Focaccia (plus three toppings)

If you're new to making bread then focaccia – which needs very little shaping – is a great place to start. We've suggested a range of toppings here, but feel free to experiment with alternatives or additions. A quarter of a teaspoon of nigella seeds looks great sprinkled over the red onion and goat's cheese topping, for example. Or you can play around with the herbs in the parsley and oil topping, substituting in hard herbs such as thyme or rosemary (you'll need less, though) instead.

Whatever toppings you do go for, follow the advice Jim Webb gave us when developing this bread. 'Focaccia isn't a fat pizza', he'd say, 'but a bread enriched with oil and some flavouring'. Use the best extra virgin olive oil you can here and be generous with it.

The oil in the bread allows for a shelf life of about three days. If you need to freshen it up, just lightly brush a slab of the bread with a bit more oil before chargrilling it on a hot, ridged griddle pan for 30 seconds or so.

———

For the starter, put the yeast and water in a large mixing bowl and stir with a wooden spoon until the yeast dissolves. Add the flour and stir until you get a porridge-like consistency. Cover the bowl with a damp cloth and leave somewhere warm for about 2 hours, until doubled in size.

In a mixer fitted with a dough hook attachment, mix the starter with the flour, sugar and olive oil. Knead on a low speed for 6 minutes, then add the salt and work on a fast speed for 2 minutes.

Brush a large bowl with oil, place the dough in it and brush the surface of the dough with more oil. Cover the bowl with a damp cloth and leave in a warm place for 1 hour, until the dough has doubled in size.

Turn the dough on to a floured work surface and stretch and flatten it into a rectangle. Try not to work it too much. Take one of the short edges of the rectangle and fold it into the centre. Take the other end and fold it over the first one to form 3 layers of dough.

330g strong white bread flour

1 tbsp soft light brown sugar

2 tbsp olive oil, plus extra for brushing

1 tbsp flaky sea salt

Starter

1½ tsp active dried yeast (or 15g fresh yeast)

420ml bottled still spring water, lukewarm

330g strong white bread flour

Take a heavy baking tray, roughly 30 x 40cm, and brush it with oil. Lift the dough on to the tray, placing it so the seam is at the bottom, and flatten it by pressing hard with your fingers. Cover with cling film and leave to rise for another hour. During this time you will need to work on the dough 3 or 4 times. Press it down with your fingertips and stretch it out gently to the edges of the baking tray each time. By the end of this process it should cover the whole tray in a layer about 2cm thick and have lots of bumps and little hills in it.

Preheat the oven to 240°C/220°C fan/Gas Mark 9. Follow one of the topping instructions opposite. Place the focaccia in the oven and bake for 10 minutes, then reduce the temperature to 210°C/190°C fan/Gas Mark 6 and continue for 15–20 minutes. Check underneath the bread to make sure it is baked through. When it is out of the oven and still hot, brush with plenty of olive oil.

Parsley and olive topping

Stir together the olive oil, garlic and parsley. Dot them over the top of the dough. Spread the pitted olives over it, pressing them into the dough, and sprinkle with salt.

2 tbsp olive oil

1 garlic clove, crushed

30g parsley, chopped

50g kalamata olives, pitted

flaky sea salt

Grape and fennel seed topping

Halve the grapes lengthwise. Mix the sugar and fennel seeds together. Stud the top of the dough with the grapes and sprinkle with the sugar and seeds.

300g seedless red grapes

50g caster sugar

2 tsp fennel seeds

Red onion and goat's cheese topping

Mix the onion with the olive oil and scatter it on top of the bread. Dot with pieces of crumbled goat's cheese and sprinkle with a little salt.

1 small red onion, thinly sliced

2 tbsp olive oil

100g goat's cheese, crumbled

flaky sea salt

Jerusalem artichoke and Swiss chard tart

1 quantity of Shortcrust pastry (page 293) or use 500g bought pastry

vegetable oil, for brushing the tin

flour, for dusting

Filling

600g Jerusalem artichokes, peeled and cut into 2cm cubes

250g Swiss chard (or spinach)

60ml olive oil

½ tsp chopped rosemary

juice of ½ lemon

1 garlic clove, crushed

220ml double cream

50ml crème fraîche

2 medium eggs

150g feta cheese, broken into pieces

salt and black pepper

Swiss chard has an earthiness that works well with Jerusalem artichokes. Its availability is a sign of how times have changed since we first published this book. We used to have to explain what chard was; now it's widely available in both rainbow-coloured and green varieties.

This tart can either be served warm from the oven or at room temperature. If you want to make it the day before, you'll just need to warm it through before serving.

———

Lightly oil a 22–24cm loose-bottomed tart tin. On a lightly floured surface, roll out the pastry to 2–3mm thick. Use the pastry to line the tin, pressing it well into the corners and the sides and allowing it to spill over the edge by at least 2cm. This excess will be trimmed later. Prick the base with a fork in a few places, then leave the tart case to rest in the fridge for at least half an hour.

Heat the oven to 190°C/170°C fan/Gas Mark 5. Cut a circle of greaseproof paper greater in diameter than the base plus the sides of the tart tin. Tuck it in the pastry case and fill up with dried beans or rice. Bake the case blind for 35 minutes, then remove the paper and the beans or rice (you can keep them and reuse indefinitely for baking blind). Return the pastry case to the oven and bake for a further 5–10 minutes, until light golden and thoroughly cooked. Remove from the oven and leave to cool.

While your pastry is resting and baking, prepare the filling. Place the artichokes in a saucepan, cover with cold water and bring to the boil with a little salt. Reduce the heat and simmer for 15 minutes, until tender. Drain and leave to cool.

Cut the chard leaves off the stalks, then roughly chop the leaves and stalks, keeping them separate. Heat the oil in a large frying pan, add the stalks and fry for 2 minutes, then add the leaves and the rosemary. Sauté for 6–8 minutes, depending on how woody the chard is. It should wilt completely. Remove from the heat, stir in the lemon juice, garlic and some seasoning and leave to cool.

Whisk together the double cream, crème fraîche, eggs and a pinch of salt and pepper. Spread the artichokes, chard and feta over the base of the pastry case, arranging them so that all the ingredients are visible. Pour the custard mixture on top. Make sure you don't fill the tart to the rim, so that bits of the filling show above the custard.

Carefully transfer the tart to the hot oven and bake for 15 minutes. Then cover loosely with foil and bake for a further 45 minutes, until the filling is set. If the top is still pale, remove the foil and leave the tart in the oven for a few extra minutes.

Take out of the oven and allow to cool slightly. Break off the excess pastry and take the tart out of the tin. Serve warm or at room temperature.

Sweet and spicy beef and pork pie

1 quantity of Shortcrust pastry (see page 293) or use 500g bought pastry

vegetable oil, for brushing the tin

flour, for dusting

Filling

50g pine nuts

120ml olive oil

400g minced beef

400g minced pork

3 tbsp tomato purée

2 tsp sugar

1 tbsp dried mint

2 tsp ground allspice (pimento)

1 tsp ground cinnamon

½ tsp ground nutmeg

1 tsp sweet paprika

½ tsp cayenne pepper or dried chilli flakes

2 onions, thinly sliced

7 eggs

10g parsley, roughly chopped

salt and black pepper

This is not your average pork pie! Rather than the meat being enclosed, suspiciously, in a sealed container of pastry, the fillings here in this open-topped pie are there to be seen. Any dish that involves braised eggs will always amount to comfort food in our book and this is no exception. It's a hearty and rustic dish, happy to be served for brunch, lunch or supper, with a simple green salad alongside.

———

Lightly oil a 22–24cm loose-bottomed tart tin. On a lightly floured surface, roll out the pastry to 2–3mm thick. Use the pastry to line the tin, pressing it well into the corners and the sides and allowing it to spill over the edge by at least 2cm. This excess will be trimmed later. Prick the base with a fork in a few places, then leave the tart case to rest in the fridge for at least half an hour.

Heat the oven to 190°C/170°C fan/Gas Mark 5. Cut a circle of greaseproof paper greater in diameter than the base plus the sides of the tart tin. Tuck it in the pastry case and fill up with dried beans or rice. Bake the case blind for 35 minutes, then remove the paper and the beans or rice (you can keep them and reuse indefinitely for baking blind). Return the pastry case to the oven and bake for a further 5–10 minutes, until light golden and thoroughly cooked. Remove from the oven and leave to cool.

You can toast the pine nuts for the filling at the same time as cooking the pastry case. Scatter them on a baking tray and leave in the oven for 8 minutes or until they go golden.

To make the filling, heat half the olive oil in a large, heavy saucepan, add the beef and break it down with a fork. Cook over a high heat for a few minutes, until coloured. Add the pork, mix well with your fork and keep on cooking over a medium heat for 15 minutes or until golden. Stir in the tomato purée and sugar and cook for another 3 minutes. Then add the mint, all the spices, 2 teaspoons of salt and a good grind of black pepper. Cook for 10 minutes over a low heat.

In the meantime, fry the onions in the remaining olive oil in a separate pan for about 10 minutes, until golden brown. Drain off most of the oil and add the onions to the cooked meat. Add the pine nuts and taste for salt and pepper.

Heat the oven to 210°C/190°C fan/Gas Mark 6. To assemble the tart, spoon half the hot meat mixture into the pastry case. Make 3 shallow holes in the mixture, then break 3 eggs, one by one, and pour them into the holes. Using a wooden spoon, stir the eggs gently in the meat – just enough to disperse them a little, while keeping areas with more egg and maintaining some distinction between white and yolk. Spoon the rest of the meat on top, create some holes in it and break in the rest of the eggs, dispersing them as before.

Put the pie in the oven and bake for about 15 minutes, until the eggs are set. If the top begins to darken too much, cover it with foil for the remaining cooking period.

Remove from the oven and break off the excess pastry with your hands. Take the pie out of the tin and serve hot or warm, garnished with the parsley.

Butternut, carrot and goat's cheese tartlets

1 small butternut squash, peeled, de-seeded and cut into 2cm dice (450g)

2 tbsp olive oil

1 tsp mustard seeds

2 large carrots, peeled and coarsely grated (180g)

35g caster sugar

30ml white wine vinegar

50ml orange juice

30g unsalted butter, melted

150g goat's cheese

1 egg yolk

120ml whipping cream

20g chives, finely chopped

40g Parmesan cheese, freshly grated

salt and black pepper

Pastry

230g plain flour

½ tsp salt

25g poppy seeds

110g butter, fridge-cold and cut into 1cm dice

60ml milk

Start by making the pastry. Sift the flour into a large bowl and add the salt and poppy seeds. Rub the butter into the flour with your fingertips, until the mixture resembles fine breadcrumbs. Add the milk and stir until the mixture just starts to form a ball. Do not mix any more. Shape the dough into a fat disc, wrap in cling film and chill for a few hours.

Preheat the oven to 190°C/170°C fan/Gas Mark 5. Mix the diced squash with 1 tablespoon of the olive oil and some salt and pepper. Put the squash into a roasting dish and cook in the oven for 15 minutes or until semi-soft. Leave to the side to cool down.

While the squash is cooking, heat the remaining oil in a large saucepan and add the mustard seeds. Cook until they start to pop, then add the grated carrots and cook, stirring frequently, for 10 minutes. Stir in the sugar, white wine vinegar and orange juice, bring to the boil and then reduce the heat to a low simmer. Cook for 20–25 minutes, stirring occasionally, until almost all the liquid has evaporated. Remove from the heat and leave to cool.

Take 6 tartlet tins, 10cm in diameter and 2cm deep, and brush them lightly with the melted butter. On a lightly floured work surface, roll out the pastry to 3–4mm thick. Cut out circles big enough to line the tins and gently press them into each one, working with your fingers around the edges to line them evenly. Cut off any excess pastry, then chill the tartlet cases for at least 30 minutes. Line the base and sides of each one with a disc of greaseproof paper and fill it with baking beans or rice. Bake blind at 190°C/170°C fan/Gas Mark 5 for 20 minutes, then remove the paper and beans or rice and return to the oven for 5–10 minutes, until golden brown. Leave to cool.

Turn the oven up to 200°C/180°C fan/Gas Mark 6. In a large bowl, combine the egg yolk with the cream, chives, grated Parmesan, a pinch of salt and a good grind of black pepper. Whisk together until the cream firms up to form soft peaks and then refrigerate.

To assemble the tartlets, divide the carrot mixture equally between the pastry cases, spreading it over the bases. Top with the butternut squash and crumble the goat's cheese over it. Place the tartlets on a baking tray and spoon over the cream mixture, filling them almost to the top. Place in the oven and bake for 8–10 minutes, until the filling is golden and set. Once the tarts are cool enough to handle, remove them from their tins. Serve warm, with a peppery salad.

Brioche

Makes 1 × 500g loaf

If you're new to working with yeasted products, brioche is the place to start. It's really easy to make and the results are hugely rewarding: deliciously buttery but with a smooth and light texture as well.

The master recipe here is for one small brioche loaf, perfect for breakfast spread with (even) more butter and jam. If you're feeling decadent, it also makes for some serious French toast, served with a spoonful of mascarpone cream (see page 291).

Alternatively, for later in the day, the dough can also be used as the base for some little 'pizzas' (see over), topped with feta, tomatoes and olives. The dough also works as an alternative to the puff pastry base for the Sweet potato galettes (see page 190).

Whatever you make, you will need to get the dough slow-proving in the fridge the day before baking.

Place the lukewarm water and yeast in the bowl of an electric mixer. If using dried yeast, leave for 10 minutes for the yeast to activate. Gently stir with your finger until the yeast dissolves. Add all the rest of the ingredients apart from the butter and start working them together with a spatula until the flour is incorporated.

Attach the bowl to the machine and work on a low speed for about 3 minutes. The dough should become smooth but will still stick to the bowl. Once it has reached this stage, scrape it off the sides of the bowl, increase the speed of the machine to medium-high and start adding the diced butter. Do this gradually, making sure that the butter is more or less incorporated into the dough before adding more. Once all the butter is in, keep the machine working until the dough is shiny, has no lumps of butter and comes away naturally from the sides of the bowl. This will take about 9 minutes, depending on your machine (the dough will be lukewarm; make sure it doesn't get hot). Once or twice during the mixing process, you might need to stop the machine, scrape the sides of the bowl clean and very(!) lightly dust with flour.

2 tbsp lukewarm water (not more than 30°C)

1 tsp active dried yeast or 1½ tsp (tightly packed) fresh yeast

190g strong white bread flour, plus extra for dusting

½ tsp salt

20g caster sugar

2 medium eggs, at room temperature, plus 1 egg, beaten, to glaze the loaf

75g unsalted butter, fridge-cold and cut into 2cm dice, plus extra, melted, for brushing the tin

Remove the dough from the mixer and place in a lightly greased bowl or plastic container that is about twice as large as the dough. Cover with cling film and leave at room temperature for 1 hour. Then transfer to the fridge and leave for 14–24 hours before using. During this time, the dough will not rise much or change significantly.

Have ready a 500g loaf tin, lightly brushed with some melted butter. Take the dough out of the fridge, place it on a work surface and dust very lightly with flour. Using your hands, knock the dough down and then shape it into a rectangle that is about the size of the tin base. Place it inside the tin, cover with cling film and leave somewhere warm for 2–3 hours, until almost doubled in height.

Preheat the oven to 190°C/170°C fan/Gas Mark 5. Brush the dough lightly with beaten egg. Put the tin on an oven tray and place in the hot oven. After about 15 minutes, the loaf should be dark brown and baked through. Stick a skewer inside to make sure it is completely dry. Remove from the oven and leave until cool enough to handle, then take out of the tin and leave to cool completely.

'Pizza' with feta, tomato and olives

Makes 6 snack-sized pizzas

There's a sweet-salty contrast here that works very well: the sweet from the brioche and tomatoes and then the salt from the feta and olives. Play around with different toppings, if you like: soft goat's cheese and salty chopped anchovies would be a great combination, with a little bit of chopped thyme. These are a lovely little lunch or snack and also travel well, if you want to take them into work or on a picnic. They are best eaten on the day they are made but can also be warmed through a day or two later.

Put the brioche dough on a lightly floured work surface and roll it out to a sheet about 2cm thick. Using a pastry cutter or the rim of a large cup, cut out 6 circles, 9–10cm in diameter. Place on a non-stick baking tray and leave to rise for 1–2 hours, depending on how warm the kitchen is. The brioche discs should double in height.

While the brioche is rising, prepare the toppings. Cut the tomatoes into quarters lengthways and then cut each quarter into 2 long pieces. Place the wedges skin-side down on a baking tray and drizzle over the oil and vinegar. Sprinkle the mint on top, along with ½ teaspoon of flaky sea salt and a good grind of black pepper. Put in the oven for up to an hour, until the tomatoes have dried out but still retain some moisture. Leave to cool.

For the caramelised onion, put the onion, oil, sugar and ¼ teaspoon of salt in a large pan and cook for 7 minutes over a high heat, stirring occasionally, until golden. Remove from the heat and stir in the crushed garlic. Leave to cool.

Preheat the oven to 190°C/170°C fan/Gas Mark 5. To assemble the brioche pizzas, brush the risen dough discs with a little beaten egg and place a generous amount of the caramelised onion in the centre. Top with lots of tomatoes, feta and olives. Remember, the size of the dough will increase substantially in the oven, so be generous! Drizzle with a little olive oil and season with salt and pepper. Bake for 15–20 minutes. Check the bottoms of the pastries to make sure they are thoroughly cooked.

Remove from the oven and leave to cool. Lightly brush with more olive oil and garnish with the parsley leaves.

1 quantity of Brioche dough (see page 185)

1 egg, lightly beaten

75g feta cheese, crumbled

40g Kalamata olives, pitted

olive oil, for drizzling

6 parsley leaves, to garnish

flaky sea salt and black pepper

Oven-dried tomatoes

300g plum tomatoes

1 tsp olive oil

1 tsp balsamic vinegar

½ tsp dried mint

Caramelised onion

1 onion, thinly sliced

1 tbsp olive oil

¼ tsp sugar

1 garlic clove, crushed

Sweet potato galettes

3 sweet potatoes (1kg)

250g puff pastry, or use ½ quantity of the Rough puff pastry (see page 295)

1 egg, lightly beaten

100ml soured cream

100g hard goat's cheese

2 tbsp pumpkin seeds

1 medium-hot chilli, finely chopped

1 tbsp olive oil

1 garlic clove, crushed

5g parsley, finely chopped

flaky sea salt and black pepper

These are lovely as a stand-alone starter or else for a light lunch, served with a plain green salad. Dot a few oven-dried tomatoes (see page 189) or wrinkly black olives through the sweet potatoes, if you like, or spoon a few teaspoons of black olive tapenade over the tarts as they come out of the oven.

Preheat the oven to 220°C/200°C fan/Gas Mark 7. Bake the sweet potatoes in their skins for 35–45 minutes, until they soften up but are still slightly raw in the centre (check by inserting a small knife). Leave until cool enough to handle, then peel and cut into slices 3mm thick.

While the sweet potatoes are in the oven, roll out the puff pastry to about 2mm thick on a lightly floured work surface. Cut out four 7 × 14cm rectangles and prick them all over with a fork. Line a small baking sheet with baking parchment, place the pastry rectangles on it, well spaced apart, and leave to rest in the fridge for at least half an hour.

Remove the pastry from the fridge and brush lightly with beaten egg. Using a palette knife, spread a thin layer of soured cream on the pastries, leaving a 5mm border all round. Arrange the potato slices on the pastry, slightly overlapping, keeping the border clear. Season with salt and pepper, crumble the goat's cheese on top and sprinkle with the pumpkin seeds and chilli. Bake for 20–25 minutes or until the pastry is cooked through. Check underneath; it should be golden brown.

Whilst the galettes are cooking, stir together the olive oil, garlic, parsley and a pinch of salt. As soon as the pastries come out of the oven, brush them with this mixture. Serve warm or at room temperature.

Roasted pepper and cannellini bruschetta

Serves 4

You'll make more red peppers and cannellini paste than you need for this bruschetta. Both toppings keep well in the fridge for 3 or 4 days, though, so you'll have a ready-made snack or light meal to hand. As an addition, black olives are great on top of the cannellini paste, or a few anchovy fillets work well chopped up and mixed through with the peppers.

———

Drain the beans and place in a large saucepan with enough cold water to cover them by twice their volume. Bring to the boil and simmer for 80–90 minutes, until they are very soft. You will need to skim the froth from the surface a few times during the cooking and might have to add some more boiling water. Drain the beans but keep the cooking liquid.

Heat the oven to 220°C/200°C fan/Gas Mark 7. To prepare the peppers, cut them into quarters and shave off the white parts and seeds. Put them in a roasting tray and toss with 2 tablespoons of the oil and a little salt. Roast in the oven for 35 minutes or until soft, then transfer the hot peppers to a bowl and cover it with cling film; this will make them easier to peel. Once they are cool enough to handle, peel the peppers, place in a container with their cooking juices and set aside. In a separate bowl whisk 60ml of the olive oil with the balsamic vinegar, 2 tablespoons of water, sugar, thyme, 2 sliced garlic cloves and a pinch of salt. Pour this over the peppers and leave for at least half an hour. If you are not using them on the day, keep the peppers refrigerated for up to a week, well immersed in the marinade.

Put the warm beans in a food processor together with 1 crushed garlic clove, the lemon juice, the remaining oil, 1 teaspoon of salt, a good grinding of black pepper and 50ml of the bean cooking liquid. Process to a smooth paste. Taste and see if you want to add any more salt, pepper or lemon juice. Leave to cool and then taste again; you will probably need to add more salt.

Put the bread slices on a baking tray, brush them with olive oil and sprinkle with a little salt. Bake for 10–12 minutes or until golden brown. While they are still hot, rub the slices with 2 peeled garlic cloves, then leave them to cool on a wire rack.

Spread a good amount of the bean purée on each toast, top generously with the marinated peppers, then garnish with the spring onions and a drizzle of olive oil.

150g dried cannellini beans, soaked overnight in plenty of cold water

2 red and 2 yellow peppers

135ml olive oil, plus extra for brushing

2 tbsp balsamic vinegar

1 tsp muscovado sugar

4 sprigs of thyme

5 garlic cloves

juice of 1 lemon

4 thick slices of Crusty white Italian loaf (see page 170) or another rustic loaf

2 spring onions, roughly sliced

salt and black pepper

Salmon and asparagus bruschetta

olive oil, for drizzling
and brushing the bread

350g salmon fillet

4 bay leaves

4 juniper berries

120ml Muscat
(or another sweet wine)

½ lemon

4 thick slices of Crusty
white Italian loaf (see page
170) or another rustic loaf

2 garlic cloves, peeled

150g asparagus spears

120g cream cheese

a few sprigs of chervil and
lemon wedges, to garnish

flaky sea salt and
black pepper

As always, feel free to experiment with the toppings here. Try adding some thinly sliced preserved lemon or chopped capers to the mix, or some wrinkly black olives. For the base, mascarpone can be used instead of the cream cheese, for a rich alternative.

Preheat the oven to 220°C/200°C fan/Gas Mark 7. Drizzle an ovenproof dish with some olive oil and place the salmon fillet in it, skin-side down. Add the bay leaves, juniper and wine, then sprinkle the fillet with a little salt. Squeeze over the lemon half and throw it in with the fish. Cover the dish with foil and bake for 15–20 minutes. The fish should be just cooked, and still lightly pink inside. Remove from the oven, take off the foil and allow to cool.

To prepare the bread, lay out the slices on a baking tray, brush with olive oil and sprinkle with salt. Bake for 10–12 minutes, until golden brown. While they are still hot, rub the slices with the peeled garlic cloves, then leave on a wire rack to cool down.

Trim off the woody ends of the asparagus. Add the asparagus to a large saucepan of boiling salted water and simmer for 2 minutes. Drain in a colander and refresh under cold water until completely cool. Drain again and leave to dry in a colander.

When the salmon has cooled sufficiently, flake it with your hands into big chunks, reserving the cooking liquor in a separate bowl.

Spread the toasts liberally with the cream cheese. Arrange the salmon and asparagus on top creatively. Spoon over some of the reserved cooking juices and finish with a good grind of black pepper and some salt. Garnish with a few sprigs of chervil and a wedge of lemon.

Olive oil crackers

There's nothing like the snap of a wafer-thin cracker to launch the beginning of a feast. These are super simple to make and are great either as they are or with dips for pre-dinner snacks. They will keep in a sealed container for up to a week.

———

In a large bowl, mix together all the ingredients except the sea salt to form a soft dough. You can do this by hand or in a mixer fitted with a dough hook. Work it until you get a firm consistency, then cover with cling film and leave to rest in the fridge for 1 hour.

Heat up the oven to 240°C/220°C fan/Gas Mark 9. Turn the dough on to a clean work surface. Have a bowl of flour for dusting ready at the side. Use a large, sharp knife to cut off walnut-sized pieces (roughly 15g each) from the dough. Roll out each piece as thinly as possible with a rolling pin, dusting with plenty of flour. They should end up looking like long, oval tongues, almost paper thin.

Place the crackers on a tray lined with baking parchment. Brush them with plenty of olive oil and sprinkle with sea salt. Bake for about 6 minutes, until crisp and golden.

250g plain flour, plus extra for dusting

1 tsp baking powder

115ml water

25ml olive oil, plus extra for brushing

½ tsp salt

1 tsp paprika

¼ tsp cayenne pepper

flaky sea salt, for sprinkling, and black pepper

Parmesan and poppy biscuits

Makes about 35

These smell divine when baking in the oven and also provide the ultimate accompaniment to a glass of red wine. They are great to make ahead for a drinks party as you can roll and freeze the dough well in advance, ready to then just be sliced and baked on the day. If you want to actually bake them in advance that's also fine: they keep well in a sealed container for 3 or 4 days. If you are keeping things informal then feel free to leave out the poppy seeds: they look great but the biscuits still work well without. If you want to dress them up, on the other hand, spoon a tiny bit of chunky pesto on top of each biscuit (once it's been baked and cooked) and then dot this with an oven-dried cherry tomato (see page 189, using cherry instead of plum tomatoes): it's a canapé that goes down very well indeed.

210g plain flour, plus plenty extra for dusting

½ tsp baking powder

½ tsp paprika

a pinch of cayenne pepper

165g unsalted butter, at room temperature

165g Parmesan cheese, freshly grated

80g poppy seeds

1 egg, beaten

salt and black pepper

Sift the flour, baking powder, paprika and cayenne into a bowl and add the salt and pepper.

Mix the softened butter with the Parmesan until they are well blended. You can do this either by hand, using a spatula, or in a freestanding mixer fitted with the paddle attachment. Add the dry ingredients and continue mixing until a soft dough is formed.

Put the dough on a well-floured work surface and divide it in half. Use plenty of flour, both on your hands and on the work surface, to roll each piece into a long log, 3–4cm in diameter. Wrap each log in cling film and place in the fridge for about 30 minutes to firm up.

Scatter the poppy seeds over a flat plate or tray. Brush the logs with the beaten egg and then roll them in the poppy seeds until covered. Refrigerate again for 1 hour (at this stage you can also wrap the logs and freeze them).

Preheat the oven to 190°C/170°C fan/Gas Mark 5. Line a baking sheet with baking parchment. Cut the logs into slices 5–8mm thick and arrange them on the tray, spaced 3cm apart. Bake for 12 minutes. The biscuits should be dark golden and smell amazing! Leave to cool completely before serving, or storing in a tightly sealed container.

Cheddar and caraway cheese straws

plain flour, for dusting

300g puff pastry, or ½ quantity of Rough puff pastry (see page 295)

1 egg, lightly beaten

100g strong Cheddar cheese, finely grated

1 tsp caraway seeds

As with the Parmesan biscuits on page 199, anything involving dough and cheese always fills the kitchen with incredible smells and has a taste to match. Feel free to use other hard cheeses: Comté also works well, for example. Or try a very light sprinkle of nigella seeds with a pinch of dried chilli flakes, instead of the caraway. These are best served on the day they are made but can also be baked ahead and warmed through the next day. You can also freeze the dough once it has been twisted into straws and cook them straight from frozen. You'll just need to leave them in the oven for a minute or two longer.

When making the cheese straws, work fast and try to keep a flow of fresh, cool air in the kitchen. Otherwise the pastry will heat up, turn sticky and be difficult to manage.

———

Dust a work surface lightly with flour and roll out the pastry to a rectangle 2–3mm thick. Trim the edges with a sharp knife in order to get a perfect rectangle, roughly 30 x 20cm. Place on a baking sheet dusted with flour and leave to rest in the fridge for 30 minutes.

Return the pastry sheet to the dusted work surface. Brush off any flour and then brush the top with the beaten egg and sprinkle over half the cheese. Press the cheese down lightly with your hands so it sticks to the pastry. Be brisk so that you don't warm up the butter in the pastry. Carefully turn the pastry over, brush off any excess flour and repeat this process on the other side.

Now cut strips about 3cm wide across the width of the pastry. Pick up a strip holding one end in each hand. Place one end on the work surface and hold still. Twist the other end on the work surface to make a tight spiral form. You will need to pull as you twist to get a long, hollow, straw shape.

Carefully transfer the straws to a baking sheet lined with baking parchment. Space them at least 3cm apart and sprinkle with the caraway seeds. Rest them in the fridge for at least 30 minutes.

Preheat the oven to 200°C/180°C fan/Gas Mark 6. Place the tray of cheese straws in the oven and bake for 20–25 minutes. Make sure you do not open the oven door for the first 15 minutes. When ready, the straws should be a beautiful light brown colour. Let them cool slightly before serving.

CHOCOLATE and HAZELNUT BROWNIE £2.10

Apple and olive oil cake with maple icing

80g sultanas

60ml water

280g plain flour

½ tsp ground cinnamon

¼ tsp salt

½ tsp baking powder

1¼ tsp bicarbonate of soda

120ml olive oil

160g caster sugar

½ vanilla pod

2 eggs, lightly beaten

3 Bramley apples, peeled, cored and cut into 1cm dice

finely grated zest of 1 lemon

2 egg whites

icing sugar, for dusting (optional)

Maple icing

100g unsalted butter, at room temperature

100g light muscovado sugar

85ml maple syrup

220g cream cheese, at room temperature

This is a huge Ottolenghi favourite – many of our customers confess that they order it just for the maple icing! It can also be made in advance and kept wrapped in the fridge for up to a week, ready to be brought back to room temperature and iced on the day of serving.

——

Grease a 20cm springform cake tin and line the base and sides with baking parchment. Place the sultanas and water in a medium saucepan and simmer over a low heat until all of the water has been absorbed. Leave to cool.

Preheat the oven to 190°C/170°C fan/Gas Mark 5. Sift the flour, cinnamon, salt, baking powder and bicarbonate of soda. Set aside.

Put the oil and sugar in the bowl of a freestanding electric mixer fitted with a paddle attachment (or use a whisk if you don't have a mixer). Slit the vanilla pod lengthways in half and, using a sharp knife, scrape the seeds out into the bowl. Beat the oil, sugar and vanilla together, then gradually add the eggs. The mix should be smooth and thick at this stage. Mix in the diced apples, sultanas and lemon zest, then lightly fold in the sifted dry ingredients.

Whisk the egg whites in a clean bowl, either by hand or with a mixer, until they have a soft meringue consistency. Fold them into the batter in 2 additions, trying to lose as little air as possible.

Pour the batter into the lined tin, level it with a palette knife and place in the oven. Bake for 1½ hours, or until a skewer inserted in the centre comes out clean. Remove from the oven and leave to cool in the tin.

Once the cake is completely cold, you can assemble it. Remove from the tin and use a large serrated knife to cut it horizontally in half. You should end up with 2 similar discs. If the cake is very domed, you might need to shave a bit off the top half to level it.

To make the icing, beat together the butter, muscovado sugar and maple syrup until light and airy. You can do this by hand, or, preferably, in a mixer, using the paddle attachment. Add the cream cheese and beat until the icing is totally smooth.

Using a palette knife, spread a 1cm-thick layer of icing over the bottom half of the cake. Carefully place the top half on it. Spoon the rest of the icing on top and use the palette knife to create a pattern. Dust it with icing sugar, if you like.

Orange polenta cake

50g plain flour

1 tsp baking powder

½ tsp salt

200g unsalted butter

200g caster sugar

3 eggs, lightly beaten

2 tsp orange blossom water

240g ground almonds

120g quick-cook polenta

Caramel topping

90g caster sugar

20g unsalted butter, diced

2 oranges, plus a possible extra one

Glaze (optional)

4 tbsp orange marmalade

1 tbsp water

Blood oranges (in season from January to April) look spectacular if you can get them for this. Regular oranges are also great, though, and this is a lovely cake to make all year round. Use quick-cook polenta here – the regular type will leave a rather gritty texture – and use the Cortas brand for the orange blossom water, if you can: some supermarket-own varieties can taste very artificial and perfume-like.

⸻

Lightly grease a 20cm round cake tin and line the base and sides with baking parchment. If using a loose-based tin, make sure the paper circle you cut for the base is large enough to go some way up the sides as well, to prevent leaking.

To make the caramel, have ready by the stove a small pastry brush and a cup of water. Put the sugar for the caramel topping in a heavy-based saucepan along with 2 tablespoons of water. Stir gently to wet the sugar through and then place on a low-medium heat. Slowly bring the sugar to the boil. While it bubbles away, brush the sides of the pan occasionally with a little of the water in the cup to get rid of any crystals that form close to the bubbling sugar. After a few minutes the water should evaporate and the sugar will start to darken. Be sure to keep your eyes on the sugar at all times as it can easily burn. As soon as it reaches a nice golden colour, remove the pan from the heat. With your face at a safe distance, add the chunks of butter. Stir with a wooden spoon and pour the caramel over the lined base of the cake tin. Carefully but quickly (so it doesn't set) tilt it to spread evenly.

Grate the zest of the 2 oranges, making sure you don't reach the white part of the skin. Set the grated zest aside. Using a small, sharp knife, slice off 1cm from the top and bottom of each orange. Standing each orange up on a board, carefully but neatly follow the natural curves of the orange with the knife to peel off the remaining skin and all the white pith. Cut each orange horizontally into roughly 6 slices. Remove the pips and lay out the slices tightly over the caramel. (You might need to peel and slice another orange to cover the whole space.)

Now make the cake batter. Heat up the oven to 190°C/170°C fan/Gas Mark 5. Sift together the flour, baking powder and salt and set aside.

In an electric mixer fitted with the paddle attachment, cream the butter and sugar together lightly. Make sure they are well combined but do not incorporate much air into the mixture. Gradually add the eggs while the machine is on a low speed. Next add the reserved orange zest and the orange blossom water, followed by the almonds, polenta and sifted dry ingredients. As soon as they are all mixed in, stop the machine.

Transfer the batter to the prepared cake tin, making sure that the oranges underneath stay in a single neat layer. Level the mixture carefully with a palette knife. Place the cake in the oven and bake for 40–45 minutes, until a skewer inserted in the centre comes out dry. Remove from the oven and leave to cool for about 5 minutes.

While the cake is still hot (warm it up a little if you forgot, otherwise the caramel will stick to the paper), place a cardboard disc or a flat plate on top. Briskly turn over and then remove the tin and the lining paper. Leave the cake to cool completely.

For the glaze, bring the marmalade and water to the boil in a small saucepan and then pass through a sieve. While the glaze is still hot, lightly brush the top of the cake with it.

Chocolate fudge cake

Serves 6–8

Chocolate, butter, sugar, eggs and a pinch of salt: so few ingredients, but so utterly rich. This cake keeps very well and you can also serve it to friends who don't eat gluten or nuts. It's perfect as it is, but some soured cream or crème fraîche is very welcome spooned alongside.

We bake this in two stages – we like the contrast of the firmer base and the more mousse-like top – but if you want to simplify the process, just pour all the mixture into the tin at the same time and increase the total baking time to about 1 hour.

240g unsalted butter, cut into small cubes

265g dark chocolate (52% cocoa solids), cut into small pieces

95g dark chocolate (70% cocoa solids), cut into small pieces

290g light muscovado sugar

60ml water

5 large eggs, separated

a pinch of salt

cocoa powder, for dusting

Preheat the oven to 190°C/170°C fan/Gas Mark 5. Grease a 20cm springform cake tin and line the base and sides with baking parchment.

Place the butter and both types of chocolate in a very large heatproof bowl – it should be big enough to accommodate the entire mix. Put the muscovado sugar and water in a small saucepan, stir to mix, then bring to the boil over a medium heat. Pour the boiling syrup over the butter and chocolate and stir well until they have melted and you are left with a runny chocolate sauce. Stir in the egg yolks, one at a time. Set aside until the mixture comes to room temperature.

Put the egg whites and salt in a large bowl and whisk to a firm, but not too dry, meringue. Using a rubber spatula or a large metal spoon, gently fold the meringue into the cooled chocolate mixture a third at a time. The whites should be fully incorporated but there is no harm if you can see small bits of meringue in the mix.

Pour 800g (about two-thirds) of the mixture into the prepared cake tin and level gently with a palette knife. Leave the rest of the batter for later. Place the cake in the oven and bake for about 40 minutes, until a skewer inserted in the centre comes out almost clean. Remove from the oven and leave to cool completely.

Flatten the top of the cake with a palette knife. Don't worry about breaking the crust. Pour the rest of the batter on top and level the surface again. Return to the oven and bake for 20–25 minutes. The cake should still have moist crumbs when checked with a skewer. Leave to cool completely before removing from the tin. Dust with cocoa powder and serve.

The cake will keep, covered, at room temperature for 4 days.

Serves 8

Caramel and macadamia cheesecake

600g good-quality
cream cheese,
at room temperature

120g caster sugar

½ vanilla pod

4 eggs, lightly beaten

60ml soured cream

icing sugar, for dusting

Base

160g dry biscuits
(HobNobs are good)

40g unsalted butter,
melted

Nut topping

150g macadamia nuts

90g caster sugar

Caramel sauce

65g unsalted butter

160g caster sugar

100ml whipping cream

There are various stages to making this but don't be intimidated: you can get well ahead so there need be no pressure. The whole cake can be made and kept in the fridge for up to 2 days before serving, or you can also make the various elements in advance and then put the cake together the day you want to eat it. Make the sauce on the day you are assembling the cake, though, as it will set too firm in the fridge and you won't be able to pour it.

———

Preheat the oven to 160°C/140°C fan/Gas Mark 3. Lightly grease a 20cm springform cake tin and line the base and sides with baking parchment.

To make the base, whiz the biscuits to crumbs in a food processor (or put them in a plastic bag and bash with a mallet or rolling pin). Mix with the melted butter to a wet, sandy consistency. Transfer to the lined tin and flatten with the back of a tablespoon to create a level base.

To make the cake batter, put the cream cheese and sugar in a mixing bowl. Slit the vanilla pod lengthways in half and, using a sharp knife, scrape out the seeds into the bowl. Whisk by hand or, more easily, with an electric mixer, until smooth. Gradually add the eggs and soured cream, whisking until smooth. Pour the mixture over the biscuit base and place in the oven. Bake for 60–70 minutes, until set; a skewer inserted in the centre should come out with a slightly wet crumb attached. Leave to cool to room temperature, then turn out of the tin. Removing the cake from its base can be a little tricky. You can leave it there and serve from the base, if you prefer. Otherwise, get a flat 20cm cake board and gently squeeze it between the base of the cake and the lining paper. As a last resort, get a couple of fish slices and someone to help you lift the whole thing on to a flat serving plate. Now chill the cake for at least a couple of hours.

To prepare the nut topping, scatter the nuts over a baking sheet and roast in the oven at 160°C/140°C fan/Gas Mark 3 for about 15 minutes, until golden. Remove from the oven and set aside. Line a baking tray with baking parchment. Place the sugar in a saucepan with a very thick base (it is important that the layer of sugar is not more than 3mm high in the pan, so choose a large one). Heat the sugar gently until it turns into a golden-brown caramel. Do not stir it at any stage. Don't worry if some small bits of sugar don't totally

dissolve. Carefully add the toasted nuts and mix gently with a wooden spoon. When most of the nuts are coated in caramel, pour them on to the lined tray and leave to set. Break bits off and chop them very roughly with a large knife. It's nice to leave some of the nuts just halved or even whole.

To make the sauce, put the butter and sugar in a thick-bottomed saucepan and stir constantly over a medium heat with a wooden spoon until it becomes a smooth, dark caramel. The butter and sugar will look as if they have split. Don't worry; just keep on stirring. Once the desired colour is reached, carefully add the cream while stirring vigorously. Remove from the heat and leave to cool.

To finish the cake, dust the edges and sides with plenty of icing sugar. Spoon the sauce in the centre, allowing it to spill over a little. Scatter lots of caramelised nuts on top. The cheesecake will keep in the fridge for 3 days.

Carrot and walnut cake

160g plain flour

½ tsp baking powder

½ tsp bicarbonate of soda

1 tsp ground cinnamon

¼ tsp ground cloves

1 egg, plus 1 extra egg yolk

200g sunflower oil

270g caster sugar

50g walnut halves, chopped

50g desiccated coconut

2 medium carrots, peeled and roughly grated (135g)

2 egg whites

a pinch of salt

Icing

175g cream cheese, at room temperature

70g unsalted butter

35g icing sugar

25g honey

30g walnut halves, chopped and lightly toasted

There have always been two separate camps in the world of carrot cake at Ottolenghi. Whilst we prefer a light and fluffy cake, Helen Goh and Sarit Packer – partners-in-crime on all things sweet – always opted for a denser and fruitier cake. We wrote, in the first edition of this book, that an update on the 'tense ceasefire' needed to wait 'until the next Ottolenghi cookbook'. It just so happens that the next book in line is a sweet one, co-written with Helen. The standoff between Helen and Yotam continues on this one matter, though, so much so that Helen has converted her much-loved (dense and fruity) carrot cake into a parsnip cake. So now everyone is happy.

————

Preheat the oven to 190°C/170°C fan/Gas Mark 5. Grease a 20cm springform cake tin and line the base and sides with baking parchment.

Sift together the flour, baking powder, bicarbonate of soda and spices. Lightly whisk the whole egg with the egg yolk.

Put the sunflower oil and caster sugar in the bowl of an electric mixer fitted with the beater attachment and beat for about a minute on a medium speed. On a low speed, slowly add the beaten egg. Mix in the walnuts, coconut and carrot and then the sifted dry ingredients. Don't over mix.

Transfer the mixture to a large bowl. Wash and dry the mixer bowl, making sure it is totally clean, then put the egg whites and salt in it and whisk on a high speed until firm peaks form. Gently fold the egg whites into the carrot mixture in 3 additions, being careful not to over mix. Streaks of white in the mixture are okay.

Pour the cake mixture into the prepared tin and bake for approximately 1 hour; it could take longer. A skewer inserted in the centre should come out dry. If the cake starts getting dark before the centre is cooked through, cover it with foil. Let the cake cool completely and then remove from the tin.

To make the icing, beat the cream cheese in a mixer until light and smooth. Remove from the mixer. Beat the butter, icing sugar and honey in the mixer until light and airy. Fold together the cheese and butter mixes. Spread on top of the cake and sprinkle with the nuts.

Teacakes

These are a signature cake in our shops, lined up in neat rows with their variously coloured toppings. Though far removed from the British fruited bun bearing the same name, these cakes are the most perfect accompaniment to, well, a cup of tea. They are light, summery and really very pretty.

We like to make our teacakes in mini bundt tins (about 10 centimetres wide and taking 150–200g of cake batter) but you can also use mini kugelhopf pans (with the same sort of capacity) as well. All sorts of shapes and sizes of tins are available in kitchen shops and online, so have a look and see what you can find. Whatever you use, it's important to really grease your tins well before they get filled. We chill ours first before brushing them generously with melted butter.

——

Peach and raspberry

180g unsalted butter,
plus extra, melted,
for greasing the tins

260g plain flour

1 tsp baking powder

½ tsp bicarbonate of soda

¼ tsp salt

160g caster sugar

2 eggs

1 tsp vanilla essence

170ml soured cream

1 peach, halved, pitted
and cut into 1cm dice

250g raspberries

icing sugar, for dusting

Glaze

200g raspberries

170g apricot jam

100ml water

Preheat the oven to 190°C/170°C fan/Gas Mark 5. Leave 6 small bundt or kugelhopf tins in the fridge for a few minutes, then remove and brush with plenty of melted butter. Return them to the fridge.

Start by sifting together the flour, baking powder, bicarbonate of soda and salt, then set aside. Cream the butter and sugar together until light and fluffy, preferably using an electric mixer. Mix the eggs with the vanilla, then gradually add to the creamed mixture, beating well until each little addition has been fully incorporated. Gently fold in a third of the flour mixture, followed by a third of the soured cream. Continue like this until both are mixed in and the batter is smooth. Fold in the diced peach.

Either pipe or spoon the mixture into the tins, filling them to about 2cm from the top. Press 4 raspberries into each cake, sinking them with your finger to just below the surface of the batter (keep the remaining raspberries to scatter over the finished cakes). Place the cakes in the oven and bake for 25–30 minutes. Poke with a skewer to make sure they are completely dry inside; it should come out clean. Remove them from the oven and leave in their tins for 10 minutes to cool slightly, then turn out on to a wire rack and leave to cool completely.

To make the glaze, place all the ingredients in a small saucepan and bring to the boil. Stir and leave to simmer for 4 minutes. Pass the hot glaze through a fine sieve, rubbing the raspberry pips with a wooden spoon to release as much of the juice as you can. Brush or drizzle the hot glaze over the cakes and leave to set (if the glaze is too thin to coat the cakes, simmer it over a moderate heat until reduced; if it is too thick, add a little water and heat gently). Pile the remaining raspberries on top of the cakes and dust with icing sugar.

Lemon and blueberry

Makes 6

Preheat the oven to 190°C/170°C fan/Gas Mark 5. Leave 6 small bundt or kugelhopf tins in the fridge for a few minutes, then remove and brush with plenty of melted butter. Return them to the fridge.

Mix together the flour and ground almonds and set aside. Using an electric mixer, or by hand, cream the butter and sugar together until pale and fluffy. Break the eggs into a cup and mix lightly with a fork. Gradually add the eggs to the butter mix, beating well until each little addition has been fully incorporated. If the mixture looks as if it has split, add a little of the almond and flour mixture and it should come back together. Once all the egg is incorporated, gently fold in the almonds and flour, followed by the lemon zest, juice and blueberries. Be gentle, so the blueberries don't break.

Take the moulds from the fridge. Either pipe or spoon the mixture into the tins, reaching all the way up to the edge. Level the mixture and clean the edges of the tins if necessary. Bake in the oven for 30–35 minutes, until a skewer inserted into the centre of a cake comes out clean. Remove them from the oven and leave them in their tins for 10 minutes, then turn out on to a wire rack and leave to cool completely.

To make the glaze, whisk the lemon juice and icing sugar together in a small bowl, adding more lemon juice or sugar if necessary to make an icing with a drizzling consistency. Spoon it liberally over the cakes or brush with a pastry brush, letting the icing drip down the sides.

280g unsalted butter, plus extra, melted, for greasing the tins

65g plain flour

280g ground almonds

280g caster sugar

5 eggs

finely grated zest of 2 lemons

100ml lemon juice

120g blueberries

Glaze

50ml lemon juice

150g icing sugar

Makes 6

Lavender and honey

225g unsalted butter,
plus extra, melted,
for greasing the tins

115g caster sugar

115g lavender honey
(or plain honey,
as an alternative)

3 eggs

245g plain flour

1 tsp baking powder

½ tsp bicarbonate of soda

½ tsp salt

½ tsp ground cinnamon

½ tsp chopped dried
lavender, plus extra
to finish

110ml soured cream

Glaze

20ml lemon juice

2 tsp honey

about 100g icing sugar

Preheat the oven to 190°C/170°C fan/Gas Mark 5. Leave 6 small
bundt or kugelhopf tins in the fridge for a few minutes, then remove
and brush with plenty of melted butter. Return them to the fridge.

Cream the butter, sugar and honey together until pale and fluffy,
preferably using an electric mixer. Break the eggs into a cup, beat
them lightly with a fork and gradually add to the creamed mixture,
beating well until each little addition has been fully incorporated.
Sift together the flour, baking powder, bicarbonate of soda, salt
and cinnamon, then stir in the dried lavender. Gently fold the flour
mixture into the creamed mix in 3 additions, alternating with
the soured cream.

Either pipe or spoon the mixture into the tins, filling them to about
1.5cm from the top. Level out the mix and clean the edges of the
tins if necessary. Place in the oven and bake for 25–30 minutes,
until a skewer inserted in the centre of a cake comes out clean.
Remove them from the oven and leave in their tins for 10 minutes,
then turn out on to a wire rack and leave to cool completely.

To make the glaze, mix the lemon juice and honey together in
a small bowl, then whisk in enough icing sugar to make a thick,
pourable glaze. Use a pastry brush or a spoon to coat the top of
the cakes, allowing the icing to drip down the sides. Sprinkle with
a little dried lavender.

Muffins

Muffins are lovely and light. The way to ensure this lightness is to not overwork the mixture. You don't want to develop the protein in the flour and you don't want to incorporate too much air into the batter. In short, don't stir too much! Stop mixing whilst there are still plenty of lumps in the mix.

Muffins are such a favourite for the home cook because, beyond this instruction, they are quick and easy to make and require very little preparation or kit.

We've offered three variations here, all good for different occasions. The plum muffin is perfect for a celebratory brunch: the compote looks wonderful but the muffins also work well as they are, without the plum topping, if you want to keep things simple. The blueberry is a classic and much loved amongst muffin-makers on account of the fruit's ability to keep its shape and remain whole when baked. The carrot, apple and pecan is a favourite amongst our breakfast or mid-morning take-out customers, with its oat-and-seed topping. With thanks to Tamar Shany for developing this last recipe.

These muffins are all best eaten the day they are made – even warm, if possible – although you can easily squeeze an extra day out of the carrot and apple muffins.

Makes 10–12

Plum, marzipan and cinnamon

480g plain flour

1 tsp baking powder

½ tsp bicarbonate of soda

1 tsp ground cinnamon

a pinch of salt

200g caster sugar

2 eggs

280ml milk

110g unsalted butter, melted

120g marzipan

finely grated zest of 2 oranges

icing sugar, for dusting

Plum compote

700g ripe red plums, pitted and cut into quarters

60g caster sugar

1 cinnamon stick

Make the plum compote first. Preheat the oven to 190°C/170°C fan/ Gas Mark 5. Place the plums in a shallow baking dish, add the sugar and cinnamon stick and mix together. Place in the oven and bake for 10–20 minutes, until the plums are soft and their skin starts to separate from the flesh (the cooking time will vary significantly, depending on the ripeness of the fruit). Remove from the oven and set aside to cool.

Sift the flour, baking powder, bicarbonate of soda, cinnamon and salt into a bowl. Put the sugar and eggs in a large mixing bowl and whisk together. Add the milk and butter (make sure it is not too hot) and whisk to combine.

Grate the marzipan on the coarse side of a grater and add this to the batter, together with the orange zest. Now add 80g of the plum compote (pulp and juices) and stir together. Set the rest of the compote aside for later.

Using a rubber spatula, gently fold the flour mixture into the wet mix until just combined (there may still be a few lumps and bits of flour; that is what you want).

Line your muffin tins with paper cases and spoon in the mixture, filling them all the way to the top. Bake for 25–30 minutes, until a skewer inserted in the centre of a muffin comes out clean. When cool enough to handle, take the muffins out of the tins and leave on a wire rack until cold.

Just before serving, dust the tops with a little icing sugar and top with the reserved plum compote.

Makes 10–12

Blueberry crumble

540g plain flour

5 tsp baking powder

½ tsp salt

2 eggs

340g caster sugar

140g unsalted butter, melted

380ml milk

finely grated zest of 1 lemon

1 Granny Smith apple (unpeeled), cut into 1cm dice

200g fresh blueberries, plus a few extra for the topping

½ quantity of Crumble (see page 291)

Preheat the oven to 190°C/170°C fan/Gas Mark 5. Line a muffin tray with paper cases.

Sift together the flour, baking powder and salt and set aside. In a large mixing bowl, lightly whisk together the eggs, sugar and melted butter (make sure it is not too hot). Whisk in the milk and lemon zest, then gently fold in the fruit.

Add the sifted dry ingredients and fold together very gently. Make sure you stir the mix just enough to combine; it should remain lumpy and rough.

Spoon the mixture into the muffin cases to fill them up. Generously cover with the crumble topping to form small domes over the batter, then dot with a few extra blueberries. Bake for 30–35 minutes or until a skewer inserted in the centre of a muffin comes out clean. Take out of the tins while still warm and allow to cool slightly before serving.

Carrot, apple and pecan

Makes 10–12

Start by making the topping. In a bowl, stir together the butter, flour and sugar. Rub with your fingertips until the butter is incorporated and you have a crumbly texture. Mix in the oats and seeds and then the oil, honey and 1 teaspoon of water. Stir everything together, resulting in a wet, sandy texture. Set aside.

Preheat the oven to 190°C/170°C fan/Gas Mark 5. Line a muffin tray with paper cases.

Sift together the flour, baking powder, cinnamon and salt. In a large mixing bowl, whisk together the eggs, oil, sugar, vanilla and grated carrot and apple. Gently fold in the pecans, sultanas, coconut and then the sifted flour mixture. Do not over mix, and don't worry if the batter is lumpy and irregular. Spoon into the paper cases and generously scatter over the topping. Bake for about 25 minutes, until a skewer inserted in the centre of a muffin comes out clean. Remove the muffins from the tins when they are just warm and allow them to cool down before serving. Their flavour will actually improve after a couple of hours.

300g plain flour

2 tsp baking powder

2 tsp ground cinnamon

a pinch of salt

4 eggs

160ml sunflower oil

280g caster sugar

2 tsp vanilla essence

3 medium carrots, peeled and coarsely grated (200g)

2 small Bramley or Granny Smith apples, coarsely grated (200g)

100g pecan halves, roughly chopped

100g sultanas

50g flaked coconut

Topping

50g unsalted butter, fridge-cold and cut into small pieces

75g plain flour

25g light muscovado sugar

50g whole rolled oats

15g sunflower seeds

25g pumpkin seeds

15g black sesame seeds

1 tsp sunflower oil

1½ tsp honey

Cupcakes

Cupcakes have come in and out of fashion over the years, and we have always been of the opinion that the only cupcakes really worth eating are ones with a seriously good icing. Our cupcakes can be made well in advance – they keep well in a sealed container at room temperature for up to 3 days – and freeze well, ready to be iced on the day of serving.

Hazelnut

Preheat the oven to 170°C/150°C fan/Gas Mark 3. Place the hazelnuts on a baking sheet and roast for 15 minutes, until lightly coloured. Remove from the oven. Once they have thoroughly cooled down, rub them in a tea towel and shake it in your hands to get rid of most of the skins. Blitz them in a food processor with half the sugar until finely chopped.

Now make the cupcakes. Increase the oven temperature to 190°C/170°C fan/Gas Mark 5. Line a muffin tray or bun sheet with 8–12 paper cases. Sift together the flour, baking powder and salt. Cream together the butter, remaining sugar, hazelnut oil and finely chopped hazelnuts until light and airy. Mix in the beaten eggs a little at a time, waiting until each addition is fully incorporated before adding the next bit. Use a spatula or large metal spoon to fold in half the sifted dry ingredients, then half the soured cream, followed by the rest of the dry ingredients and then the remaining cream. Spoon the mixture into the cupcake cases, filling them to within 5mm of the rim. Bake for 20–25 minutes, until a skewer inserted in the centre comes out clean. Remove from the oven and leave to cool.

Make the icing only once the cupcakes are cold. Beat the cream cheese and mascarpone together until they are smooth and light. In a separate bowl, beat the butter and icing sugar together, either with an electric mixer or by hand, for at least 5 minutes (if the whisk doesn't reach the bottom of the bowl you might need to do this by hand). The mixture should turn almost white and become fluffy and light. Fold in the cream cheese mixture and then use a spatula to sculpt a wavy topping on each cupcake.

45g unblanched hazelnuts

150g caster sugar

180g plain flour

1¼ tsp baking powder

⅓ tsp salt

150g unsalted butter

1 tbsp hazelnut oil

2 small eggs, lightly beaten

150ml soured cream

Icing

150g cream cheese, at room temperature

150g mascarpone cheese, at room temperature

80g unsalted butter, at room temperature

100g icing sugar

Makes 12

Chocolate

2 eggs

115ml soured cream

80ml sunflower oil

20ml black treacle

20g unsalted butter, melted

60g caster sugar

60g light muscovado sugar

120g plain flour

35g cocoa powder

1 tsp baking powder

½ tsp bicarbonate of soda

¼ tsp salt

40g ground almonds

200g dark chocolate, cut into small pieces

Icing

165g dark chocolate, cut into small pieces

135ml whipping cream

35g unsalted butter, diced

1 tbsp Amaretto liqueur

Heat the oven to 190°C/170°C fan/Gas Mark 5. Line a muffin tray or a bun sheet with 12 paper cases.

Whisk together the first 7 ingredients in a large mixing bowl until they are just combined. Don't over mix. Sift together the flour, cocoa, baking powder and bicarbonate of soda. Add them to the wet mix, along with the salt and almonds, and fold together gently. Fold in the chocolate pieces.

Spoon the batter into the cupcake cases, filling them up completely. Bake for about 20–25 minutes; if you insert a skewer in one, it should come out with quite a bit of crumb attached. Remove from the oven and leave to cool, then take the cupcakes out of their tins.

While the cupcakes are in the oven, start making the icing. It will take time to set and become spreadable. Place the chocolate in a heatproof bowl. Put the cream in a small saucepan and heat almost to boiling point, then pour it over the chocolate. Use a rubber spatula to stir until all the chocolate has melted. Add the butter and Amaretto and beat until smooth.

Transfer the icing to a clean bowl and cover the surface with cling film. Leave at room temperature until the cupcakes have fully cooled down and the icing has started to set. You want to catch it at the point when it spreads easily but isn't hard. Do not rush it by refrigerating!

Spoon a generous amount of icing on top of each cupcake and shape with a palette knife.

Pear and Amaretto crumble cake

melted butter, for greasing
the tins

½ Bramley apple,
peeled and cut into
1.5cm dice (100g)

1 pear, peeled and cut
into 1.5cm dice (150g)

30g toasted walnut halves,
roughly chopped

finely grated zest
of 1 lemon

2 tbsp Amaretto liqueur

210g plain flour

¾ tsp baking powder

¾ tsp ground cinnamon

⅓ tsp ground cloves

45g ground almonds

3 eggs

180ml sunflower oil

230g caster sugar

⅓ tsp salt

120g Crumble
(see page 291)

These next two cakes work well served either with
a cup of tea in the afternoon or after a big meal,
with some vanilla ice cream. Yotam will find any excuse
to add a bit of alcohol to all sorts of sweet things but
the combinations – pear and Amaretto here and then
prunes and Armagnac in the sticky chocolate loaf –
really are classic.

For both cakes, you can make them in one large loaf
or round tin instead of two, if you like. Just increase the
baking time by 5–10 minutes. Both cakes also keep well,
in a sealed container at room temperature, for up to
2 days (for the pear cake) and 4 days (for the chocolate).
They also freeze well, wrapped in aluminium foil.

———

Preheat the oven to 190°C/170°C fan/Gas Mark 5. Grease 2 small
(500g) loaf tins with melted butter and line the base and sides with
baking parchment.

Mix the chopped apple and pear with the walnuts, lemon zest and
Amaretto liqueur. In a separate bowl, sift together the flour, baking
powder, cinnamon and cloves. Add the ground almonds.

Separate 2 of the eggs, keeping the whites separate while mixing
the yolks with the third egg. Using an electric mixer, beat together
the oil and sugar for about a minute (this can also be done by hand,
mixing briskly with a spatula). On a low speed, slowly add the yolk
and egg mix. Quickly add the sifted dry ingredients, followed by the
fruit mix. Stop the machine as soon as everything is incorporated.

Whisk the egg whites with the salt until it forms firm peaks, then
gently fold it into the cake mix, using a spatula or metal spoon.
Again, be careful not to over mix. Streaks of white in the mixture
are okay.

Divide the cake mix between the tins and scatter the crumble on
top. Bake for 40–45 minutes, until a skewer inserted in the centre
comes out clean (it might take a bit longer, depending on the
moisture content of the fruit). If the cakes start going dark before
the centre is cooked, cover them with foil. Remove from the oven
and leave to cool, then remove the cakes from the tins.

Sticky chocolate loaf

Makes 2 small loaves
(Serves 4–6)

This is a rich cake – the Armagnac, the prunes, the treacle – but don't let this fool you: it's as moreish as any chocolate cake gets.

Agen prunes are the best variety to use here: they're much juicier and more tender than some other varieties and play a key role in the cake's general gooeyness.

―――

Preheat the oven to 190°C/170°C fan/Gas Mark 5. Butter 2 small (500g) loaf tins and line the base and sides with baking parchment.

Place half the prunes in a small saucepan and add the Armagnac or Cognac. Warm very slightly, then set aside.

Put the remaining prunes in a blender or food processor and blend together with the buttermilk or yoghurt and oil until you get a light, shiny paste, a bit like mayonnaise. Transfer to a large mixing bowl and, using a hand whisk, mix in the egg, both types of sugar and the treacle.

Sift together the flour, baking powder, bicarbonate of soda, salt and cocoa powder. Fold them gently into the prune mix with a spatula. Fold in the chopped chocolate and divide the mixture equally between the prepared tins. Level the surface with a spatula. Cut each soaked prune in half with scissors and use your fingers to press them below the surface of the cakes. Place in the oven and bake for 45–50 minutes, until a skewer inserted in the centre comes out clean.

While the cakes are in the oven, make the syrup. Mix the water and sugar in a small saucepan and place on the heat. As soon as the water begins to simmer and the sugar is completely dissolved, remove from the heat and set aside for 10 minutes to cool down slightly. Finally, stir in the Armagnac or Cognac (you can also add any liquid left from soaking the prunes).

As soon as the cakes are out of the oven, pierce them through in a few places with a skewer and use a pastry brush to soak them with the warm syrup. Let them cool down completely before removing from the tins.

220g Agen prunes, pitted

100ml Armagnac
or Cognac

60ml buttermilk or yoghurt

60ml sunflower oil

1 egg

30g caster sugar

60g soft light brown sugar

40ml treacle

115g plain flour

½ tsp baking powder

½ tsp bicarbonate of soda

a pinch of salt

15g cocoa powder

150g dark chocolate,
chopped

Syrup

80ml water

80g caster sugar

2 tbsp Armagnac
or Cognac

Pistachio shortbreads

8 cardamom pods

200g unsalted butter

25g ground rice

240g plain flour

½ tsp salt

35g icing sugar

60g shelled pistachio kernels

1 egg, lightly beaten

2 tbsp vanilla sugar

These are particularly good with coffee but are also lovely served after supper, alongside a set milk pudding or some ice cream. The dough can be made and rolled in advance and then frozen, ready to be baked whenever you want a fresh batch. Once cooked, they also keep well, in a sealed container, for up to a week. The whole cardamom pods can be replaced by ground cardamom, if you have some: you'll just need ¼ teaspoon. Vanilla sugar can either be bought or else very simply made by sticking any used vanilla pods in a jar of caster sugar and leaving them there for a few days, until the sugar is ready to use.

Use a pestle and mortar to crush the cardamom pods, then remove the skins and work the seeds to a fine powder.

Using an electric mixer with the beater attachment fitted, mix together the butter, ground rice, flour, salt, ground cardamom and icing sugar. Run the machine until they turn into a paste and then stop the mixer at once. You don't need to incorporate much air (you could also do this by hand using a large plastic scraper; a strong wrist is required!).

Turn out the dough and, dusting with a little flour, roll it with your hands into a log 3–4cm in diameter. Wrap in cling film and leave in the fridge for at least an hour.

While the dough is chilling, chop the pistachios finely with a sharp knife, but not as fine as ground almonds. Or, if using a food processor, pulse them a few times until ground with some chunkier bits remaining. Scatter the pistachios on a flat tray.

Brush the log with the beaten egg and roll it in the ground pistachios. Wrap back in cling film and leave in the fridge to set for at least 30 minutes.

Preheat the oven to 170°C/150°C fan/Gas Mark 3. Remove the cling film and cut the log into slices 5mm–1cm thick. Lay them out on a baking tray lined with baking parchment, spacing them at least 2cm apart. Dust with the vanilla sugar.

Bake the biscuits for roughly 20 minutes. They must not take on too much colour but should remain golden. Remove from the oven and allow to cool completely before storing in a sealed jar. They will keep for up to a week.

BAKING AND PÂTISSERIE

Pistachio and ginger biscotti

Makes 25

This is a softer, friendlier version of the traditionally tooth-breaking biscuit. It still counts as biscotti, though, because it's twice-baked. The name comes from the Latin *panis biscotus* – twice-baked bread. Traditionally, the biscuits were so rusk-like and dry that people dipped them in their coffee or wine to soften up before munching. We have very strong feelings against dunking but we know that others feel similarly strongly on the opposing camp, so feel free, if you're a 'dunker', to continue this time-honoured practice.

These keep well in a sealed container, for up to 2 weeks. The dough can also be frozen after the first bake. Divide it into 2 or 3 before freezing so that you can defrost a piece at a time and then slice and bake. Thanks to Helen Goh (who has a phobia about dunking but who 'chases' each bite of biscotti with a sip of tea!).

80g unsalted butter

110g caster sugar

2 eggs, lightly beaten

1 tbsp brandy

finely grated zest of 1½ oranges

150g plain flour, plus extra for dusting

½ tsp ground ginger

¼ tsp salt

80g shelled pistachio kernels

60g stem ginger in syrup, drained and roughly chopped

Line a baking tray with baking parchment.

Using an electric mixer (or a good spatula and both your hands), cream the butter and sugar together until they lighten in colour and texture. Gradually add the eggs, beating well after each addition. Stir in the brandy and orange zest, followed by the flour, ground ginger and salt. Lastly, fold in the pistachios and stem ginger.

Lightly dust the lined baking tray with flour and spoon the mixture on to the tray. Leave to rest in the fridge for about 30 minutes so it firms up a little. Preheat the oven to 190°C/170°C fan/Gas Mark 5.

Take the dough out of the fridge and, using your hands and a bit of extra flour, form a log shape about 25cm long. It does not need to be perfect, as the mix will spread during baking. Bake for 20 minutes, then remove from the oven and leave to cool. At this point the log will be partially baked and still quite soft. Adjust the oven temperature to 150°C/130°C fan/Gas Mark 2.

Once the log has cooled down, use a serrated knife to cut it across into slices 1cm thick. Lay them flat on the baking tray and return to the oven for about 40 minutes, until crisp. Remove and leave to cool. Store in a sealed container.

White chocolate and cranberry biscuits

90g plain flour

¼ tsp salt

½ tsp baking powder

½ tsp bicarbonate of soda

100g unsalted butter, at room temperature

1 tsp vanilla essence

110g soft brown sugar

25g caster sugar

1 egg, lightly beaten

80g whole rolled oats

60g white chocolate, chopped into chocolate-chip-sized pieces

75g dried cranberries

The dried cranberries here make these particularly popular around Thanksgiving and Christmas. We like to make them year-round, though, sometimes substituting the cranberries with either dried blueberries or sour cherries.

They keep well in a sealed container for up to 5 days. If you're getting ahead for the festive period, take the biscuits up to the stage where they are shaped into small balls and then freeze them. They can then be cooked straight from frozen (with an extra minute or two added to the baking time), whenever you want a fresh batch.

Preheat the oven to 190°C/170°C fan/Gas Mark 5. Sift together the flour, salt, baking powder and bicarbonate of soda and set aside.

Put the butter, vanilla and sugars in a large mixing bowl and beat with a wooden spoon until the mixture is lighter in colour and texture. Gradually add the egg, making sure each addition is fully incorporated before adding more. Add the flour mixture and the oats, then the chocolate and cranberries. Do not continue mixing once the dry ingredients are blended in.

Chill the mixture slightly to help you shape the biscuits. Scoop out a bit of the mix with a spoon and use your hands to roll it into a ball, somewhere between the size of an olive and a walnut. Press the balls lightly on to baking trays lined with baking parchment. Make sure you space them a good 6–7cm apart (they will spread more than you expect!). Place in the oven and bake for about 10 minutes, until they are a good brown colour. Remove from the oven and allow to cool on the trays before serving.

Cranberry and
white choc
Dige

Almond and orange Florentines

vegetable oil, for brushing

2 egg whites

100g icing sugar

260g flaked almonds

finely grated zest
of 1 orange

Having some leftover egg whites provides a great excuse to make these. They're very quick and easy, you'll have all the ingredients you need already sitting in your cupboard and the results are lace-like, light and lovely. They don't have the caramel chewiness and stickiness of traditional Florentines but it's precisely this simplicity that appeals to us. If you want to nod a bit more to tradition, though, brush a thin layer of dark chocolate on the base of each biscuit once they're out of the oven and have cooled.

With or without the chocolate, they'll keep in a sealed container for up to 4 days. Don't leave them sitting out too long, though, as they'll lose their crispness. Thanks to Jim Webb for these.

Preheat the oven to 170°C/150°C fan/Gas Mark 3. Line a heavy baking tray with baking parchment and brush lightly with vegetable oil. Next to you have a small bowl of cold water.

Put the egg whites, icing sugar, flaked almonds and orange zest in a bowl and gently mix them together. Dip your hand in the bowl of water and pick up portions of the mix to make little mounds on the lined tray, well spaced apart. Dip a fork in the water and flatten each biscuit very thinly. Try to make them as thin as possible without creating too many gaps between the almond flakes. They should be about 8cm in diameter.

Place the baking tray in the oven and bake for about 12 minutes, until the biscuits are golden brown. Check underneath one biscuit to make sure they are cooked through.

Allow to cool, then gently, using a palette knife, remove the biscuits from the baking sheet. Store in a sealed jar.

Champagne chocolates

60g milk chocolate

200g dark chocolate

150g unsalted butter

80ml champagne
(or prosecco or cava,
as an alternative)

40ml good-quality brandy

to finish

150g dark chocolate,
for coating

50g cocoa powder,
for dusting

Anything that involves opening a bottle of bubbles to use under 100 millilitres either means you're making the most decadent of petits fours, you're going to be doubling the recipe and freezing half the batch, or you're going to have a splendidly fun time finishing up the fizz.

In all seriousness, though, these are great to make with half-drunk bottles of champagne (or prosecco or cava) the day after a party. Get the best-quality chocolate you can, and some good-quality brandy.

These will keep well in the fridge for up to a week.

———

Take a cake tin roughly 14cm square and line it with cling film. Using a sharp knife, chop both kinds of chocolate into small pieces and place them in a heatproof bowl large enough to accommodate all the ingredients. Warm the chocolate for a couple of minutes in a microwave or over a pan of simmering water until it is semi-melted; be careful not to heat it much. Cut the butter into small pieces and keep it separate.

Pour the champagne and brandy into a small saucepan and place on the stove until they warm up to around 80°C; they should be hot to the touch but not boiling. Pour the alcohol over the chocolate and stir gently with a rubber spatula until it melts completely. Stir in the butter in a few additions, then continue stirring until the mixture is smooth. Pour it into the lined tray and place in the fridge for at least 3 hours, until it has set firm.

Place the chocolate for coating in a heatproof mixing bowl and put it over a pan of simmering water. Stir occasionally and, as soon as the chocolate has melted, remove the bowl from the steam bath. Scatter the cocoa powder over a flat plate.

Turn the chilled chocolate block out of the tin on to a sheet of baking parchment and remove the cling film. Use a very sharp, long knife to cut it into roughly 2cm squares. Clean the knife in hot water after every time you cut.

Using 2 skewers or forks, dip the squares in the melted chocolate, wiping off any excess on the side of the bowl. Quickly roll the squares in the cocoa powder and place on a clean tray. Allow the chocolates to set in the fridge, but make sure you leave them out at room temperature for at least half an hour before serving.

Sour cherry amaretti

Makes about 20

This is our version of the popular little almond Italian biscuit. They have a softer and chewier inside, which makes them particularly moreish. They're perfect eaten as they are, served with coffee, or else chopped and sprinkled over ice cream. It comes full circle if you made your own ice cream in the first place and are looking for a way to use up your leftover egg whites.

The tart contrast provided by the dried sour cherries works well here, but these can be replaced with dried apricots or dried blueberries, if you like, or else omitted altogether. If you want to enhance the flavour, you can make your own ground almonds by finely grinding almonds that have been blanched, peeled and lightly roasted. Either way, be sure to stick to the instructed '3 drops' of natural almond extract and start with the purest extract you can. Anything else (in terms of quantity and quality) will spread with it an artificial aroma.

Once baked and cooled, these keep in a sealed container for 10 days and can also be frozen for a longer period.

180g ground almonds

120g caster sugar

finely grated zest of 1 lemon

3 drops of natural almond extract

a pinch of salt

60g dried sour cherries, roughly chopped

2 egg whites

2 tsp honey

plenty of icing sugar, for rolling

———

Preheat the oven to 190°C/170°C fan/Gas Mark 5. Put the ground almonds, sugar, lemon zest, almond extract and salt in a large bowl and rub with your fingertips to disperse the zest and essence evenly. Add the cherries and set aside.

Using a manual or electric whisk, beat the egg whites and honey until they reach a soft meringue consistency. Gently fold the meringue into the almond mixture. At this stage you should have a soft, malleable paste.

With your hands, form the mixture into 20 irregular shapes. Roll them in plenty of icing sugar, then arrange them on a baking tray lined with baking parchment. Place in the oven and bake for about 12 minutes. The biscuits should have taken on some colour but remain relatively pale and chewy in the centre. Leave to cool completely before indulging, or storing them in a sealed jar.

Prune and brandy truffles

24 Agen prunes

200g dark chocolate, for coating

4 tbsp cocoa powder, for dusting

Ganache filling

150g dark chocolate

20g unsalted butter

100ml double cream

4 tsp glucose syrup

4 tsp brandy

These are a seriously impressive way to end a meal, either passed around the table or served at a drinks party as a canapé 'pudding'. With both dark chocolate and brandy in the filling, they have pretty much everything you need in order to call it a day. They're great throughout the year but particularly well suited to festive feasts, when most of the ingredients should be close to hand.

These keep well in the fridge, in a sealed container, for up to 2 weeks. Take them out of the fridge half an hour before serving, though: you don't want them to be fridge-cold.

With thanks to Khalid Assyb for creating these.

To make the ganache filling, chop up the chocolate and butter into very small pieces and place in a heatproof bowl. Put the cream and glucose into a small saucepan and bring to the boil, watching carefully. As soon as they boil, pour them over the chocolate and butter. Stir gently with a rubber spatula until you get a smooth, shiny mix (if the chocolate doesn't melt fully, you can 'help' it by placing the bowl over a saucepan of simmering water for a few seconds). Stir in the brandy until well blended. Place a sheet of cling film over the surface of the ganache and leave to set overnight at room temperature. Alternatively, you can set it in the fridge, but you will need to take it out in advance and let it come to room temperature before using.

Once the ganache has set, split each prune down one side with a knife and carefully remove the stone. Spoon some ganache into each prune to fill it up. Close to form a little parcel and then chill for at least half an hour.

To coat the prunes, roughly chop the dark chocolate and place in a bowl set over a saucepan of simmering water, making sure the bowl does not touch the water. Stir gently until melted, then remove from the pan. Scatter the cocoa powder in a flat dish.

Using 2 forks, dip the prunes in the melted chocolate, wiping off any excess chocolate on the side of the bowl. Roll them straight in the cocoa powder and place on a clean plate. Allow to set, preferably in a cool place, or otherwise in the fridge. Don't serve them fridge-cold.

Raspberry and oat bars

Base

120g plain flour

⅓ tsp baking powder

100g unsalted butter, diced

60g caster sugar

a pinch of salt

80g whole rolled oats

Filling

220g raspberry jam, bought or homemade

Topping

70g flaked almonds

70g pecan halves, roughly chopped

70g hazelnuts, roughly chopped

70g Brazil nuts, roughly chopped

100g unsalted butter

75g caster sugar

40ml milk

1 tsp vanilla essence

Raspberry jam, rolled oats, chopped nuts, milk: it's for good reason that these are a popular 'grab-and-go' breakfast bar option for those rushing out of the door in the morning. A batch keeps well in a sealed container at home for up to 3 days; a slice also keeps well in your on-the-move tupperware for a mid-morning or afternoon snack. Play around with the jams, if you like: strawberry and apricot also work well.

———

Preheat the oven to 190°C/170°C fan/Gas Mark 5. Lightly grease a 20cm square tin and line it with baking parchment.

To make the base, sift together the flour and baking powder. Add the butter, sugar and salt and rub everything together with your fingertips to form crumbs. Stir in the oats. Spread this mixture over the base of the prepared tin; don't press down too much, so the base remains light. Bake for 20 minutes or until light brown. Remove from the oven and allow to cool a little, then spread with the jam.

For the topping, place the nuts in a large bowl. In a small saucepan, heat up the butter, sugar, milk and vanilla. Stir until the sugar has dissolved, then pour the mixture over the chopped nuts and stir together. Pack the nut mix evenly over the jam and return to the oven for 30 minutes, until the nuts have turned a nice golden brown.

Leave to cool, then remove from the tin and slice into bars or squares.

Granola bars

Granola bars have undergone something of an image change. What used to be seen as rather a hippy sort of food then became the go-to 'nutrient-packed' snack of the chia-seed-eating hipsters. For all that they've gone in and out of fashion, our bars – an absolute must-have for many a long-term customer – have carried on rolling with the same punches: rolled oats, roasted nuts, runny caramel. Kids also love them, whether they're destined for hippy or hipster-dom. Once cooked, these keep well in a sealed container for up to 5 days.

———

Preheat the oven to 160°C/140°C fan/Gas Mark 3. Lightly grease a 20cm square tin and line it with baking parchment.

Scatter the pecans on a baking tray and roast for 8 minutes. Remove from the oven and increase the temperature to 180°C/160°C fan/Gas Mark 4.

Half-fill a small bowl with hot water and add the apricots and cherries. Leave to soak for about 10 minutes and then drain through a colander.

In a large mixing bowl, stir together all the ingredients apart from the butter, honey and sugar. Put these last 3 in a small saucepan and bring to a light simmer. Leave to cook to a light brown colour, watching the whole time so the caramel doesn't spill over or go too dark. Once light brown, pour it over the dry ingredients and stir to mix everything together. Spoon the mixture into the lined tin and pack it down lightly with a palette knife or spoon.

Bake for about 22 minutes, until lightly coloured on top. The bar will still be soft when removed from the oven but will firm up as it cools down. Take out of the tin and cut into individual bars. Eat straight away or store in a sealed container.

45g pecan halves

45g dried apricots, very roughly chopped

45g dried sour cherries

45g pumpkin seeds

30g sesame seeds

30g ground almonds

190g whole rolled oats

1¼ tsp ground cinnamon

a pinch of salt

95g unsalted butter

85g honey

95g Demerara sugar

Brownies

For all that baking is a precise science, you also need to use your common sense and know your oven. What might take 22 minutes in one oven can take 18 or 19 or 24 in another. You need to have the confidence to pull something out of the oven or leave it in for a little bit longer if you think it needs it. Nowhere is this more the case than when cooking brownies, where the difference between a couple of minutes in the oven can be the difference between perfectly gooey and overcooked and dry. We say this not to terrify you: we simply care passionately about the gooeyness of your brownies. So seriously do we take this passion that we've penned what we think of as The Golden Brownie Rules.

You'll know that your brownies are perfectly cooked when you stick a skewer into your cooked brownie and it comes out covered with lots of gooey crumbs: not as gooey and wet as when the mixture went into the oven, obviously, but also not with crumbs that are dry. The mixture should be thick and slightly sticky to the touch, with a tendency to set once cooled down a bit. The brownie should also have risen slightly – between 10 and 20 per cent – in the oven and its surface should be totally dry.

The brownies will continue to set once they are taken out of the oven and set aside to cool. It's always better to bring them out slightly underdone rather than overdone. If it turns out they are too underdone and uncooked, you can always chill them in the fridge to set. If they are overdone, they've crossed the threshold into the realm of cake and there's just no going back.

———

Not rules, but still useful to know:

Our brownie recipes are for a 22cm square tin but you can either use any tin or dish with a similar surface area, or else a 25cm round cake tin.

Once cooked, brownies keep well in a sealed container for up to 4 days. They can also be frozen. They won't keep their molten gooeyness but they still work well, particularly as bite-sized brownies. A bit of firmness, in this case, will be really appreciated.

Makes 8–10

Toffee

200g unsalted butter, plus extra, melted, for greasing

280g plain flour

½ tsp salt

300g dark chocolate, broken into pieces

2 eggs

220g caster sugar

1 tsp vanilla essence

140g apricot, banana or raspberry jam

Butter toffee

25g unsalted butter, plus extra, melted, for greasing

75g caster sugar

There is a reason why toffee apples are still around: the pairing of sweet fruit with butter toffee is irresistible. Choose whichever jam you want swirled through the surface of the brownie: apricot and raspberry jam are obviously more widely available than banana jam, but it's the sort of thing you stumble across at a farmers' market, or you can easily make your own with a bunch of over-ripe bananas. Have a look online: there are lots of recipes.

Start by making the butter toffee. Lightly brush an oven tray (not the one you will use to bake the brownies in) with melted butter. Put the butter and sugar for the toffee in a heavy-based saucepan and place over a medium heat. Stir constantly with a wooden spoon until the mixture turns a dark caramel colour (at one point it might seem the mixture has split; it will come back together when you stir vigorously). Carefully pour the toffee on to the buttered tray and leave aside until it sets.

When you are ready to make the brownies, brush a 22cm square baking tin with melted butter and line with baking parchment. Preheat the oven to 190°C/170°C fan/Gas Mark 5. Sift together the flour and salt.

Put the butter and chocolate in a heatproof bowl and place over a saucepan of simmering water, making sure the water does not touch the base of the bowl. Leave to melt, stirring from time to time. As soon as the butter and chocolate have melted, remove the bowl from above the water. This is important! You need to avoid getting the mix very hot.

In a large bowl, lightly whisk together the eggs, sugar and vanilla. Work them just until combined, a few seconds only, as there is no need to incorporate any air into the eggs. Fold in the melted chocolate mixture and then the sifted flour. Break the toffee into small pieces and fold them in as well.

Pour the mix into the lined tin. Drop the jam in spoonfuls into the mixture and swirl it around with a knife.

Place on the centre shelf of the oven and bake for roughly 25 minutes. Make sure you check the instructions on page 253 before deciding to remove the brownie from the oven. Once out, allow it to cool down completely before removing from the tin (you might even need to chill it first). Cut into any shape you like and keep in an airtight container for up to 5 days.

Makes 8–10

Macadamia and white chocolate

200g macadamia nuts

200g unsalted butter, plus extra, melted, for greasing

280g plain flour

½ tsp salt

300g dark chocolate, broken into pieces

2 eggs

230g caster sugar

1 tsp vanilla essence

2 tsp instant coffee

200g white chocolate, broken into pieces (or use chocolate chips)

This is an almost guaranteed way to get people talking with their mouths full. 'Oh my goodness', friends will say, 'these are soooooooooo good'. And the smaller the squares you cut them into, the more people will eat. There is some unspoken rule that it's okay to eat five bite-sized brownies rather than sit in the corner devouring one big slab.

Preheat the oven to 190°C/170°C fan/Gas Mark 5. Spread the nuts out in an ovenproof dish and roast for 5 minutes, then remove from the oven.

Follow the brownie instructions in the recipe on page 254 up to the stage where you fold in the toffee, adding the instant coffee to the eggs, vanilla and sugar. Instead of the toffee, fold in the white chocolate and half the nuts. Pour the mix into the lined tin and top with the remaining nuts.

Continue as in the first brownie recipe.

Khalid's chocolate and chestnut bars

Makes 8–10

These pull off the trick of being both delicate and light and completely decadent and rich. It's the flour-free nature of the chocolate part of the bar that makes it so light, but then all the things inside – the chestnuts, the dried figs, the chopped white chocolate – make it so full of substance. For an extra dimension of decadence, soak the figs in rum or brandy before adding them to the mix. Gluten-free biscuits also work instead of the digestives.

The best chestnuts for this are the ready cooked and peeled ones that come vacuum-packed or in a tin. Don't use those cooked in syrup: they'll be too sweet. Once baked, these keep well in a sealed container for up to 3 days. They also freeze well.

Thanks to Khalid Assyb for these.

———

Preheat the oven to 170°C/150°C fan/Gas Mark 3. Lightly grease a 20cm square tin and line it with aluminium foil or baking parchment.

For the base, place the biscuits in a large bowl and crush with your hands or a rolling pin. Add the melted butter and mix together to make a sandy paste. Scatter this mixture in the tin and press hard on to the base until level. Leave in the fridge to set.

Meanwhile, put the dark chocolate and butter in a heatproof bowl set over a saucepan of simmering water and leave to melt. Stir occasionally with a wooden spoon and remove from the pan as soon as they melt so that they don't get too hot.

Use an electric mixer to whisk the eggs, yolk and sugar together until thick and pale (if it doesn't scare you, you could also do it with a hand whisk). Gently fold the chocolate mixture into the eggs, followed by the chopped chestnuts, figs and white chocolate. Spread evenly over the biscuit base and bake on the middle shelf of the oven for 15–20 minutes. A skewer inserted in the bar should come out with lots of gooey crumb attached, the same as when you make brownies (see page 253 for a full description). Make sure you don't go beyond this point. Remove from the oven, leave to cool, then refrigerate for a few hours until set.

Take the bar out of the tin and peel off the foil or paper. Cut into bars or squares and dust lightly with cocoa powder. Let them come to room temperature before serving.

225g dark chocolate

150g unsalted butter, diced

2 eggs, plus 1 extra egg yolk

45g caster sugar

120g cooked peeled chestnuts, roughly chopped

120g dried figs (the soft, ready-to-eat type), stalks removed, roughly chopped

120g white chocolate, roughly chopped

cocoa powder, for dusting

Base

190g digestive biscuits

90g unsalted butter, melted

Macaroons

Making your own macaroons at home is very gratifying and not as challenging as you might imagine. Ours, made at home, probably won't look as precisely even and elegant as those sold in dedicated French pâtisseries but they will, however, taste just as wonderfully soft and sweet, without any added colourings and flavourings. They are a great way to use up egg whites and, chances are, you'll have the remainder of the ingredients needed already in your cupboards.

You can make the macaroons well ahead of when you want to eat them: without their filling, they keep well in a sealed container for up to a week and they also freeze incredibly well. In fact, freezing will cause them to soften a little once sandwiched together, which is just the effect you are after. Once filled, they are best eaten within 2 days. They should be stored in the fridge but brought back to room temperature before serving.

———

General method

See the individual macaroon recipes for ingredients.

Heat up the oven to 190°C/170°C fan/Gas Mark 5. Using a fine sieve, sift the icing sugar and ground almonds into a clean, dry bowl.

Place the egg whites and caster sugar in the bowl of a freestanding electric mixer and start whisking on full speed until the whites have formed a thick, aerated meringue, firm but not too dry. Remove the bowl from the machine, take a third of the meringue and fold it gently into the sifted almond and sugar mix. Once incorporated, add another third of the meringue and continue similarly until all the meringue has been added and the mix appears smooth and glossy.

Take a sheet of baking parchment and 'glue' it on to a baking sheet by dotting the tray in a few places with a tiny amount of the macaroon mix. Now you need to use the mix to create uniform shallow discs, about the size of a two-pound coin. In our kitchens we pipe the macaroon mix on to the lined tray using a piping bag fitted with a small nozzle. This requires a bit of experience but you can try it.

To assist you, draw little circles on the paper, spaced well apart. This will guide you in achieving consistently sized macaroons. Then either pipe or spoon little blobs of the macaroon mix on to the lined tray. Alternatively, take a bowl of icing sugar, dip your fingers in it and shape the macaroons with your hands.Now hold the tray firmly and tap its underside vigorously. This should help to spread and smooth out the biscuits. Leave the macaroons out and uncovered for 15 minutes before baking.

To bake, place the macaroons in the preheated oven and leave for about 12 minutes. They might take longer, depending on your oven. The macaroons are ready when they come freely off the paper when lifted with a palette knife. Remove from the oven as soon as they reach this stage, so that you don't overbake them, and leave aside to cool down completely.

To assemble the macaroons, use a small spoon or a piping bag to deposit a pea-sized amount of the filling on the flat side of half the biscuits. Sandwich them with the other half, squeezing them together gently. Leave at room temperature to set within a couple of hours, or chill them to hasten the process. Just remember not to serve your macaroons cold from the fridge.

Salty peanut and caramel

Makes about 20

The combination of salted peanuts and caramel might seem like an obvious one now, but it seemed enormously novel when Carol Brough first made these for us. Dulce de leche – literally translated as 'candy made from milk' can be bought in supermarkets, or you can make your own by covering a sealed can of condensed milk with boiling water and then leaving it on a medium simmer for about 3 hours. If you do this, be sure to keep an eye on the water levels and keep them topped up: there is a danger of the can exploding if it is not covered with water at all times.

———

To make the macaroons, follow the instructions on page 260, using all the ingredients listed apart from the chopped peanuts. These you add after you have laid out (or piped) the macaroons on the baking tray and before the 15-minute rest. Just dot each biscuit with a few pieces of chopped peanut, leave them to rest, then bake.

To make the filling, mix the peanuts with the dulce de leche, stir in a small pinch of salt, then taste. You want to get a sweetness that is balanced by a fair amount of saltiness, a bit like peanut butter.

110g icing sugar

60g ground almonds

2 egg whites (60g)

40g caster sugar

20g natural roasted peanuts, roughly chopped

Caramel filling

30g natural roasted peanuts, finely chopped

100g dulce de leche

salt

110g icing sugar

60g ground almonds

2 egg whites (60g)

40g caster sugar

5 large basil leaves,
finely chopped

finely grated zest of 1 lime

Buttercream filling

100g unsalted butter,
at room temperature

45g icing sugar

finely grated zest and juice
of 1 lime

5 large basil leaves,
finely chopped

Lime and basil

Fresh, zesty and light green: these have got 'summer
garden party' written all over them.

————

To make the buttercream filling, place the butter and icing sugar
in a mixing bowl and beat them together with a rubber spatula
until pale in colour and light in texture. Add the lime juice and
zest and the basil and beat them in until fully incorporated.
Cover the buttercream with cling film and leave in a cool place,
but not the fridge.

To make the macaroons, follow the instructions on page 260,
using all the ingredients listed. Fold the basil and lime zest into
the mix at the final stage, after the almonds and icing sugar are
fully incorporated into the meringue.

Makes about 20

110g icing sugar

50g ground almonds

12g cocoa powder

2 egg whites (60g)

40g caster sugar

Ganache filling

65g dark chocolate

15g unsalted butter

50ml double cream

2 tsp dark rum

Chocolate

Possibly the perfect way to end a meal, served with
a black coffee.

————

Start by making the ganache filling. Chop up the chocolate into tiny
pieces and the butter into small dice. Place them in a heatproof bowl.
Pour the cream into a small saucepan and bring to the boil, watching
it carefully. As soon as it boils, pour it over the chocolate and butter.
Stir gently with a rubber spatula until you get a smooth mix (if the
chocolate doesn't melt easily, help it by placing the bowl over a pot
of simmering water and stirring). Stir in the rum until well blended.

Place a sheet of cling film over the surface of the ganache and
leave to set somewhere cool for a couple of hours. Don't put it
in the fridge. It should not get too hard, as you need to spoon
it between the macaroons.

To make the macaroons, follow the instructions on page 260,
using the ingredients listed and adding the cocoa powder to
the icing sugar and ground almonds when sifting them.

Meringues

Enormously oversized and often brightly coloured, meringues have long been associated with the Ottolenghi window displays.

Our repertoire has expanded – we do a range of little bite-sized meringues, for example, and we top fruity cake slices with meringue. There's also a bunch of mess-like desserts that we serve in the restaurants, and then there are our 'classic' passion fruit meringue tartlets which, on their own, are solely responsible for bringing into our shops sweet-toothed brigades from far and near. For all the variants, though, the classics – the large ones topped with either finely chopped pistachios or freeze-dried raspberry – remain hugely popular.

As well as using up all of your leftover egg whites, meringues are another baker's favourite because of how well they keep, in a sealed container, for up to 3 weeks. They also freeze very well. If you don't spend your life making ice cream or custard and don't happen to have 300 grams of egg whites to hand, you can now buy handy cartons of pure egg whites in most supermarkets.

Don't attempt to make these unless you have a good free-standing electric mixer. They need whisking on a high electric speed for a good 10 minutes so it's just not possible to do this by hand or even with a hand-held mixer.

Pistachio and rosewater

Makes 12 large
meringues

600g caster sugar

300g egg whites
(about 10)

2 tsp rosewater

60g pistachio kernels,
finely chopped

Preheat the oven to 220°C/200°C fan/Gas Mark 7. Spread the sugar evenly over a large oven tray lined with baking parchment. Place the tray in the oven for about 8 minutes or until the sugar is hot (over 100°C). You should be able to see it beginning to dissolve at the edges.

While the sugar is in the oven, place the egg whites in the bowl of a freestanding electric mixer fitted with the whisk attachment. When the sugar is almost ready, start the machine on high speed and let it work for a minute or so, until the whites just begin to froth up.

Carefully pour the sugar slowly on to the whisking whites. Once it has all been added, add the rosewater and continue whisking on high speed for 10 minutes or until the meringue is cold. At this point it should keep its shape when you lift a bit from the bowl and look homogenously silky (you can now taste the mixture and fold in some more rosewater if you want a more distinctive rose flavour).

Turn down the oven temperature to 130°C/110°C fan/Gas Mark ¾. To shape the meringues, line a baking tray (or 2, depending on their size) with baking parchment, sticking it firmly to the tray with a bit of meringue. Spread the pistachios over a flat plate.

Have ready 2 large kitchen spoons. Use one of them to scoop up a big dollop of meringue, the size of a medium apple, then use the other spoon to scrape it off on to the plate of pistachios. Roll the meringue so it is covered with nuts on one side and then gently place it on the lined baking tray. Repeat to make more meringues, spacing them well apart on the tray. Remember, the meringues will almost double in size in the oven.

Place in the preheated oven 110°C and leave there for about 2 hours. Check if they are done by lifting them from the tray and gently prodding to make sure the outside is completely firm, whilst the centre is still a little soft. Remove from the oven and leave to cool. The meringues will keep in a dry place, at room temperature, for quite a few days.

Cinnamon and hazelnut

We use the Swiss meringue method here, which involves dissolving the sugars in the egg whites before whipping them up. Doing this enables the brown sugar to mix properly with the whites, creating a uniform mix. Thanks to Carol Brough for making these work, after many trials and tribulations.

———

Preheat the oven to 130°C/110°C fan/Gas Mark ¾.

Fill a medium saucepan with water and bring it to a light simmer. Place the egg whites and both sugars in a heatproof bowl large enough to sit on top of the pan. Put it over the simmering water, making sure it doesn't actually touch the water, and leave it there for about 10 minutes, stirring occasionally, until the mixture is quite hot (40°C) and the sugars have dissolved into the whites.

Pour into the bowl of a freestanding electric mixer and whip up on high speed, using the whisk attachment. Work the meringue for about 8 minutes or until the mix has cooled down completely. When ready, it should be firm and glossy and keep its shape when you lift a bit with a spoon.

Sprinkle the cinnamon over the meringue mix and use a rubber spatula to fold it in gently.

Line a flat baking tray (or 2, depending on their size) with baking parchment. You can stick the edges to the tray with a few blobs of the meringue mix. This will hold the paper in place whilst you shape the meringues.

Have ready 2 large kitchen spoons. Use one of them to scoop up a generous spoonful of the meringue and the other to scrape this out on to the tray (leave plenty of room between the meringues for them to expand in the oven; they can almost double in size). Using the spoons, shape the meringues into spiky dollops, the size of medium apples, and sprinkle with the chopped hazelnuts. Place in the preheated oven and bake for anything from 1¼–2 hours, depending on the oven and the size of your meringues. To check, poke them gently inside and look underneath. The meringues should be nice and dry underneath and still a little soft in the centre.

Remove from the oven and leave to cool. Stored in a dry place, but not the fridge, the meringues will keep for a few days.

Makes 10 large meringues

200g egg whites (about 7)

260g caster sugar

140g dark brown muscovado sugar

½ tsp ground cinnamon

30g unskinned hazelnuts, roughly chopped

Tartlets

The five recipes here all call for tartlet cases that are made up from about a third or a quarter of the full quantity of sweet pastry (see page 293). The leftover pastry can be frozen for a rainy day. It's nice to choose two or three different fillings and then offer your guests a selection to pick from.

If you don't have six tartlet tins that are each about 6 centimetres wide, use a small muffin tin with similar proportions instead. Whatever the diameter of your tins, just make sure you adjust the size of your pastry discs: they need to be wide enough to cover the base and sides of the mould and rise up 2 or 3 millimetres above the rim.

If you want to make and bake and then freeze the tartlet cases, that's fine: they keep well in the freezer. But once filled, the tarts are best eaten the day they are made.

Makes 6

40g unsalted butter, melted, for brushing

¼–⅓ quantity of Sweet pastry (see page 293)

plain flour, for dusting

Pre-baked cases

Start by brushing your tartlet tins with a thin layer of melted butter, then leave to set in the fridge.

Meanwhile, prepare a wide, clean working surface and have ready a rolling pin and a small amount of flour. Lightly dust the work surface, place the pastry in the middle and roll out the sweet pastry thinly, turning it around as you go. Work quickly so it doesn't get warm. Once the pastry is no more than 2–3mm thick, cut out 6 circles using a pastry cutter or the rim of a bowl. Line the buttered tins by placing the circles inside and gently pressing them into the corners and sides. Leave to rest in the fridge for at least 30 minutes.

Preheat the oven to 170°C/150°C fan/Gas Mark 3. Line each pastry case with a circle of scrunched-up greaseproof paper or a piece of cling film. It should come 1cm above the edge of the pastry (paper muffin cases are another great solution). Fill them up with rice or dry beans, then place in the oven and bake blind for about 25 minutes. By then they should have taken on a golden-brown colour. If they are not quite there yet, remove the beans and lining paper and continue baking for 5–10 minutes. Remove from the oven.

Keep the baking beans or rice and the paper holding them for future use. Remove the tart cases from the tins while they are still slightly warm and leave them on the side to cool down completely.

Fresh berries

6 pre-baked tartlet cases
(see page 270)

Mascarpone cream
(see page 291)

50g strawberries, halved
or quartered

50g raspberries

50g blueberries

icing sugar, for dusting
(optional)

Just make a batch of these and fast-track your way to
pretending that summer garden parties are exactly the
sort of thing you put on the whole time. They need to be
served within 6 hours of assembling, preferably sooner.

___

Use a piping bag or a spoon to fill the tart cases three-quarters
full with the mascarpone cream. Be creative when topping up
generously with the fresh berries. You can throw them on in
a beautiful mess or arrange them meticulously – a matter of
personality. Dust with icing sugar, if you like, then chill. Serve within
6 hours, but preferably at once.

White chocolate and raspberry

40g raspberries

180g white chocolate,
chopped into tiny pieces

20g unsalted butter,
cut into 5mm dice

90ml double cream

6 tsp raspberry jam,
bought or homemade (see
page 288)

6 pre-baked tartlet cases
(see page 270)

Some combinations can't be messed with: step forward
white chocolate and raspberry.

___

Crush the fresh raspberries with a fork and then pass them through
a fine sieve to remove the pips. Set the smooth coulis aside.

Put the white chocolate and the butter in a heatproof bowl. Heat the
cream in a small saucepan and bring to the boil, watching it constantly.
As soon as it comes to the boil, pour it over the chocolate and butter
and stir gently with a rubber spatula. Continue until all the chocolate
has melted and you are left with a smooth, shiny ganache.

Immediately, before the ganache begins to set, spoon the raspberry
jam into the tartlet cases. Carefully pour in the ganache; it should
almost reach the rim (if the ganache does begin to set, heat it gently
over a pan of hot water before pouring). Be very gentle now and
don't shake the cases.

Spoon a tiny amount of the raspberry coulis – not more than
½ teaspoon – into the centre of each tart. Use the tip of a knife
or a skewer to swirl the coulis around. Carefully transfer the tarts
to the fridge and leave them there to set. Remove at least
30 minutes before serving.

Lemon meringue

There are very good lemon curds available, if you want to cut yourself some slack, but homemade is great.

———

Preheat the oven to 220°C/200°C fan/Gas Mark 7. Spoon the cold lemon curd into the tart cases, filling them three-quarters full. Leave aside, preferably in the fridge.

To make the meringue, spread the sugar over an oven tray lined with baking parchment. Place in the hot oven for 5–6 minutes. The sugar should become very hot but mustn't begin to dissolve. Remove from the oven. Reduce the temperature to 170°C/150°C fan/Gas Mark 3.

At the last minute of heating up the sugar, place the egg whites in the bowl of a freestanding electric mixer. Whisk on high speed for a few seconds, until they begin to froth up. Now carefully pour the hot sugar on to the whisking whites in a slow stream. Once finished, continue whisking for a good 15 minutes, until the meringue is firm, shiny and cold.

Use 2 spoons or a piping bag to dispense the meringue on top of the curd and create a pattern. At this point you can either leave the meringue totally white or you can place it in the oven for 1–3 minutes to brown the top very lightly. Serve at once or chill for up to 12 hours.

½ quantity of Lemon curd (see page 290) chilled for at least 6 hours

6 pre-baked tartlet cases (see page 270)

120g caster sugar

2 egg whites

Dark chocolate

The raspberry jam in the base of these is a nice surprise against the richness of the chocolate. A spoonful of tahini or peanut butter also works well, for a grown-up version of a Reese's peanut butter cup.

———

Preheat the oven to 190°C/170°C fan/Gas Mark 5. Put the chocolate and butter in a bowl, set it over a pan of simmering water and leave to melt. Whisk the egg and yolk with the sugar until thick and pale yellow, then fold this into the melted chocolate.

If using the jam, put a spoonful in the base of each tartlet case. Fill them up with the chocolate mix; it should reach right up to the rim. Place in the oven and bake for 5 minutes. Cool a little, then remove the tartlets from their tins and allow them to cool down completely.

Lightly dust with cocoa powder and serve at room temperature.

150g dark chocolate, broken up

100g unsalted butter, diced

1 egg, plus 1 extra egg yolk

30g caster sugar

60g raspberry jam, bought or homemade (see page 288) (optional)

6 pre-baked tartlet cases (see page 270) – baked 5 minutes less than suggested and left in their tins

cocoa powder, for dusting

Banana and hazelnut

45g unskinned hazelnuts

90g unsalted butter

100g icing sugar

40g plain flour

2 egg whites

½ tsp vanilla essence

50g mashed banana

2 tsp lemon juice

6 pre-baked tartlet cases
(see page 270) – baked
5 minutes less than
suggested and left in
their tins

50g smooth apricot jam

50g dark chocolate,
broken into pieces
(optional)

Another classic flavour combination here, with the
banana, hazelnuts and chocolate.

⸺

Heat the oven to 170°C/150°C fan/Gas Mark 3. Scatter the
hazelnuts in an oven tray and roast for 12 minutes. Remove and
allow to cool down.

While you wait for the nuts, make some burnt butter. Put the butter
in a medium pan and cook over a moderate heat. After a few
minutes, it should start to darken and smell nutty. Take off the
heat and leave to cool slightly.

Set aside 10g of the nuts. The rest (plus their skins) put in a food
processor, together with 70g of the icing sugar. Work to a fine
powder and then add the flour. Pulse together to mix. Add the egg
whites and work the machine very briefly, just to mix them in. Repeat
with the vanilla and the butter. It is important to stop the machine
as soon as the ingredients are incorporated.

Mix the mashed banana with the lemon juice and the remaining
icing sugar. Spoon about 2 teaspoons of this mixture into each
pre-baked tart case (still in its tin). Top with the hazelnut batter.
It should come to within 2–3mm of the top. Place in the oven and
bake for 20–22 minutes, until the hazelnut filling is completely set.
You can check this with a skewer. Remove the tarts from the oven
and cool slightly, then carefully remove them from their tins.

Put the apricot jam in a small saucepan, stir in a tablespoon of
water and bring to the boil. Remove from the heat and brush lightly
over the tart tops. Roughly chop the reserved nuts and scatter
them on the jam.

If using the chocolate, put it in a heatproof bowl and place over a
pan of simmering water. Stir gently just until the chocolate melts.
Use a spoon to drizzle the tarts gently with the chocolate, trying to
create thin, delicate lines. Do not drizzle too much, so the chocolate
doesn't take over.

Semolina and raspberry tart

vegetable oil, for brushing the tin

plain flour, for dusting

250g Sweet pastry (see page 293) or use bought pastry

80g unsalted butter

180ml whipping cream

345ml milk

60g caster sugar

½ vanilla pod

60g semolina

1 egg

200g raspberries

50g apricot jam (optional)

icing sugar, to finish

Semolina conjures up lots of fond memories of growing up in the Middle East. Syrup-soaked semolina cakes were the stuff of dreams and then, on the savoury side, couscous and (from Yotam's Italian grandmother) semolina gnocchi. We are aware, however, that those who grew up elsewhere often have rather different memories of semolina. We implore you to give this ingredient another chance, though: it is wonderfully light and comforting.

This tart is best served within a few hours of making it. You can, however, refrigerate it for up to 24 hours after baking and cooling, remove from the fridge for an hour or so, glaze, top with the fresh raspberries and serve.

Lightly brush an 18cm loose-based cake tin with a tiny amount of oil, then set aside.

Make sure you have a clean work surface dusted with a bit of flour. Using a rolling pin, roll the pastry out into a rough disc, 2–3mm thick. Work quickly, turning the pastry around as you go. Once you have reached the right thickness, cut the pastry into a circle large enough to cover the tin and most of the sides comfortably. Carefully line the tin, patching up any holes with excess pastry if necessary. When the pastry is in place, use a sharp knife to trim it so you have a neat edge, roughly 3cm high. Place in the fridge to rest for 30 minutes.

Preheat the oven to 190°C/170°C fan/Gas Mark 5. Cut out a circle of baking parchment large enough to cover the base and sides of the cake tin. Place it inside the case and fill up with dry beans or rice so the sides of the pastry are totally supported by the beans and won't collapse during baking. Bake the case blind for 25–35 minutes or until it is very light brown. Remove from the oven and take out the beans or rice (you can keep them for future tarts).

To make the filling, put the butter, cream, milk and sugar in a saucepan. Slit the vanilla pod open lengthwise with a sharp knife and scrape out all the flavoursome seeds. Drop the seeds and the scraped pod into the pan. Place the pan on the stove and bring to the boil. Let it simmer while you whisk in the semolina in a slow stream. Continue whisking until the mix comes back to the boil and thickens up like porridge. Remove from the heat and whisk in the egg. Remove the vanilla pod.

Pour the semolina mixture into the pastry case and level it with
a wet palette knife. Push half the raspberries inside, allowing them
to show on the surface. Bake for 20–25 minutes, until the filling is
slightly golden. Remove from the oven and cool slightly before
removing the tart from the tin.

Put the apricot jam in a small pan with a tablespoon of water and
bring to the boil. Strain it through a sieve and brush over the tart.
Finish with the remaining raspberries and a dusting of icing sugar.

Individual plum clafoutis

Makes 6

We break away from tradition here. Whereas the French clafoutis batter is usually poured over fresh pitted cherries in a large ovenproof dish and then baked to make a rustic, soufflé-like dessert, we make stand-alone little cakes here. Feel free to revert back to tradition, though, and make one large round clafoutis. You'll need a 20cm round or oval baking dish to create a communal plate from which everyone can help themselves to a warm pudding. Whether the portions are individual or shared, this is lovely served warm with vanilla ice cream or else at room temperature with coffee.

These are best eaten on the day they are made.

———

Preheat the oven to 190°C/170°C fan/Gas Mark 5. Take 6 small baking dishes or tins, roughly 10cm in diameter and 2cm deep (ceramic ramekins are a good solution here), and brush them lightly with vegetable oil. Line with baking parchment discs that come 1.5cm above the edge of each dish.

Halve the plums, remove the stones and cut each half into 3–4 wedges. Arrange half the fruit over the base of the lined dishes and set the rest aside.

To make the batter, whisk the egg yolks with half the sugar until thick and pale. You can do this by hand or with an electric mixer. Use a rubber spatula to fold in first the flour and then the vanilla essence, cream and salt. Slit the vanilla pod open along its length with a sharp knife and scrape out all the seeds, then add them to the batter.

Whisk the egg whites with the remaining sugar until they form stiff, but not dry, peaks. Fold them gently into the batter. Pour the batter over the plums to reach about three-quarters of the way up the paper cases. Place in the oven for 15–20 minutes. Take out and quickly arrange the remaining plums on top, slightly overlapping. Continue to bake for about 5 minutes, until a skewer inserted in the centre comes out dry. Allow to cool slightly before removing from the tins. Dust with a little icing sugar, if you like, and serve.

vegetable oil, for brushing the tins

4 ripe red plums

3 eggs, separated

70g caster sugar

70g plain flour

1 tsp vanilla essence

150ml double cream

a pinch of salt

½ vanilla pod

icing sugar, to finish (optional)

Brioche galette

Serves 4–6

This makes a substantial treat for an afternoon tea or, served with lightly sweetened crème fraîche, a 'wow' of a dessert to round off a meal. You need to make the dough a day in advance so that it can be rolled and left to prove. If you are getting organised, the mascarpone cream and crumble can also be made then. That way everything can be at the ready to be assembled and baked close to when you want to serve it. It is best eaten warm.

———

After the brioche dough has been in the fridge for 14–24 hours, transfer it to a lightly floured work surface and use a rolling pin to roll it into an oval about 2cm thick (it doesn't need to be perfect). Transfer to a heavy-duty baking tray lightly dusted with flour. Using a pastry brush, lightly brush the rim of the brioche with a small amount of water. Fold in the edge to form a border 1cm thick. Prick all over the centre of the dough with a fork. Cover loosely with cling film and leave somewhere warm until it has risen by about half its volume.

Preheat the oven to 190°C/170°C fan/Gas Mark 5. When the brioche has risen sufficiently, brush the edges with a little milk. Spread the centre with the mascarpone cream, being careful not to press down too hard. Scatter the plum slices over the cream and then arrange the berries on top. Brush the berries with the melted butter. Mix the crumble with the almonds and cinnamon and sprinkle on top.

Bake in the preheated oven for 25–30 minutes. Check the base by lifting with a palette knife to make sure it is evenly coloured. Transfer to a wire rack and leave to cool slightly.

Just before serving, scoop out the inside of the passion fruit and drizzle it over the fruits.

1 quantity of Brioche dough (see page 185)

plain flour, for dusting

milk, for brushing

⅓ quantity of Mascarpone cream (see page 291)

1 red plum, halved, pitted and cut into slices about 2mm thick

150g mixed berries (e.g. raspberries, blackcurrants, blueberries)

30g unsalted butter, melted

¼ quantity of Crumble (see page 291)

15g flaked almonds

1 tsp ground cinnamon

1 ripe passion fruit

Larder

———

Green tahini sauce

150ml tahini paste

150ml water

80ml lemon juice

2 garlic cloves, crushed

½ tsp salt

30g parsley, finely chopped if making by hand

With or without the parsley, this is one of our go-to fridge staples. It keeps well for a good week or so and will add a creamy richness to anything it's drizzled over: from wedges of roasted butternut squash or aubergine to a simply baked fillet of cod in a tomato sauce. On slices of roast lamb or cubes of grilled chicken, or in a pita stuffed with any or all of the above, a drizzle of tahini is a fast-track guarantee to deliciousness. Once chilled, the sauce will thicken so you'll just need to loosen it with a bit of whisking and possibly a splash more water. You want the consistency to be thick but runny, almost like honey.

Try to get hold of one of the many Middle Eastern brands of tahini (Lebanese is the most widely available), if you can: they don't have any of the clagginess or bitterness that those from other regions can.

———

In a bowl, thoroughly whisk the tahini, water, lemon juice, garlic and salt together. The mixture should be creamy and smooth. If it is too thick, add more water. Stir in the chopped parsley, then taste and add more salt if needed.

If using a food processor or a blender, process together all the ingredients except the parsley until smooth. Add more water if needed. Add the parsley and turn the machine on again for a second or two. Taste for seasoning.

Labneh

Labneh is an Arab cheese or spread made by straining yoghurt. You can buy it in specialist Middle Eastern shops but it's also very easy and rewarding to make: start with natural goat's milk yoghurt, if you can, or else natural full-fat cow's milk yoghurt works very well. Don't start with a set or Greek variety, though: it won't work as well.

The process is not complicated – you just 'hang' the yoghurt in a muslin over a jar or bowl that is large enough so that the base of the cheese is not touching the base of the jar or bowl – but the labneh takes 2 days to make. If you need to speed things along, though, you can always squeeze the muslin from time to time to help release the liquid from the cheese. This can bring the time down to about 8 hours if you want to get it going first thing and serve it the same evening.

Once made, the labneh keeps well in the fridge for up to a week and can be used as a spread. You can also roll it into small balls and then lightly dip them in za'atar to dot through all sorts of salads (see the recipe for Couscous and mograbiah with oven-dried tomatoes on page 94). If you go for this option, you can store the balls in an airtight container, completely covered with olive oil, where they will keep very well for up to a month.

1 litre natural goat's milk yoghurt (or full-fat cow's milk yoghurt)

¾ tsp salt

200–300ml olive oil

10–15g dried mint

a good grind of black pepper

Line a large bowl with a piece of muslin or other fine cloth. In another bowl, mix the yoghurt and salt well. Transfer the yoghurt to the muslin, pick up the edges of the cloth and tie them together well to form a bundle. Hang this over your sink or over a large bowl and leave for 48 hours. By this time the yoghurt will have lost most of its liquid and be ready to use as a spread.

To go the whole hog, leave it hanging for a day longer. Remove the labneh from the cloth and place in a sealed container in the fridge. Once it is thoroughly chilled, preferably after 24 hours, roll the cheese into balls, somewhere between the size of an olive and a walnut.

Take a sterilised jar about 600ml in capacity (see Preserved lemons, page 286, for how to sterilise jars). Pour some of the oil inside and gently lay the balls in the oil. Add some more oil and continue with the balls until all the cheese is inside and immersed in the oil. Seal the jar and keep until needed. Before serving, scatter the mint and pepper on a flat plate and roll the labneh balls in it.

Preserved lemons

6 unwaxed lemons

6 tbsp flaky sea salt

2 sprigs of rosemary

1 large red chilli

juice of 6 lemons

olive oil

We often say that we like 'bursts of flavour' in food that is otherwise comforting. We like the ability for a dish to both comfort (through its familiarity) and also delight (through an element of surprise). This surprise, or burst of flavour, can come in many ways: through a sprinkle of the astringent and lemony spice sumac on some simple scrambled eggs, for example, or some sweet-sour Iranian dried barberries stirred through the mix for a frittata or a rice-based salad. The biggest flavour bomb of them all, though, is preserved lemon skin, either finely chopped or sliced into thin strips. Preserved lemon works well with all sorts of dishes – a must with any oily fish, great with grilled meats, a nice change on top of roasted vegetables – so have a play around and experiment. Be warned, though: once you get into the habit of adding these to your food, they become somewhat addictive.

In the shops, we get our mustard in lovely tall Kilner jars, which we then use to store our preserved lemons when we make up a batch. The jars are widely available to buy in household shops, though, if you can seek a couple out. Once you get into the habit, you can just have a batch constantly on the go ready to use whenever you want. The preserving process takes a few weeks but then you have the benefit of an end result that doesn't go off.

———

Before starting, get a jar just large enough to accommodate all the lemons tightly. To sterilise it, fill it up with boiling water, leave for a minute and then empty it. Allow it to dry out naturally without wiping it so it remains sterilised.

Wash the lemons and cut a deep cross all the way from the top to 2cm from the base, so you are left with 4 quarters attached. Stuff each lemon with a spoonful of salt and place in the jar. Push the lemons in tightly so they are all squeezed together well. Seal the jar and leave for at least a week.

After this initial period, remove the lid and press the lemons as hard as you can to squeeze as much of the juice out of them as possible. Add the rosemary, chilli and lemon juice and cover with a thin layer of olive oil. Seal the jar and leave in a cool place for at least 4 weeks. The longer you leave them, the better the flavour.

Ruth's mayonnaise

Yotam always travels to visit his parents with a large Tupperware jar, which has a round red lid. The jar goes out empty and comes back full of his mother's legendary mayonnaise. The ingredients are not particularly novel but the measures have been perfected over the years and the addition of the coriander makes this very special indeed. No grilled chicken or cheese and tomato sandwich in the Ottolenghi household is complete without it. The mayonnaise keeps well in a sealed container in the fridge for up to 2 weeks.

1 egg

¾ tbsp Dijon mustard

2 tsp caster sugar

½ tsp salt

3 garlic cloves, peeled

2 tbsp cider vinegar

500ml sunflower oil

15g fresh coriander, leaves and stalks

The best way to make this mayonnaise is by using a stick blender. You could also use a food processor or liquidiser, or make it by hand, using a whisk. If doing it by hand, you need to crush the garlic and chop the coriander finely before you start.

If using a stick blender, put the egg, mustard, sugar, salt, garlic and vinegar in a large mixing bowl. Process a little and then start adding the oil in a slow trickle. Keep the machine working as you pour in a very light stream of oil. Once the mayonnaise starts to thicken, you can increase the stream until all the oil is fully incorporated. Now add the coriander and continue processing until it is all chopped and properly mixed in. Transfer to a clean jar and chill. The mayonnaise will keep in the fridge for up to 2 weeks.

Passion fruit jam

300g passion fruit pulp
(roughly 10 passion fruit)

150g caster sugar

A batch of this is very useful to keep in the fridge (where it lasts well for at least 2 weeks), ready to pour over your morning yoghurt or granola. It's also heaven poured over ice cream and crushed meringues – a passion fruit Eton mess – or all sorts of cakes and puddings. Cheesecake, pavlova: anything sweet, really! Nice and ripe passion fruits are a must here: the ones where the skin is dark brown and has started to shrivel.

—

Halve the passion fruit and use a spoon to scoop out the pulp straight into a small saucepan. Add the sugar, stir well with a wooden spoon and put over a low heat. Bring to a slow simmer and cook for about 5 minutes, stirring frequently and taking great care that it doesn't stick to the bottom of the pan. When ready, it should be as thick as honey. To make sure, chill a little bit of the jam in a bowl in the fridge and check its consistency.

Once ready, pour into a clean jar, leave to cool completely, then seal and store in the fridge. The jam will keep for at least 2 weeks.

Raspberry jam

300g raspberries

100g caster sugar

Somewhere between a jam and a coulis, this is a lovely one to pour over your morning yoghurt or granola, or serve with all sorts of puddings. It has a tartness that makes it a perfect match for a slice of dark chocolate cake served with some crème fraîche or ice cream. Add a couple of whole star anise to the jam whilst it is cooking, if you like, or else half a vanilla pod, sliced open and seeds scraped. Doing so adds a nice extra dimension to the tart sweetness.

—

Put the raspberries and sugar in a small, heavy-bottomed saucepan and stir them together. Put over a low heat, bring to a light simmer and cook for 7–8 minutes. Remove from the heat, transfer to a bowl, cover the surface with cling film, leave to cool and then refrigerate.

Lemon curd

200ml lemon juice
(4–6 lemons)

finely grated zest
of 4 lemons

200g caster sugar

4 eggs, plus 4 extra
egg yolks

180g unsalted butter,
cut into cubes

There is something very satisfying about making your
own lemon curd. It's also very simple to make and you'll
probably already have the ingredients to hand. It lasts
well in the fridge for up to 4 days. We love to spread a
thin layer in crêpes – a riff on the classic 'lemon and sugar'
– or between the layers of a stack of ricotta pancakes.

———

Put all the ingredients in a large, heavy-based saucepan, leaving out
roughly half the butter. Place over a medium heat and, using a hand
whisk, whisk constantly while you cook the curd. Reduce the heat
if it starts sticking to the bottom of the pan. Once the curd reaches
boiling point, you will notice large bubbles coming to the surface.
Continue whisking vigorously for another minute and then remove
from the heat.

Off the heat, add the remaining butter and whisk until it has melted.
Pass the curd through a sieve and into a plastic container. Cover the
surface with cling film, allow it to come to room temperature and
then chill for at least 6 hours, preferably overnight, for it to firm up
well. It will keep in the frige for up to 4 days.

Vanilla essence

4 vanilla pods
500ml water
120g caster sugar

There are lots of good varieties of vanilla essence for sale
but none as good as the one you make yourself. It keeps
in the fridge for up to a month.

———

Use a small, sharp knife to slit the vanilla pods open along their
length, then scrape the seeds out with the tip of the knife. Place
the seeds and pods in a medium saucepan, cover with the water
and sugar and bring to the boil. Boil rapidly for about 15 minutes,
until the essence has reduced to a third of its original volume.
Pour into a jar and leave to cool, then seal with a tight-fitting lid.
Keep refrigerated for up to a month.

Mascarpone cream

A spoonful of this is positively heavenly alongside all sorts of puddings: a slice of chocolate cake, peach and raspberry teacakes, simply roasted fruit or a bowl of fresh berries. It's one of those sides that you'll see vying for centre stage. The vanilla essence can be substituted with ¼ teaspoon ground star anise, if you like.

110g mascarpone cheese

110ml crème fraîche

¼ tsp vanilla essence (see page 290)

25g icing sugar

———

Put the mascarpone in a mixing bowl and loosen it up with a whisk. Add the rest of the ingredients and continue whisking until the cream thickens up again. It should be able to hold its shape when lifted with a spoon. Chill until ready to use.

Crumble

Sprinkle this on top of some ready-to-roast fruit or, less conventionally, mix with grated cheese and scatter over the fennel and cherry tomato gratin (see page 71).

300g plain flour

100g caster sugar

200g unsalted butter, fridge-cold and cut into small cubes

———

Put the flour, sugar and butter in a bowl and mix with your hands or an electric mixer fitted with the beater attachment to work it to a uniform breadcrumb consistency. Make sure there are no lumps of butter left. If using a mixer, watch it carefully. Within a few seconds, a crumble can turn into a cookie dough. (If this unpleasant scenario happens, roll it out thinly, cut out cookies, bake them and half dip in melted chocolate.)

Transfer the crumble to a plastic container. It will keep in the fridge for up to 5 days, or for ages in the freezer.

Granola

60g whole unskinned
almonds

40g Brazil nuts

40g cashew nuts

300g whole rolled oats

60g pumpkin seeds

60g sunflower seeds

100g dried apricots,
roughly chopped

60g dried cranberries

60g dried blueberries

Syrup

¼ tsp salt

3 tbsp water

2 tbsp rapeseed oil

2 tbsp sunflower oil

120ml maple syrup

120ml honey

Play around with the nuts, fruit and seeds here, depending on what you have and what you like. Just keep the total net weight the same. The oats can also be replaced with quinoa or buckwheat flakes if you want the granola to be gluten-free.

———

Preheat the oven to 160°C/140°C fan/Gas Mark 3. Roughly chop all the nuts and put them in a large mixing bowl. Add the oats and seeds and set aside.

Mix together all the syrup ingredients in a small saucepan. Place over a low heat and stir while you warm the syrup gently. Once it is warm, pour it over the seeds, nuts and oats and stir well with a wooden spoon.

Line a large baking tray with baking parchment and spread the granola over it evenly. It should form a layer no more than 1cm thick. If it is too thick, consider using 2 trays. Bake for 40 minutes, turning and mixing the granola 2 or 3 times. When ready, it will have taken on a dark, honey-like colour. Don't worry if it is soft; once it is cool it will turn crunchy. Remove from the oven. While the granola is still warm, but not hot, stir in the fruit. Leave to cool on the tray and then transfer to a sealed container. It will keep for up to 2 weeks.

Shortcrust pastry

Having a block of pastry in the freezer will always make you feel like a real home cook. We use this shortcrust pastry for our Jerusalem artichoke and Swiss chard tart (see page 180) as well as our Sweet and spicy beef and pork pie (see page 182), but it can be filled with all sorts of whatever you have in the fridge to be used up.

300g plain flour

½ tsp salt

160g unsalted butter, fridge-cold and cut into 1cm dice

70ml ice-cold water

———

Put the flour and salt into a bowl and add the butter. Rub it in by hand, or using a mixer fitted with the beater attachment, until you reach a fine breadcrumb texture. A third easy option is to use a food processor.

Add the water and continue working just until the dough comes together. Stop at once. Shape the pastry into a disc roughly 4cm thick, wrap it in cling film and chill for at least 2 hours.

The pastry will keep in the fridge for 5 days and for at least a month in the freezer. Defrost in the fridge overnight.

Sweet pastry

The sweet pastry is just as versatile as the shortcrust: we use it for all of our little tartlets as well as our larger Semolina and raspberry tart (see page 276), but the world is your oyster when you've a block in the fridge and the day is a fine one for baking.

330g plain flour

100g icing sugar

finely grated zest of ½ lemon

¼ tsp salt

180g unsalted butter, fridge-cold and cut into small cubes

1 egg yolk

2 tbsp cold water

———

Put the flour, icing sugar, lemon zest and salt in a bowl and add the butter. Rub it in with your hands or, more easily, using a mixer fitted with the beater attachment. Or you can do the job in a food processor. In all cases, you need to mix the ingredients until you get a coarse breadcrumb consistency, making sure there aren't any large lumps of butter left.

Add the egg yolk and water and mix just until the dough comes together, being careful not to mix any longer than necessary. You might need to add a tiny amount of extra water.

Remove the dough from the mixing bowl and knead very lightly for a few seconds only, just to shape it into a smooth disc, 5–6cm thick. Wrap in cling film and chill until ready to use. The pastry will keep in the fridge for a week and at least a month in the freezer.

Rough puff pastry

We know that making your own puff pastry is not
something we all do every time a recipe calls for it.
All that rolling and folding and chilling! But do try it if
you haven't done so before: the results are outstandingly
satisfying and you'll get a heap of respect from those
you're feeding.

If you choose to start with ready-made puff, either go
for an all-butter variety or else brush with plenty of
melted butter before baking.

300g plain flour

1 tsp salt

180g unsalted butter,
frozen

140ml ice-cold water

Sift the flour and salt into a large mixing bowl. Use a coarse cheese
grater to grate 80g of the frozen butter into the flour. Lightly mix
together. Add the cold water and, using a knife, stir the flour and
water together until a dough starts to form. Now use your hands
to bring it together into a ball. You may need to add a little more
water if some dry bits remain in the bowl. Press the dough into a
neat square, wrap it in cling film and chill for 30 minutes.

Using a rolling pin, roll out the pastry on a lightly floured work
surface into a rectangle with a long edge that is 3 times its width.
Grate the remaining butter and spread it evenly over two-thirds of
rectangle. Take the third that is not scattered with butter and fold
it over on to the middle of the buttered part. Then fold the 2 layers
over the remaining single layer. You will be left with 3 layers of
pastry and 2 layers of butter separating them.

Turn the pastry by 90 degrees. Dust your work surface lightly
with flour and roll out the pastry again into a long rectangle with
the same proportions as before. The 2 short edges will reveal
the 3 layers of pastry and 2 layers of butter.

Take one of the short sides and fold it over to reach the middle
of the remaining part of the pastry. Fold the remaining third on
top of the first one to get 3 layers on top of each other. Wrap
the pastry in cling film and rest in the fridge for 30 minutes.

Roll the pastry again into a rectangle with the short edges
displaying the seams. Fold into 3 as before. Rest in the fridge
again for 30 minutes.

Repeat the process one last time and then wrap and chill for at
least an hour.

The pastry will keep in the fridge for up to 4 days and in the freezer
for a month.

Index

aioli 159
almond and orange Florentines 242–3
amaretti, sour cherry 246–7
Amaretto and pear crumble cake 232
apple
  apple and olive oil cake with maple
    icing 204–5
  blueberry crumble muffin 222
  carrot, apple and pecan
    muffins 224–5
apricot, dried
  Camargue red rice and quinoa with
    orange and pistachios 93
  couscous with dried apricots and
    butternut squash 96
  granola 292
  granola bars 251
Arak, buttered prawns with tomato,
  olives and Arak 160–1
artichoke, baked artichokes and broad
  beans 54
asparagus
  asparagus and samphire 50–1
  chargrilled asparagus, courgette and
    manouri 48–9
  fried scallops with saffron potatoes,
    asparagus and samphire 159
  salmon and asparagus
    bruschetta 194–5
aubergine
  aubergine-wrapped ricotta gnocchi
    with sage butter 44–5
  burnt aubergine with yellow pepper
    and red onion 42–3
  grilled aubergine and lemon
    soup 108
  marinated aubergine with tahini and
    oregano 40–1
  roasted aubergine with saffron
    yoghurt 46–7
  roasted butternut squash with
    burnt aubergine and pomegranate
    molasses 60–3

bacon, Puy lentils with sour cherries,
  bacon and Gorgonzola 97
baking times 169
banana and hazelnut tartlets 274–5
bars
  granola bars 251
  Kahlid's chocolate and chestnut
    bars 257
  raspberry and oat bars 250
basil
  Etti's herb salad 38
  lime and basil macaroons 262
  roasted aubergine with saffron
    yoghurt 47
bean(s) see broad bean; butterbean;
  cannellini bean; French bean
beef
  beef and lamb meatballs baked in
    tahini 120
  roasted beef fillet (plus three
    sauces) 118–19

sweet and spicy beef and pork
  pie 182–3
beetroot, roasted red and golden 78–9
berries
  brioche galette 281
  fresh berry tartlets 272
bigga 170–1
biscotti, pistachio and ginger 238–9
biscuits
  Parmesan and poppy biscuits 198–9
  white chocolate and cranberry
    biscuits 240–1
blenders 168
blueberry
  blueberry crumble muffins 222–3
  fresh berry tartlets 272
  granola 292
  lemon and blueberry teacakes 217
brandy and prune truffles 248–9
bread
  crusty white Italian loaf 170–1
  focaccia (plus three toppings) 176–9
  green olive loaf 172–3
  sour cherry and walnut stick 174–5
  see also bruschetta
brioche 185–7, 188–9
  brioche galette 280–1
  'pizza' with feta, tomato and
    olives 188–9
broad bean
  baked artichokes and broad
    beans 54
  radish and broad bean salad 32–3
broccoli 13
  chargrilled broccoli with chilli and
    garlic 56–7
  purple sprouting broccoli and salsify
    with caper butter 58
broccolini, sweet broccolini with tofu,
  sesame and coriander 55
brownies 252–6
  macadamia and white chocolate
    brownies 256
  toffee brownies 254–5
bruschetta
  roasted pepper and cannellini
    bruschetta 192–3
  salmon and asparagus
    bruschetta 194–5
bulgar, sardines stuffed with bulgar,
  currants and pistachios 156–7
butter
  caper butter 58
  sage butter 44–5
butterbean with sweet chilli sauce and
  fresh herbs 91
buttercream, basil 262
butternut squash
  butternut, carrot and goat's cheese
    tartlets 184
  couscous with dried apricots and
    butternut squash 96
  roasted butternut squash with
    burnt aubergine and pomegranate
    molasses 60–3

cakes
  apple and olive oil cake with maple
    icing 204–5
  carrot and walnut cake 212–13
  chocolate fudge cake 208–9
  orange polenta cake 206–7
  pear and Amaretto crumble
    cake 232
  sticky chocolate loaf 233
  see also brownies; cupcakes; muffins
cannellini bean and roasted pepper
  bruschetta 192–3
caper(s)
  caper butter 58
  chargrilled cauliflower with tomato,
    dill and capers 68–9
caramel
  caramel and macadamia
    cheesecake 210–11
  caramel sauce 210–11
  caramel toppings 206–7
  salty peanut and caramel
    macaroons 261
carrot
  butternut, carrot and goat's cheese
    tartlets 184
  carrot, apple and pecan
    muffins 224–5
  carrot and peas 86–7
  carrot and walnut cake 212–13
cauliflower
  cauliflower and cumin fritters 66–7
  chargrilled cauliflower with tomato,
    dill and capers 68–9
celeriac, sweet and sour celeriac and
  swede 81
celery
  grilled mackerel with green olive,
    celery and raisin salsa 146–7
  whole wheat and mushrooms with
    celery and shallots 98
Champagne chocolates 244–5
chard
  peaches and spec with orange
    blossom 29
  red lentil and chard soup 106
  roasted red and golden beetroot 78
cheese
  Cheddar and caraway cheese
    straws 200–1
  Puy lentils with sour cherries, bacon
    and Gorgonzola 97
  see also labneh; Parmesan
cheesecake, caramel and
  macadamia 210–11
cherry
  granola bars 251
  Puy lentils with sour cherries, bacon
    and Gorgonzola 97
  sour cherry amaretti 246–7
  sour cherry and walnut stick 174–5
  sweet and sour celeriac and
    swede 81
chestnut, Kahlid's chocolate and
  chestnut bars 257

chicken
  harissa-marinated chicken with red grapefruit salad 128–9
  roast chicken with saffron, hazelnuts and honey 132–3
  roast chicken with sumac, za'atar and lemon 130–1
  roast chicken and three-rice salad 134–5
chickpea
  chickpeas and spinach with honeyed sweet potato 99
  harira (lamb, chickpeas and spinach) 107
chilli and garlic with chargrilled broccoli 56–7
chocolate
  banana and hazelnut tartlets 274
  Champagne chocolates 244–5
  chocolate cupcakes 230–1
  chocolate fudge cake 208–9
  chocolate ganache 248, 262
  chocolate icing 230
  chocolate macaroons 262
  dark chocolate tartlets 273
  Kahlid's chocolate and chestnut bars 257
  prune and brandy truffles 248–9
  sticky chocolate loaf 233
  see also white chocolate
choka (smoky tomato sauce) 119
cinnamon
  cinnamon and hazelnut meringues 266–7
  mixed mushrooms with cinnamon and lemon 74–5
  oxtail stew with pumpkin and cinnamon 124–5
  plum, marzipan and cinnamon muffins 220–1
clafoutis, individual plum 278–9
compote, plum 220–1
coriander
  Etti's herb salad 38
  marinated rack of lamb with coriander and honey 112–13
  marinated turkey breast with cumin, coriander and white wine 138–9
  sweet broccolini with tofu, sesame and coriander 55
courgette
  chargrilled asparagus, courgette and manouri 48–9
  courgette-wrapped lamb kebabs 116–17
couscous
  couscous with dried apricots and butternut squash 96
  couscous and mograbiah with oven-dried tomatoes 94–5
crackers, olive oil 196–7
cranberry
  granola 292
  white chocolate and cranberry biscuits 240–1

cream, Mascarpone 281, 291
cream cheese
  caramel and macadamia cheesecake 210–11
  cream cheese icing 212, 229
  maple icing 204–5
  salmon and asparagus bruschetta 194
creaming 168
crumble 291
  blueberry crumble muffin 222–3
  brioche galette 281
  fennel, cherry tomato and crumble gratin 70–1
  pear and Amaretto crumble cake 232
cucumber and poppy seed salad 36–7
cumin
  cauliflower and cumin fritters 66–7
  marinated turkey breast with cumin, coriander and white wine 138–9
cupcakes 228–31
  chocolate cupcakes 230–1
  hazelnut cupcakes 229
currant(s), sardines stuffed with bulgar, currants and pistachios 156–7

dill
  chargrilled cauliflower with tomato, dill and capers 68–9
  Etti's herb salad 38
dressings 85, 134–5
  orange blossom 29
duck, seared duck breasts with blood orange and star anise 140–1

elderflower, gooseberry & ginger 121, 122
electric mixers 168
endive
  caramelised endive with Serrano ham 64–5
  peaches and spec with orange blossom 29
equipment 168

fennel
  fennel, cherry tomato and crumble gratin 70–1
  fennel and feta pomegranate seeds and sumac 34–5
  grape and fennel seed topping 179
  seafood, fennel and lime salad 144–5
feta
  courgette-wrapped lamb kebabs 116–17
  fennel and feta pomegranate seeds and sumac 34–5
  Jerusalem artichoke and Swiss chard tart 180
  'pizza' with feta, tomato and olives 188–9
  Portobello mushrooms with pearl barley and preserved lemon 76

fig
  figs with young pecorino and honey 30–1
  Kahlid's chocolate and chestnut bars 257
  lamb cutlets with walnut, fig and goat's cheese salad 114–15
fish
  chargrilled salmon with red pepper and hazelnut salsa 158
  grilled mackerel with green olive, celery and raisin salsa 146–7
  grilled mackerel with sweet potato pickle and mint yoghurt 148–9
  pan-fried sea bass on pita with labneh, tomato and preserved lemon 154
  pan-fried sea bream with green tahini and pomegranate seeds 155
  salmon and asparagus bruschetta 194–5
  sardines stuffed with bulgar, currants and pistachios 156–7
  seared tuna with pistachio crust and papaya salsa 150–1
Florentines, almond and orange 242–3
focaccia (plus three toppings) 176–9
food philosophy 13–14
French bean and mangetout with hazelnut and orange 52–3
fritters, cauliflower and cumin 66–7

galettes
  brioche galette 280–1
  sweet potato galettes 190–1
ganache, chocolate 248, 262
garlic
  chargrilled broccoli with chilli and garlic 56–7
  gremolata 124–5
ginger
  baked okra with tomato and ginger 59
  gooseberry, ginger and elderflower 121, 122
  pistachio and ginger biscotti 238–9
  spiced red plum, ginger and rhubarb relish 121, 122
glazes
  marmalade glaze 206–7
  for teacakes 216–18
gnocchi, aubergine-wrapped ricotta gnocchi with sage butter 44–5
goat's cheese
  butternut, carrot and goat's cheese tartlets 184
  lamb cutlets with walnut, fig and goat's cheese salad 114–15
  red onion and goat's cheese topping 179
gooseberry, ginger and elderflower 121, 122
Gorgonzola, Puy lentils with sour cherries, bacon and Gorgonzola 97
granola 292

granola bars 251
grape and fennel seed topping 179
grapefruit, harissa-marinated chicken with red grapefruit salad 128–9
gratin
Danielle's sweet potato gratin 88–9
fennel, cherry tomato and crumble gratin 70–1
green tahini sauce 284
recipes using 33, 41, 155
gremolata 124–5

ham, caramelised endive with Serrano ham 64–5
harira (lamb, chickpeas and spinach) 107
harissa-marinated chicken with red grapefruit salad 128–9
hazelnut
banana and hazelnut tartlets 274–5
chargrilled salmon with red pepper and hazelnut salsa 158
cinnamon and hazelnut meringues 266–7
French beans and mangetout with hazelnut and orange 52–3
hazelnut cupcakes 229
roast chicken with saffron, hazelnuts and honey 132–3
herbs
butterbeans with sweet chilli sauce and fresh herbs 91
Etti's herb salad 38–9
honey
chickpeas and spinach with honeyed sweet potato 99
figs with young pecorino and honey 30–1
lavender and honey teacake 218
marinated rack of lamb with coriander and honey 112–13
roast chicken with saffron, hazelnuts and honey 132–3
horseradish
crushed new potatoes with horseradish and sorrel 80
rocket and horseradish sauce 119

icing
chocolate icing 230
cream cheese icing 212, 229
maple icing 204–5

jam
passion fruit jam 288
raspberry jam 288
Jerusalem artichoke
Jerusalem artichoke and rocket soup 109
Jerusalem artichoke and Swiss chard tart 180–1
roast potatoes and Jerusalem artichokes with lemon and sage 90

kebabs, courgette-wrapped lamb 116–17
kosheri 100–1

labneh 285
couscous and mograbiah with oven-dried tomatoes 94–5
pan-fried sea bass on pita with labneh, tomato and preserved lemon 154

lamb
beef and lamb meatballs baked in tahini 120
courgette-wrapped lamb kebabs 116–17
harira (lamb, chickpeas and spinach) 107
lamb cutlets with walnut, fig and goat's cheese salad 114–15
marinated rack of lamb with coriander and honey 112–13
lavender and honey teacake 218
lemon
grilled aubergine and lemon soup 108
lemon and blueberry teacakes 217
lemon curd 273, 290
lemon meringue tartlets 273
mixed mushrooms with cinnamon and lemon 74–5
roast chicken with sumac, za'atar and lemon 130–1
roast potatoes and Jerusalem artichokes with lemon and sage 90
see also preserved lemon
lentil(s)
kosheri 100–1
Puy lentils with sour cherries, bacon and Gorgonzola 97
red lentil and chard soup 106
lime
lime and basil macaroons 262
lime sauce 67
seafood, fennel and lime salad 144–5
loaf cakes, sticky chocolate loaf 233
loaves
crusty white Italian loaf 170–1
green olive loaf 172–3

macadamia
caramel and macadamia cheesecake 210–11
macadamia and white chocolate brownies 256
macaroons 258–62
chocolate macaroons 262
lime and basil macaroons 262
salty peanut and caramel macaroons 261
mackerel, grilled mackerel with green olive, celery and raisin salsa 146–7
mangetout and French beans with hazelnut and orange 52–3
mango, seared tuna with pistachio crust and papaya salsa 150
manouri, chargrilled asparagus, courgette and manouri 48–9
maple
maple icing 204–5
roasted potato with pecan and maple 85
marinades 41, 115, 142
harissa marinade 128–9
marmalade glaze 206–7
marzipan, cinnamon and plum muffins 220–1
Mascarpone cream 281, 291
mash, parsnip and pumpkin 84
mayonnaise, Ruth's 287
meatballs
beef and lamb meatballs baked in tahini 120

turkey and sweetcorn meatballs with roasted pepper sauce 136–7
meringues 263–7
cinnamon and hazelnut meringues 266–7
lemon meringue tartlets 273
pistachio and rosewater meringues 264–5
mint yoghurt 148–9
mograbiah
barbecued quail with mograbiah salad 142–3
couscous and mograbiah with oven-dried tomatoes 94–5
moulds 168
mozzarella, marinated romano peppers with buffalo mozzarella 72
muffins 219–25
blueberry crumble muffins 222–3
carrot, apple and pecan muffins 224–5
plum, marzipan and cinnamon muffins 220–1
mushroom
mixed mushrooms with cinnamon and lemon 74–5
Portobello mushrooms with pearl barley and preserved lemon 76–7
whole wheat and mushrooms with celery and shallots 98
mustard and watercress sauce 119

nut(s)
granola 292
granola bars 251
raspberry and oat bars 250
see also hazelnut; macadamia

oat(s)
granola bars 251
raspberry and oat bars 250
okra, baked okra with tomato and ginger 59
olive oil crackers 196–7
olive(s)
buttered prawns with tomato, olives and Arak 160–1
green olive loaf 172–3
grilled mackerel with green olive, celery and raisin salsa 146–7
Kalamata olives 90, 161, 179, 189
parsley and olive focaccia topping 179
'pizza' with feta, tomato and olives 188–9
roast potatoes and Jerusalem artichokes with lemon and sage 90
onion
burnt aubergine with yellow pepper and red onion 42–3
caramelised onion 189
red onion and goat's cheese topping 179
orange
almond and orange Florentines 242–3
Camargue red rice and quinoa with orange and pistachios 92–3
French beans and mangetout with hazelnut and orange 52–3
orange polenta cake 206–7
seared duck breasts with blood orange and star anise 140–1

orange blossom dressing 29
oxtail stew with pumpkin and
   cinnamon 124–5

papaya salsa 150–1
Parmesan
   fennel, cherry tomato and crumble
      gratin 71
   Parmesan and poppy biscuits 198–9
parsley
   burnt aubergine with yellow pepper
      and red onion 42
   Etti's herb salad 38
   green tahini sauce 284
   gremolata 124–5
   mixed mushrooms with cinnamon
      and lemon 74–5
   parsley and olive focaccia
      topping 179
parsnip and pumpkin mash 84
passion fruit jam 288
pastry 184
   pre-baked tartlet cases 270, 272–4
   rough puff pastry 294–5
   shortcrust pastry 180–1, 182–3, 293
   sweet pastry 276–7, 293
pea
   baked artichokes and broad
      beans 54
   carrot and peas 86–7
pea shoots, carrot and peas 86–7
peach
   peach and raspberry teacake 216
   peaches and spec with orange
      blossom 28–9
peanut, salty peanut and caramel
   macaroons 261
pear and Amaretto crumble cake 232
pearl barley, Portobello mushrooms
   with pearl barley and preserved
   lemon 76–7
pecan
   carrot, apple and pecan
      muffins 224–5
   roasted sweet potato with pecan and
      maple 85
pecorino, figs with young pecorino and
   honey 30–1
pepper (bell)
   burnt aubergine with yellow pepper
      and red onion 42–3
   butterbean with sweet chilli sauce
      and fresh herbs 91
   chargrilled salmon with red pepper
      and hazelnut salsa 158
   chilled red pepper soup with soured
      cream 104–5
   harissa marinade 128
   roasted pepper and cannellini
      bruschetta 192–3
   turkey and sweetcorn meatballs with
      roasted pepper sauce 136–7
pepper (romano), marinated romano
   peppers with buffalo mozzarella 72
pickle, sweet potato 148–9
pie, sweet and spicy beef and
   pork 182–3
pistachio
   Camargue red rice and quinoa with
      orange and pistachios 92–3
   pistachio and ginger biscotti 238–9
   pistachio and rosewater
      meringues 264–5

pistachio shortbreads 236–7
   sardines stuffed with bulgar, currants
      and pistachios 156–7
   seared tuna with pistachio crust and
      papaya salsa 150–1
pita, pan-fried sea bass on pita with
   labneh, tomato and preserved
   lemon 154
'pizza' with feta, tomato and
   olives 188–9
plum
   brioche galette 281
   individual plum clafoutis 278–9
   plum, marzipan and cinnamon
      muffins 220–1
   plum compote 220–1
   spiced red plum, ginger and rhubarb
      relish 121, 122
polenta, orange polenta cake 206–7
pomegranate
   fennel and feta pomegranate seeds
      and sumac 34–5
   pan-fried sea bream with green tahini
      and pomegranate seeds 155
pomegranate molasses, roasted
   butternut squash with burnt aubergine
   and pomegranate molasses 60–3
poppy seed
   cucumber and poppy seed
      salad 36–7
   Parmesan and poppy biscuits 198–9
pork
   roast pork belly (plus two
      relishes) 121–3
   sweet and spicy beef and pork
      pie 182–3
potato
   crushed new potatoes with
      horseradish and sorrel 80
   fried scallops with saffron potatoes,
      asparagus and samphire 159
   roast potatoes and Jerusalem
      artichokes with lemon and sage 90
prawn
   buttered prawns with tomato, olives
      and Arak 160–1
   seafood, fennel and lime
      salad 144–5
preserved lemon 286
   pan-fried sea bass on pita with
      labneh, tomato and preserved
      lemon 154
   Portobello mushrooms with pearl
      barley and preserved lemon 76–7
prune
   prune and brandy truffles 248–9
   sticky chocolate loaf 233
pumpkin
   oxtail stew with pumpkin and
      cinnamon 124–5
   parsnip and pumpkin mash 84
purple sprouting broccoli and salsify
   with caper butter 58
Puy lentil(s) with sour cherries, bacon
   and Gorgonzola 97

quail, barbecued quail with mograbiah
   salad 142–3
quinoa, Camargue red rice and quinoa
   with orange and pistachios 92–3

radish and broad bean salad 32–3
raisin, olive and celery salsa 146–7

raspberry
   fresh berry tartlets 272
   peach and raspberry teacake 216
   raspberry jam 288
   raspberry and oat bars 250
   semolina and raspberry tart 276–7
   white chocolate and raspberry
      tartlets 272
red lentil and chard soup 106
relishes
   gooseberry, ginger and elderflower
      relish 121, 122
   spiced red plum, ginger and rhubarb
      relish 121, 122
rhubarb, spiced red plum, ginger and
   rhubarb relish 121, 122
rice
   Camargue red rice and quinoa with
      orange and pistachios 92–3
   kosheri 100–1
   roast chicken and three-rice
      salad 134–5
   Tamara's stuffed vine leaves 102–3
ricotta, aubergine-wrapped ricotta
   gnocchi with sage butter 44–5
rocket
   Camargue red rice and quinoa with
      orange and pistachios 93
   chargrilled asparagus, courgette and
      manouri 48–9
   Etti's herb salad 38
   figs with young pecorino and
      honey 30–1
   harissa-marinated chicken with red
      grapefruit salad 128–9
   Jerusalem artichoke and rocket
      soup 109
   marinated romano peppers with
      buffalo mozzarella 72
   rocket and horseradish sauce 119
rosewater and pistachio
   meringues 264–5
rough puff pastry 294–5

saffron
   fried scallops with saffron potatoes,
      asparagus and samphire 159
   roast chicken with saffron, hazelnuts
      and honey 132–3
   saffron yoghurt 46–7
sage
   roast potatoes and Jerusalem
      artichokes with lemon and sage 90
   sage butter 44–5
salads
   barbecued quail with mograbiah
      salad 142–3
   cucumber and poppy seed
      salad 36–7
   Etti's herb salad 38–9
   harissa-marinated chicken with red
      grapefruit salad 128–9
   lamb cutlets with walnut, fig and
      goat's cheese salad 114–15
   radish and broad bean salad 32–3
   roast chicken and three-rice
      salad 134–5
   seafood, fennel and lime
      salad 144–5
salmon
   chargrilled salmon with red pepper
      and hazelnut salsa 158

salmon and asparagus
bruschetta 194–5
salsa
green olive, celery and raisin
salsa 146–7
papaya salsa 150–1
red pepper and hazelnut salsa 158
tomato salsa 154
salsify and purple sprouting broccoli
with caper butter 58
salty peanut and caramel
macaroons 261
samphire
asparagus and samphire 50–1
fried scallops with saffron potatoes,
asparagus and samphire 159
sardines stuffed with bulgar, currants
and pistachios 156–7
scallop, fried scallops with saffron
potatoes, asparagus and samphire 159
sea bass, pan-fried sea bass on pita
with labneh, tomato and preserved
lemon 154
sea bream, pan-fried sea bream
with green tahini and pomegranate
seeds 155
seafood, fennel and lime salad 144–5
semolina and raspberry tart 276–7
sesame
asparagus and samphire 50–1
roasted butternut squash with
burnt aubergine and pomegranate
molasses 63
sweet broccolini with tofu, sesame
and coriander 55
shallots, whole wheat and mushrooms
with celery and shallots 98
shortbreads, pistachio 236–7
shortcrust pastry 293
sorrel, crushed new potatoes with
horseradish and sorrel 80
soup
chilled red pepper soup with soured
cream 104–5
grilled aubergine and lemon
soup 108
Jerusalem artichoke and rocket
soup 109
red lentil and chard soup 106
spec and peaches with orange
blossom 28–9
spinach
chargrilled cauliflower with tomato,
dill and capers 68
chickpeas and spinach with honeyed
sweet potato 99
harira (lamb, chickpeas and
spinach) 107
squid, seafood, fennel and lime
salad 144–5
starters 177
stew, oxtail stew with pumpkin and
cinnamon 124–5
sticky chocolate loaf 233

sultana
apple and olive oil cake with maple
icing 204
carrot, apple and pecan muffins 225
sumac
fennel and feta pomegranate seeds
and sumac 34–5

roast chicken with sumac, za'atar and
lemon 130–1
swede, sweet and sour celeriac and
swede 81
sweet potato
chickpeas and spinach with honeyed
sweet potato 99
Danielle's sweet potato gratin 88–9
roasted potato with pecan and
maple 85
sweet potato galettes 190–1
sweet potato pickle 148–9
sweet and sour celeriac and swede 81
sweetcorn and turkey meatballs with
roasted pepper sauce 136–7
Swiss chard and Jerusalem artichoke
tart 180–1
syrup
granola 292
sticky chocolate loaf 233

tahini
beef and lamb meatballs baked in
tahini 120
green tahini sauce 284
marinated aubergine with tahini and
oregano 40–1
pan-fried sea bream with green tahini
and pomegranate seeds 155
tahini sauce 120
tartlets 270–5
banana and hazelnut tartlets 274–5
butternut, carrot and goat's cheese
tartlets 184
dark chocolate tartlets 273
fresh berries tartlets 272
lemon meringue tartlets 273
pre-baked cases 270, 272–4
white chocolate and raspberry
tartlets 272
tarts
Jerusalem artichoke and Swiss chard
tart 180–1
semolina and raspberry tart 276–7
teacakes 214–18
lavender and honey teacake 218
lemon and blueberry teacake 217
peach and raspberry teacake 216
tins 168
greasing and lining 169
toffee brownies 254–5
tofu, sesame and coriander with sweet
broccolini 55
tomato
baked okra with tomato and
ginger 59
burnt aubergine with yellow pepper
and red onion 42
buttered prawns with tomato, olives
and Arak 160–1
chargrilled asparagus, courgette and
manouri 48–9
chargrilled cauliflower with tomato,
dill and capers 68–9
chickpeas and spinach with honeyed
sweet potato 99
choka (smoky tomato sauce) 119
courgette-wrapped lamb
kebabs 116–17
couscous and mograbiah with
oven-dried tomatoes 94–5
fennel, cherry tomato and crumble
gratin 70–1

harira (lamb, chickpeas and
spinach) 107
oven-dried tomatoes 189
oxtail stew with pumpkin and
cinnamon 124–5
pan-fried sea bass on pita with
labneh, tomato and preserved
lemon 154
'pizza' with feta, tomato and
olives 188–9
roast potatoes and Jerusalem
artichokes with lemon and sage 90
spicy tomato sauce 100
tomato salsa 154
truffles, prune and brandy 248–9
tuna, seared tuna with pistachio crust
and papaya salsa 150–1
turkey
marinated turkey breast with cumin,
coriander and white wine 138–9
turkey and sweetcorn meatballs with
roasted pepper sauce 136–7

vanilla essence 290
vermicelli, kosheri 100–1
vine leaves, Tamara's stuffed 102–3

walnut
carrot and walnut cake 212–13
lamb cutlets with walnut, fig and
goat's cheese salad 114–15
sour cherry and walnut stick 174–5
watercress
peaches and spec with orange
blossom 29
watercress and mustard sauce 119
wheat, whole wheat and mushrooms
with celery and shallots 98
white chocolate
Kahlid's chocolate and chestnut
bars 257
macadamia and white chocolate
brownies 256
white chocolate and cranberry
biscuits 240–1
white chocolate and raspberry
tartlets 272

yoghurt
crushed new potatoes with
horseradish and sorrel 80
Jerusalem artichoke and rocket
soup 109
labneh 285
lime sauce 67
mint yoghurt 148–9
saffron yoghurt 46–7
Tamara's stuffed vine leaves 102–3
yoghurt sauce 99

za'atar, roast chicken with sumac, za'atar
and lemon 130–1

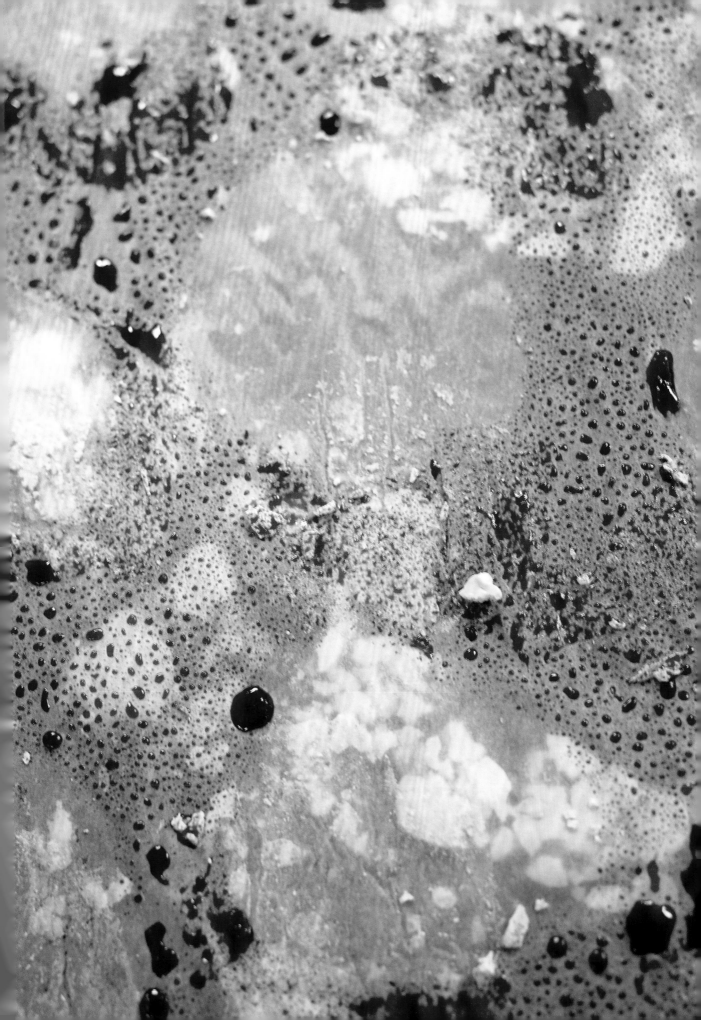

The Ottolenghi people

Trying to tell the Ottolenghi story always ends up being the story of the individuals who have participated in forming it. We can only mention here a few of the many who contributed over the years. We are deeply thankful to all the others.

First, Noam Bar, who is a senior partner in the company and has the exceptional combination of an acute business understanding and the ability to grasp the vision and drive us all forward with it.

Second, Cornelia Staeubli, a partner and general manager, the people's person and the one who, incredibly, holds it all together, physically and spiritually.

Then (in rough order of appearance at Ottolenghi): Jim Webb – creative force, manager of all projects, a man of infinite talents; Khalid Assyb – grand chef de pâtisserie; Lingchee Ang – master of the pastries and the pastry counter; Mariusz Uszakiewicz – head baker, ex-footballer and original thinker; Tamar Shany – gifted chef and star of all musicals; Nicole Steel – service provider of the year and the one with the most leaving dos; Francis Pereira – the real manager of Notting Hill; Daniela Geatti – manager, and mother of the first Ottolenghi baby; Alejandra Chavero – the one who brought Ottolenghi standards to Mexico with a big smile; Diana Daniel-Thomas – miraculously manages to put our accounts in order; Reka Fabian – person of details and great devotion; Dan Lepard – the magician who always sorts out our bread; Etti Mordo – passionately original chef with rare execution; Colleen Murphy – head pastry chef, head chef and our token East Ender; Tricia Jadoonanan – gifted, good humoured and a commander of many manly chefs; Marketa Kratochvilova – the brilliantly artistic arranger of the display; Emma Christian – efficient catering princess; Danielle Postma – creative culinary star with many admirers; Ramael Scully – the calmest and one of the most consistently inspired chefs; Jason Chuck – a sportsman and a chef who never gets dirty; Erica Rossi – Italian energy bomb and Camden town beloved; Maria Oskarsson – the only person in the world who managed to get into Cornelia's shoes; Helene Sauvage – assistant manager and a Notting Hill star with French elegance; Nguyo Milcinovic – our evening star and Scully's right hand man; Tal Kimchi – great kitchen organiser and a multi-talent; Karl Allen – the customers' favourite manager; Carol Brough – patient cake maker and inventor; Helen Goh – creator, perfectionist and analyst of a rare kind; Nir Feller – fiery foodie and bohemian; Marina Dos Santos – the one who brought us Continental chic and restaurant zeal; Gerard Viccars – meticulous and conscientious chef, plus a few tattoos; Sara Lee – the quality guard and promoter of wonderful packed products; Arek Karas – ultimate problem solver and computer wiz; Sara Fereidooni – a serious manager with an infectious charm; Basia Murphy – living proof that you can be an effective manager and smile; Itamar Strulovich – a rising talent of food and wit; Sarit Packer – merry mistress of the pastry department.

Acknowledgements

Big thanks to Alex Meitlis and Tirza Florentin, not so silent partners, whom, in two opposite departments, had a huge part in moulding Ottolenghi.

We would like to thank Amos Oppenheim for his limitless trust and generosity. His constant smile is deeply missed. And thank you to the others who had early faith: Tamara Meitlis, Ariela Oppenheim, David Oppenheim, Itzik and Ilana Lederfeind, Danny Florentin, Keren Margalit and Yoram Ever-Hadani.

For making this book happen, infinite thanks to Felicity Rubinstein and Sarah Lavelle; for making it so breathtakingly beautiful, thanks to Axel Feldmann, Sam Wolfson, Richard Learoyd and Adam Laycock; and for taking care of the details, thanks to Jane Middleton.

For the spectacular dishes and plates used in the photography, we are indebted to Lindy Wiffen from Ceramica Blue. And thanks to Gerry Ure for smiling through the hassle.

For precious assistance in making the recipes work: Jim Webb, Alison Quinn, Claudine Boulstridge, Marianne Lumb and Philippa Shepherd.

And more warm thanks, for many different reasons, to: Charley Bradley, Leigh Genis, Dino Cura, Paul and Ossi Burger, Adrien von Ferscht, Tamasin Day-Lewis, Patricia Michelson, Sarah Bilney, Binnie Dansby, Patrick Houser, Caroline Waldegrave, Jenny Stringer, Viv Pidgeon, Max Clark, Sue Spaull, Gail Mejia, Dariusz Przystasz, Przemek Suszek, Karen Handler-Kremmerman, Dorit Mintzer, Sigal Baranowitz, Pete and Greta Allen, and Jenny and Tony Taylor.

Thank you to all our devoted suppliers, without whom the wheels of the machine would not be turning.

And most humble thanks to all the Ottolenghi customers, the ultimate source of our pleasure and livelihood.